SMASHING

MOBILE WEB
DEVELOPMENT

SMASHING

MOBILE WEB DEVELOPMENT

GOING MOBILE WITH HTML5, CSS3 AND JAVASCRIPT

Greg Avola

and

Jon Raasch

A John Wiley and Sons, Ltd, Publication

PUBLISHER'S ACKNOWLEDGMENTS

Some of the people who helped bring this book to market include the following:

Editorial and Production
VP Consumer and Technology Publishing Director: Michelle Leete
Associate Director–Book Content Management: Martin Tribe
Associate Publisher: Chris Webb
Executive Commissioning Editor: Craig Smith
Assistant Editor: Ellie Scott
Development Editor: Sydney Jones
Copy Editor: Debbye Butler
Technical Editors: Jon Raasch and Greg Avola
Editorial Manager: Jodi Jensen
Senior Project Editor: Sara Shlaer
Editorial Assistant: Leslie Saxman

Marketing
Associate Marketing Director: Louise Breinholt
Marketing Manager: Lorna Mein
Senior Marketing Executive: Kate Parrett

Composition Services
Compositor: Indianapolis Composition Services
Proofreader: Wordsmith Editorial
Indexer: Potomac Indexing, LLC

For my Grandparents, who have inspired me to always reach for excellence.

For my loving wife, who has given me strength and support to always follow my dreams.

For my parents, who laid the framework of my growth and are my role models.

ABOUT THE AUTHORS

Greg Avola is a co-founder and CTO for a social startup, Untappd, that helps users track, recommend, and discover new beers, breweries, and beer venues. The Untappd mobile app was built using the HTML5/CSS/JS technologies that are discussed throughout this book.

Jon Raasch is a front-end developer and designer who has been programming for the web for more than 15 years. Using modern programming techniques, he designs user interfaces that are dynamic and engaging and make full use of full engine spiderability. By integrating design, development, and branding, he makes websites that are as accessible to users as they are to Googlebot.

CONTENTS

INTRODUCTION

When I was first was approached about writing a book for mobile web development, I was bit confused. While mobile websites are easy to build and you can load them with exciting features using HTML5 and CSS3, the focus of the mobile development has been on the native front with iOS and Android. If you offer a service or product, the first question everyone asks you is, "Do you have an app?"

However, with the increasing demand for native applications comes the higher cost it takes to develop them and support them. Users want an easier and faster way to make high quality cross-platform applications. Several years ago, when native application began to surface, it was impossible to match the quality and experience in a mobile browser.

Fast forward to 2012: Mobile browsers have finally caught up to their native counterparts. With rich features in HTML5, CSS3, and JavaScript, developers are able to create experiences close to, and even better, than those that native applications deliver. The best part is your ability to take the code and apply it to multiple devices. Finally, there is no need bring on additional developers to your organization to construct applications for every platform.

While the topic of native application is, and will continue to be, very popular, the HTML5 space is growing every day. With more and more people having access to mobile devices, HTML5/CSS/JS Web applications can move your product, service, or business to mobile space without breaking the bank.

While the topic of this book is building a sample mobile web app, you will learn about standards and best practices to apply to your creations. The book has information for all skill levels, for those who are just starting to build, to those who have built many mobile web apps in the past.

So if you want to create a mobile application, do you need to learn Objective-C and Java? Absolutely not. With HTML5/CSS3 and JavaScript you can create unique experiences all powered by the biggest app store, *the browser*.

The goal of the book is to give developers a top-down perspective of mobile web developing from local testing, development, and production enhancements and tweaks. *Smashing Mobile Web Development* focuses on the giving you an understanding of the technologies at your disposal and provides a real-life demo that can be used to be help with your application or idea. While mobile web application development might sound scary, learning a good foundation will allow you to become a seasoned developer crafting your applications to multiple devices on day 1.

This book is divided into four parts:

PART I: INTRODUCTION TO HTML5/JS/CSS

Part I starts off giving some historical background of HTML5, CSS3 and JavaScript and how they have been, and are applied to mobile devices. We break down the most used technologies in each area, including manifest cache, geolocation, and CSS3 – Rounded Corners. In addition, each section shows example code to help you get stated. We also talk about mobile UI frameworks such as jQuery Mobile and jQTouch.

Learning about the technologies provides a good background. But you also need to also know which devices the technologies support and their limitations. In Part I, we also discuss the operating systems and browsers that will power your mobile web application. While mobile browsers have come a long way, it's important to know how to deal with the various browser versions and the smaller screen-size to make sure your application behaves gracefully.

Finally, we provide some examples of companies that have embraced the mobile web-experience and what technologies they used to accomplish their mobile goals. These sites will give you a good idea of how closely web app developers can mimic the native experience.

PART II: APPLICATION SETUP AND INFRASTRUCTURE

In Part II, we begin to set up the frameworks on developing and deploying the sample application called Corks. Corks is a web-based mobile application that allows you to track and cellar your wine. You build it in this book using jQuery Mobile.

We discuss segregation of environments (development vs. production) and how to set up your local network to begin testing your mobile application using tools such as MAMP, XAAMP, and device simulators. In addition, we provide some examples of hosting options for your mobile application and talk about ways to reduce bandwidth using content delivery services (CDNs).

Finally, you learn about building mobile wireframes, which outlines the creation the sample application Corks. We outline the features, layout, and the structure of the application. You learn how important this stage is to your development cycle.

PART III: DEVELOPMENT

Part III covers a wide variety of HTML5, CSS, and JavaScript functions as you build out the functionality of the application. We discuss how to use geolocation to find wine locations and discuss ways to use Twitter to pull in conversations around any wines you have cellared.

Finally, you dig in the power of Web SQL, or web databases and local storage to keep your application persistent. This will help application users keep data even if the browser is not running the device.

PART IV: PERFORMANCE AND PRODUCTION

Last but not least, Part IV covers performance tuning. You start by reviewing best practices for optimization as well as generalized approaches for improving performance in all browsers. You also learn about tweaks you can make to the application to extend its use for your projects.

START BUILDING MOBILE WEB APPLICATIONS

This book discusses how to build, test, and maintain mobile web applications using HTML5, CSS3, and JavaScript technologies to deliver a rich and engaging user experience.

Smashing Mobile Web Development is geared towards front-end developers, but anyone with a grasp of HTML, CSS, and JavaScript can benefit from this book. Since *Smashing Web Development* focuses on using the latest and greatest technologies, having a basic understanding of JavaScript will greatly help you through the book. However, each code sample is explained thoroughly in order that any frontend developer can understand the material.

So let's start building mobile web applications and go cross-platform today!

INTRODUCTION TO HTML5/ JS/CSS

1

INTRODUCTION TO MOBILE WEB DEVELOPMENT

ABOUT 10 YEARS AGO, few people had a mobile phone, and if they did, the phone did not have a mobile web browser. Fast-forward to 2012. Almost 30 percent of the world's population now has some mobile device that enables them to browse the Internet, chat, or send text messages (source: `http://www.wired.com/gadget lab/2011/11/smartphones-feature-phones/`). Millions of people depend on their phones, not only as a device in which to hold conversations, but also to search, discover, and learn about new things while on the go.

With the total population of smartphones rising, businesses should be conscious about this opportunity to reach new customers. Once considered a luxury device, the smartphone is now readily available on most mobile networks at a reasonable price. In some areas, such as the United States, people use their cell phones as

their main phone lines instead of the once common landlines.

More and more people are browsing the web from their mobile phones, and businesses need to find a way to reach new customers by making their websites, now commonly known as "web apps," mobile friendly. Most companies develop websites for a desktop experience first; it's hard for them to go back and rebuild the same experience for the mobile platform.

This chapter discusses relevant background information about devices and design patterns for your mobile web app. It's important to understand these concepts at the start so you don't have to backtrack and redevelop your application to make it conform to the design standards for each operating system.

You also learn some new techniques to conquer device orientation, viewports, and custom fonts within mobile web application. Understanding these topics is essential to creating a great experience for your users. In addition, this chapter explores other popular mobile applications to provide guidance on the best practices and inspirations for your mobile web app.

Most people commonly think that it's very difficult to build a mobile website. The fact is that a mobile web browser has many tools and features that most people don't know exist. At the conclusion of this book, you will understand the concepts behind mobile web development and be able to design and develop your own web app using the latest technologies very easily.

MOBILE WEB EXAMPLES

You can learn and draw inspiration from a plethora of mobile websites. Sometimes it's even hard to see the difference between mobile web apps and native applications. The following examples demonstrate what you can do with the mobile web.

- **Facebook:** Facebook's user interface (UI) changed a lot over the last six to eight months, but its developers are committed to providing the best user experience no matter what device is being used. With a combination of CSS and HTML5 elements, Facebook developers were able to mask their native iPhone app to look similar to their web app. Facebook uses the geolocation element in HTML5 to grab your location and help you check into your favorite spots. To help the website load faster, the user uses caching on the browser HTML5. I touch on these features later in the book and explain how to use them in your own applications. The difference between the Facebook web app and native applications is so minimal that many users can't tell the difference. When this occurs, you know you've done your job right.

- **Twitter:** Twitter's UIs also changed significantly since launching in 2008. In fact, when the service first launched there was no official mobile app to use this service. Developers used the Application Programming Interface (API) from Twitter to develop the first Twitter applications that became popular on the market. Realizing that sharing 140 characters is important on both the desktop and the mobile device, Twitter changed the strategy to begin to develop mobile apps and websites to increase growth. What transpired was a brand-new mobile website that mimics the experience of browsing Twitter on a desktop computer. Twitter uses HTML5 features like off-line access, which gives you the capability to view tweets when you aren't connected to the Internet. They also use CSS3 transitions to ease navigation between pages. Also, just like Facebook, Twitter allows you to tag your location when you tweet, thus using the HTML5 geolocation feature. Since Twitter wasn't a mobile application when it first launched, it does have to compete with a bunch of native mobile applications maybe by third parties. This has allowed Twitter to acquire many companies to help build their current platform.

- **Foursquare:** Already having a flagship product in their native iPhone application, foursquare decided to make a simple web app to help people find information about the places they go. Foursquare uses HTML5 geolocation and input types that enable users to automatically call venues by clicking the phone number listed in the description.

■ **Financial Times:** Financial Times was originally a native application in the App Store when it decided it wanted to charge a subscription fee outside of iTunes. Because that didn't comply with the iTunes Terms Of Service, it had to be removed from the App Store. Instead of trying to work with iTunes, Financial Times decided to make their own HTML5 web app, which worked on every single platform. There was no need to develop a different platform for every phone. The Financial Times app pushed the boundaries of web applications by using HTML5 local storage, which allowed them to store and cache content in the background. It also incorporated off-line elements, enabling users to browse the web app when they aren't connected to the Internet.

■ **Yelp:** Similar to foursquare, Yelp provides a mobile website that allows users to quickly access a favorite spot, and get ratings, directions, and more information about restaurants. Yelp uses geolocation as well, including Google maps, to see what places are nearby. It also uses touch events to highlight rows when you select them, which is similar to native experience.

■ **Untappd:** Okay. I'm a little biased, because I created Untappd. Still, I think it's a great use of mobile technologies in the platform. Unlike other applications, Untappd was developed as a mobile first. This allowed us to see what we could and couldn't do with the platform. It also allowed us to reach multiple devices on day one. This helped us grow the platform and the service by gathering feedback from multiple users on multiple devices. Untappd uses local storage geolocation and other HTML5/CSS3 that attempt to blend the line between native and web.

UNDERSTANDING NATIVE VERSUS WEB PLATFORMS

Many people do not understand the difference between the native and web application. The main difference is that a native application is downloaded from an App Store and is written in different languages than web applications. Every device has its own proprietary language that is used to power the phone. For example, on the iPhone the language of choice is Objective-C; with Android devices, you program via Java. This is one of the downsides of native applications, because it requires you to hire a developer to build two different applications. That can be very costly. A common myth is that web applications don't look anything like their counterparts in the native world; yet with modern technologies, including HTML5 ESS3, and JavaScript, you have the power and the tools to make your applications look and feel native.

PROS AND CONS OF NATIVE VERSUS WEB PLATFORMS

Table 1-1 lists many of the pros and cons associated with the web or native platform. :

Table 1-1   Advantages and disadvantages of native platforms

Pros	Cons
Exposure and accessibility via an App Store	High cost to develop, upgrade, and support
Access to native features such as the Camera, Contacts, and network conditions	Code is deployable to one platform only
Monetization and revenue	Dependence on App Store restrictions and submissions

When choosing between a native and a web app, it's important to figure out your strategy for the application. If you're open to charging users for your application as a service, a native platform might work. There are many ways to get around this, including subscription fees; however, the base application will always be available on the web for free. However, some applications inhibit different pricing models that can charge at every level.

On the con side, developing an application for a native platform is very costly to build and to maintain. A common misconception is that once the application is built, you're done putting money into the application. This is wrong, because you have to continually update your application and that requires keeping a developer on retainer. Another negative side to native is its dependence upon the App Store or marketplace. When submitting your app to a store or marketplace, you are subject to all the restrictions that the company decides to place on applications. This means that at any time the employer application can stop you from making money and stop people from downloading your application. In addition, most App Store only give a portion of sales on your app. For example, Apple App Store and Google Play both take 10 percent of sales and the rest goes to the developer. While this may seem small, overtime this can grow at a rapid rate.

Table 1-2 lists the pros and cons associated with using the web platform for your apps.

Table 1-2   Advantages and disadvantages of mobile web platforms

Pros	Cons
Cheap, fast, and easy to build.	Performance tends to be an issue with intensive website pages running in the mobile browser.
Can be deployed to multiple platforms / devices, with the same code base.	Debugging and testing becomes hard to do on a mobile device.
Easy to perform maintenance.	Hard to monetize since there is no App Store.
Access to native features via third-party solutions, such as PhoneGap.	Even with PhoneGap, not all native functions are available.

Developing an application for the web can be rewarding. Making use of HTML5, CSS3, and JavaScript allows you to develop your application easily. Since these are common languages, the price of the application will be decreased. In addition, one application can be used across multiple platforms. This means your web app can work on an iPhone, Android, or BlackBerry device—all with one code base.

A downside to creating apps on the web platform is in the area of debugging and testing. Testing your web app in a desktop browser may lead to quick fixes on bugs; however, testing in a mobile emulator provides a more accurate assessment of how your web app performs. For example, with the desktop web browser the performances match the speed of the computer; on a mobile phone, however, your resources are strictly limited. Things like CSS3 transitions, which are a great way to show navigation between pages, require a great deal of memory to process. Pay attention to memory allocation; it is possible your web application will crash some browsers. While you have this situation with native applications, every Web Browser appears to perform different while native OS controls may be consistent across devices. For example, the web browsers in Android 4.0.x and Android 4.1 are very different and require different levels of debugging to get your content to display correctly.

In addition, the on-click event on the desktop web browser performs much faster than a tap on a mobile device. This is because the mobile browser sometimes waits to see if you're actually tapping a button or dragging your finger up and down the screen. This can cause a small delay when you tap links, buttons, and other attributes on your mobile web app. Luckily, there are workarounds to fix this problem. (I discuss them later in this book.). There are also other tips to make your web app feel more native including Home Screen and Full App modes on iOS and Android. These allow your web application to run without the chrome of the browser window.

WEB-TO-NATIVE SOLUTIONS

Some third-party solutions allow you to bring your web application to the native platform. This enables you to access native features that you aren't able to get when using your web browser. The camera is the most common feature that you aren't able to access via the web. Mobile Safari users are not allowed to upload files to the web browser; however, this restriction is lifted on other platforms. This inconsistency leads to problems when developing your application. It's important not that you can use file input types on Android to upload files file your file system, but it can't capture a current photo from your camera.

One of the most popular third-party solutions is called PhoneGap. This is the only open source mobile framework that supports seven platforms: iOS, Android, BlackBerry, webOS, Windows Phone 7, Symbian, and Bada. PhoneGap breaks down their API support into 10 different native APIs. This allows users to easily connect to the operating system and access the camera network, notifications, storage, files, and a whole lot more. The documentation is straightforward, easy to use, and can help you transition your web application to a native platform.

Many applications out there use PhoneGap to deliver their native platform to the consumer. One example is Untappd—where it took its web application and transformed it into a streamlined new application that allows users to take pictures of their beer and include them when they check in. Untappd was able to port its application to Android and iOS within a matter of months. The responses from the application were so tremendous, registrations for the month they released their native app were 10 times the norm. With PhoneGap, you can deploy your code to 10 different platforms. However, not every feature is consistent across every platform. PhoneGap has a great chart that explain all the features (`http://phone gap.com/about/feature`) of each platform. It's important to note that while you can use the same code to deploy to 10 different platforms, deployment of these apps to their stores might require additional software and steps. PhoneGap attempts to solve this problem by offering PhoneGap Build, which allows you to send your application code to PhoneGap Build which then provides you with app-store ready files. You can find more about PhoneGap build at `http://build.phonegap.com`.

Other solutions out there provide the same experiences as PhoneGap, but in our experience, PhoneGap has the best documentation for anyone to pick up and start coding. Pretty soon, people will be calling you an ILS Android developer when all you've done is code in HTML5, JS, and CSS3.

DEVICES AND OPERATING SYSTEMS

When developing for mobile, every developer must understand the number of devices an app needs to support. On a native platform, you can restrict devices based on the operating system that it's running on. On a mobile app, however, you don't have that luxury. You can detect the type of browser the user has; but you still might not know which device he or she is running. This is why it's very important to understand the different types of devices and operating systems. That knowledge will make your life a whole lot easier when developing for mobile.

- **iOS:** The iOS platform is a writer operating system from Apple. As of this time, the most current release is IOS 5.0.1. iOS runs on the iPod touch, iPhone, and iPad. One of the great things about the iOS platform is it is limited to two screen resolution sizes. All iOS devices come preinstalled with Mobile Safari, a WebKit browser. On Mobile Safari, any file upload control is disabled, preventing the user from uploading any files on a website. Prior to version 5, developers could not use overflow scroll elements, which are commonly used to create fixed top and bottom navigational bars. With the most recent release, web applications have become much more native with this new CSS element. Between October and November 2011, iOS market share rose from 26% to 43% (`http://techcrunch.com/2012/01/09/ios-marketshare-up-from-26-in-q3-to-43-in-octnov-2011/`).

- **Android:** The Android platform is available on a wide range of phones and is copyrighted by Google. It is an open source operating system, which means many phone designers and developers can take it and customize it to their own needs. A prime example of this is the Amazon Fire, which runs a custom build of Android, codename "Gingerbread," which is version 2.33. At the time of writing this book, the latest release was codename "Ice Cream Sandwich," version 4.0. All Android devices come with a standard WebKit browser. In version 1.5, developers could use overflow scroll elements to maintain a static header and footer. On the negative side, Android has multiple devices that run on this platform. With large and small screen resolutions, virtual and physical keyboards, and a native Back button, designing and developing for the Android platform can be a daunting task. Luckily, the Android emulator enables you to view your app at multiple screen sizes and with various operator versions. The emulator provides a great way to see what your app looks like on a phone. Android holds approximately 47% of the market share as of third quarter 2011. It's also important to note that since Android is an open-source platform, phone manufactures take the code and create custom versions of it to fit their devices and the service provider. This creates greater fragmentation, which can result in two different types of operating systems on the same phone. Google does offer the Samsung Galaxy, which is known by the developer community as "Vanilla Android" which means that is not altered in any way by the device creator. This fragmentation leads to many phones not being able to update to newest version. The majority of Android devise are still on 2.3.x which is almost two full version releases behind the latest release (Ice Cream Sandwich) at 4.0.x.

- **BlackBerry:** BlackBerry is often considered the third most popular smartphone. Like Android, BlackBerry has many different devices with many different screen sizes. Many BlackBerry devices have a physical keyboard with trackball. Recently, the company introduced touchscreen devices with virtual keyboards. As of BlackBerry OS6, all BlackBerry devices come loaded with a WebKit browser, which makes life a lot easier when developing for this platform. Prior to this version, all BlackBerry devices came with a non-WebKit browser. That said, most web apps today do not support anything lower than BlackBerry OS6.

- **WebOS:** WebOS is a platform that was designed and developed by Palm. Palm was acquired by HP in 2009 and has been committed to developing new phones to challenge Android, iOS, and BlackBerry. In 2011, HP decided to provide webOS as an open-source operating system with the hope that it would be an alternative to the Android for phone manufacturers. The most current version of webOS is 3.0.4. As of WebOS 2.0, all HTML5/CSS3 features are present in their WebKit browser.

- **Windows Phone:** In 2010, Microsoft wanted in on the mobile phone market and introduced a brand-new phone based on their operating system, called Windows Phone. The operating system that powers the phone is Windows CE. Unfortunately, this meant that the browser installed on the phone with Internet Explorer 7, while the current release is Internet Explorer 9. This left web developers struggling with how to design and develop for the platform because of lack of support for HTML5 and CSS3. In February 2011, Microsoft announced the release of the next version of the Windows Phone, codenamed "Mango." This update was significant because it allowed developers to access HTML5 and CSS3 features in the browser. However, with the newest version of Windows, phone developers are still unable to access some CSS3 features, including gradients. In third quarter 2011, the Nelson report of U.S. market share for Windows Phone 7 was only 1.2%.

The devices in this list are not the only ones out there, but they are the most common. When developing your mobile app for devices, the key thing to determine is whether the mobile device has support for modern browsers. Without this, you lack the basic HTML5 and CSS3 features that will make your app stand out. As we discuss later, there are many ways to determine users' browser agents and redirect them to a low-resolution version of your website if need be.

DESIGN AESTHETICS

The premise of mobile web development theory is to keep one code base across multiple platforms. Still, it is important to look at different design aesthetics that power the differences between each device. By paying attention to the details and designing your app to look and feel like a native app on a platform, you provide a much better experience for your users.

DIALOG BOXES

When designing for mobile web, you need to account for the bandwidth limitations of cellular networks. Certain processes may take no time at all to complete on a desktop web browser, but everything is different on a mobile device. As a best practice, always display the progress of some action on the screen. This can be done with a loading symbol or other methodologies. Without seeing this loading box, users may get discouraged with your app if they do not know whether it is currently loading.

IOS DESIGN PATTERNS

With iOS, typically most applications have two navigation bars: one at the top indicating the page you're currently on, and a navigation bar at the bottom, which has links to different pages. Prior to iOS5, there was no way to keep your top and bottom navigation bars static when the user scrolled the inner content between them. Now, by using the CSS3 property, `overflow-scroll: touch`, developers have the option to create native-like scrolling within their web applications.

ANDROID DESIGN PATTERNS

On Android devices, the general design pattern is to have an action bar at the top of the screen followed by a navigation bar immediately below it. Android devices typically lack a bottom navigation bar like those on iOS. This is because most Android devices have native buttons on the bottom part of their devices. When the navigation bar is placed on the bottom of the screen, Android users tend to hit them by mistake when pressing the native buttons on the actual device.

VIEWPORTS

Typically with a webpage on a mobile device, users are going to pinch and zoom to their heart's delight. When developing mobile applications, you use an HTML meta tag called `viewport`. This enables you to set a maximum or minimum width, depending on screen resolution, so the user cannot pinch and zoom on your web app. The viewport is set at the `<HEAD>` in an HTML document and supports the properties discussed in the following list:

- **Width:** The pixel width of your web application. The default value is 980. (Example: `width=320`)
- **Height:** The pixel height of your web application. (Example: `height=320`)
- **Maximum-scale:** A floating-point number between 0 and 10 to which defined that largest scale on your web application. The default value is 0.25. (Example: `maximum-scale=0.25`)
- **Minimum-scale:** A floating-point number between 0 and 10 to which defined that smallest scale on your web application. The default value is 1.6. (Example: `minimum-scale=1.6`)

- **Initial-scale:** A floating-point number between the minimum-scale and maximum-scale. (Example: `initial-scale=1.0`)
- **User-saleable:** A Boolean result that defines if the user is able to scale the size of the screen (for example, by pinch or zoom). The default value is True. (Example: `user-saleable=False`)

It's important to note that all width and height settings can be defined by `device-width`, which enables the HTML5 to adapt the width to the device's screen size. Following is an example of a `viewpoint` tag that can be used in a mobile web application.

```
<meta name="viewport"
content="width=device-width; initial-scale=1.0; maximum-scale=1.0;
 minimum-scale=1.0;
user-saleable=false;"/>
```

The preceding code sets the document's width to be the device's screen resolution. This is useful because users may decide to load the application onto a device such as a tablet, which has a large screen resolution. The scale is set to `1`, which means it will scale to the device width. A good way to visualize scale is to consider it a multiplier against your width. (See Figure 1-1.)

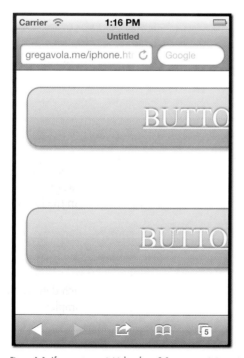

Figure 1-1: If you set your initial scale to 2.0, your app is increased by two.

The user-saleable property, by default, is set to True. For most web applications, you don't want the user to be able to pinch and zoom the content. This is because most native applications do not use this particular property; and their interface design scales to the current device. After all, if you correctly set your initial-scale, there is no need for a user to pinch and zoom on the app: Everything scales to the screen width. It's important to note that this viewport applies only to the initial page load, and can be changed by the user. Once the user reloads the device it returns to the last-known zoom.

ORIENTATIONS

Most modern mobile devices provide numerous ways to view a web page. Luckily for developers, the operating system of the phone rotates the web browser depending on if the phone is in a horizontal or portrait mode. It's the responsibility of the developer, however, to handle these events and make changes to CSS as needed.

```
<script type="text/javascript" language="Javascript">
        var supportsOrientationChange = "onorientationchange" in window,
            orientationEvent = supportsOrientationChange ? "orientationchange" :
"resize";
 window.addEventListener(orientationEvent, function() {
            alert('We just detected a screen resolution change!');
        }, false);
</script>
```

This code adds a document listener for a specific event that occurs across mobile browsers. Unfortunately, this event is not standard so you need to detect which event is on the device you're using. The first line the JavaScript allows you to detect if the events onorientation change are valid in the current window. If the browser supports this event, then use it; otherwise, the event name will be orientationchange or resize.

After you determine the name of the events of the device, set an event listener. It's enough to know that the browser logs certain events for JavaScript to pick up and perform an action upon. In this situation, when the device is rotated, the browser emits an event that JavaScript picks up. Every time this event takes place, you are displaying an alert that indicates it has detected an orientation change. In the previous example, you can replace this alert with something that is more useful based on your situation.

FONTS

With older browsers, fonts are pre-installed as part of the operating system. Currently, the standard fonts vary across mobile devices. With modern browsers, developers have a wide range of tools to display different fonts, depending on the design of their web app. These tools use JavaScript to replace the contents of an HTML element to a special property that is controlled by CSS to display the custom fonts.

For example, Google Web Fonts API provides an easy way to quickly change the default font to something that matches your style and theme. Google Web Fonts have a large range of fonts to choose from.

```html
<html>
  <head>
    <link rel="stylesheet" type="text/css"
href="http://fonts.googleapis.com/css?family=Tangerine">
    <style>
      body {
        font-family: 'Tangerine', serif;
        font-size: 48px;
      }
    </style>
  </head>
  <body>
    <div>This is test of Google Web Fonts!</div>
  </body>
</html>
```

In this example, a CSS file from Google, with a query string indentifying what type of font you would like to use is loaded in the HEAD section. When opening that link in your browser, you get the following syntax:

```css
@font-face {
  font-family: 'Tangerine';
  font-style: normal;
  font-weight: normal;
  src: local('Tangerine'),
url('http://themes.googleusercontent.com/static/fonts/tangerine/v3/
HGfsyCL5WASpHOFnouG-RD8E0i7KZn-EPnyo3HZu7kw.woff') format('woff');
}
```

Google uses a CSS3 property called @font-face, which allows your HTML document to contain special fonts that are not locally installed on the users' machine or device. Once loaded, the special fonts display on the supporting browser. For mobile devices, I recommend that you download these fonts to cache on your own site to maximize performance. It's important to note the Google Fonts API is compatible with all modern browsers, including Internet Explorer 6 and higher. It's important note that iOS supports only SVG fonts (which Google Fonts supports). However, other font libraries may not be supported. While Google Fonts is easy and supported, you can only use fonts that they have, so you can't have custom fonts that you may have purchased or downloaded elsewhere.

> *A great resource for* @font-face *is the fontsquirrel @font-face generate tool* (http://www.fontsquirrel.com/fontface/generator/) *which can help you generate the syntax for* @font-face *in your CSS file.*

SUMMARY

In this chapter we discussed an overview of mobile devices, platforms and different ways of interacting with the browser. In addition we discussed:

- Mobile web and native platforms
- Native versus web pros and cons
- Custom fonts
- OS design patterns

2

OVERVIEW OF MOBILE TECHNOLOGIES

IN THE WORLD OF TECHNOLOGY, something is always on the horizon. The use of smartphones and mobile browsers is on the rise, and new technologies that make that experience better are launching every day. The whole mindset of mobile web developers has changed from designing websites for users with a mouse to designing them for the pointer finger.

In this chapter, you learn all about the new technologies that are enabling this type of development. I touch on HTML5 features that enable users to find locations, detect network access, manage local databases, and access session and local cache. These features allow you to offer better functionality and experience to your users.

I also discuss CSS3 and the new properties that allow your mobile web app to look and feel native with properties such as box shadow, rounded corners, gradients, and background sizes to handle large resolution displays. A common misperception about mobile web development is that you need a graphic designer to design your site, but you can achieve a professional looking design by using some new CSS3 elements.

Finally, you can transition into the use of JavaScript frameworks that work well with mobile web browsers, including jQuery, Sencha Touch, XUI, and others. The chapter also talks about some utilities, such as Modernizr, iScroll, and JavaScript Template libraries, all of which you can use to help make developing your app a breeze.

HTML

Prior to HTML5, the standard HTML specification was dated December 24, 1999. The version was 4.01; however, most people just call it HTML. HTML5 has changed the whole landscape of web browsing. HTML5 brings new features to developers that were not available previously via a native browser. For example, development technologies, such as Flash, enable you to deliver things like video and interactive forms to the consumer. HTML5 you can use special tags to bring video to your webpage, without requiring the user have Flash on their device. This works well for iOS Mobile Devices, which do have Flash installed on their devices. The other benefits is that you don' t have to learn a new language to put video on your website, you can just use the HTML5 `<video>` tag.

HTML 5 introduces new attributes and elements that help define HTML documents through semantic tags. Prior to this point, anyone reading just the tags of an actual HTML document would not know where the header or the footer is. HTML 5 changes this by adding header, footer, and content tags that are easy to access and read by browsers and consumers.

In addition to semantic tags, HTML 5 brings other new features to the user in the form of databases, geolocation, and enhanced caching. These allow developers to access more features of the mobile device than they could in previous versions of HTML. And because HTML 5 is now standard, it is accessible from almost every mobile web browser.

KEY HTML5 FEATURES

While there are a lot of new features in HTML5 can power your application, there are a couple of key items that you will want to use in your mobile web application. These features allow you to push the boundaries of the browser, from caching files for offline storage to grabbing the user's location to send them local results. Depending on your application needs, you might use them all!

Using Geolocation Features

In the last couple of years, accessing a user's location information has become an important part of almost every web app or service. Developers gain the user locale to help developers do many things, including deliver local information, driving directions, and much more. HTML5 makes it simple to obtain location information and offers a few custom options, depending on what your application needs.

Geolocation from the web browser is very different than geolocation from the actual native device. According to the specification, geolocation from the web browser should use whatever is the best positioning method in the current situation. In theory, this should always be the GPS chip in the phone; however, in some cases the web browser detects location for mother elements, including cell towers and Wi-Fi signals. To learn how to use the functionality of HTML5, check out Table 2-1.

Table 2-1   Geolocation Methods in HTML5

Method	Description
`Navigator.getPosition(success, fail, options)`	Enables the developer to get the user's current location
`Navigator.watchPosition(success, fail, options)`	Enables the developer to determine if the user's location changes over a period of time

Location Method Options

Both `getPosition` and `watchPosition` enable you to pass in particular options depending on your need:

- `enableHighAccuracy` **(Boolean: true or false)**—If you set this property to `true`, you get the most accurate location. The downside of enabling this function is that it decreases battery life over time.
- `timeout (Integer, milliseconds)`—By default, there is no timeout in a geolocation request. If a location cannot be provided, it is good practice to set a `timeout` parameter in an integer to define the milliseconds before the function times out. Once a timeout occurs, the `fail` function of the method is called.
- `maximum (Integer, milliseconds)`—This option enables you to set the maximum age of your geolocation request. If the cached location that is called and the geolocation function is older than this value, a new location will be provided. Otherwise, the cached location will be supplied.

Location Callback Functions

If `geolocation` is successful, it calls `success` and passes it a `position` object that contains the attributes as shown in Table 2-2.

Table 2-2   Options Parameters for getPosition and watchPosition

Attribute	Type	Description
`Position.coords.latitude`	Double	Represents the latitude, in decimal degrees.
`Position.coords.longitude`	Double	Represents the longitude, in decimal degrees.
`Position.coords.altitude`	Double	Represents the height of the position, in meters.
`Position.coords.accuracy`	Double	Represents the accuracy level of the latitude and longitude. The higher the number, the more accurate the results.
`Position.coords.altitudeAccuracy`	Double	Represents the accuracy level of the accuracy.

continued

Table 2-2 (continued)

Attribute	Type	Description
Position.coords.heading	Double	Represents the direction of travel of the device. This is specified in degrees. If the implementation cannot provide this information, this attribute is returned as NULL.
Position.coords.speed	Double	Represents the velocity of the current device. If the implementation cannot provide this information, this attribute is returned as NULL.

If the implementation fails, the `fail` function is called and passes the object `err.code` and `err.message`, which contains the options described in Table 2-3.

Table 2-3 Error Responses for getPosition and watchPosition

Attribute (err.code)	Attribute (err.message)	Description
error.code.1	PERMISSION_DENIED	This error code is returned when users decline to share their permission with the website.
error.code.2	POSITION_UNAVAILBLE	Represents that a location could not be determined. This typically means that one or more of the location providers in the call produced error messages.
error.code.3	TIMEOUT	Represents that the location request has timed out. This can be returned only if you set a timeout option in your implementation of the method.

Using navigator.getPosition() to Locate a User Once

If your application requires you to gain the location of a user at a single point in time, this method provides you the tools you need to get that location.

```html
<html>
      <body onload="start();">            <div id="content"></div>
</body>
</html>
<script>
function start()
{
=if (navigator.geolocation) {
var options = {
enableHighAccuracy: true
};
```

```
navigator.geolocation.getCurrentPosition(onSuccess, onError, options);
}
else
{
var content = document.getElementById("content");
content.innerHTML("Geolocation is not enabled on your browser");
}
}

// success function
function onSuccess(position){
var content = document.getElementById("content");
var message = "";
var lat = position.coords.latitude;
var lng = position.coords.longitude;
        content.innerHTML = "Your latitude is: <strong>" +lat +"</strong>
and your longitude is: <strong>" + lng + "</strong>";
}
function onError(error){
        var content = document.getElementById("content");
        var message = "";
                (error.code) {
                case 0:
                        message = "Something went wrong: " + error.message;
                        break;
                case 1:
                        message = "You denied permission to this page to
retrieve a location.";
                        break;
                case 2:
                    message = "The browser was unable to determine a location:
" +
error.message;
                    break;
                case 3:
                    message = "The browser timed out before retrieving the
location.";
                    break;
        }
        content.innerHTML = message;
}
</script>
```

This script applies all the logic covered in the preceding sections to outline the correct implementation of the geolocation.getPosition method. The script requests users to obtain their location, and then displays the latitude and longitude in the DIV with the ID of content. If there is an error of any kind, the code determines the cause of the error through a switch on the err.code property and displays the error message to the user.

Using navigator.watchPosition() to Continuously Locate a User

Unlike `getPosition`, which gives you a one-time position of the user, `watchPosition` provides continuous updates of a user's location. The implementation can be used if your application wants to detect whether the user has physically moved and needs to capture movements. `watchPosition` has the same options and methods as `getCurrent`, but the setup uses a different syntax:

```
var watchID = navigator.geolocation watchPosition(success, fail, options);
```

When using `watchPosition`, it is a good practice to set a timeout in your options; otherwise, your method will keep running and draining the user's battery. `watchID` uses a numeric ID that is represented with your `watchPosition` function. You can use this variable to terminate the implementation with the following:

```
navigator.geolocation.clearWatch(watchId);
```

When the implementation of `watchPosition` is successful, behaves the same way as `getPosition`. `watchPosition` will also often return a more accurate result than `getPosition`. This is because the first result is often more of a rough estimation, which gets refined over time with `watchPosition`. However, it is more battery intensive for obvious reasons.

Setting Storage Options

With HTML5, developers have better tools for storing data; even when the web browser is closed, a mobile device is restarted. HTML5 storage has two implementations that give developers storage options that live inside the DOM of the web browser. You can use these implementations to save passwords, application settings, authentication tokens, HTML caching, and more.

Using the localStorage and sessionStorage objects

The `localStorage` object stores data that is not removed until the developer initiates the removal or the user clears his or her browser cache. You should use `localStorage` whenever you save application settings that you don't want to be removed when users end their session, such as closing the web browser or rebooting their phone.

With `sessionStorage`, the data is not persistent and is removed once the browser or tab is closed. You cannot use `sessionStorage` when a file is run locally. When you want to store items that are meant to expire, such as counters or checkout carts, this solution provides you the flexibility of not having to delete the keys on exit.

Both `localStorage` and `sessionStorage` store values in key/value system and have the same methods and syntax. The only difference is that you use the `localStorage` versus `sessionStorage` namespace depending on your needs.

Both objects have three methods: `setItem`, `getItem`, and `removeItem`, which set, get, and remove the key that you are initializing. To save a value to a key in `localStorage`, write the following code:

```
localStorage.setItem("key", "value");
```

When you want to obtain the value for a key, use the `getItem` method, as shown in following code:

```
var yourKey = localStorage.getItem("key");
```

It's good practice to always check if the key is initialized in `localStorage` before setting or deleting it. Here's the code to do that:

```
if (localStorage.getItem("books"))
{
        // Great, "books" exists as a key in our local Storage object
        var bookTitle = localStorage.getItem("book");
        document.write("The Book Title is: " + bookTitle):
}
else
{
        // Looks like "books" could not be found, so we are adding it
        localStorage.setItem("books", "Smashing Magazine");
}
```

The preceding code checks to see if the `"book"` key exists. If it does, it extracts the value of the key using `getItem`, and then prints out the results to the browser window. If it doesn't exist, it uses the `setItem` method to initialize the key of `"books"` to the value of `"Smashing Magazine"`. Alternatively, if you want to remove the key, if it exists, you could use the following code:

```
if (localStorage.getItem("books"))
{
        // Great, "books" exists as a key in our local Storage object, let's removing
        localStorage.removeItem("books");;
}
```

Taking Advantage of the Application Cache

One disadvantage of a mobile web application is that it requires users to download all the files they need every time they load the web app. The HTML5 Application Cache enables you to store your files on the users' devices so they don't have to download your app every time they launch it. The capability to perform this level of caching on a mobile device provides three key benefits:

- **Offline browsing:** The application loads resources from the cache, so there is no need to connect to a server to download them, which allows the application to be used offline.
- **Performance and speed:** Because no data connection is required to download files, the speed and performance of your application increase.
- **Reduced Bandwidth on your server:** Since the files are loaded, the server will not have to serve files for every request unless they are changed.

In order to use application cache in your application, you need to create a file called `Cache Manifest`. In this file, you outline sections that tell the browser what files to cache and which ones require a network connection. To include this file, you must append it as an attribute in your HTML tag, like the example shown here:

```
<html manifest="mycachefile.cache">
..
</html>
```

The cache file can be a local or absolute file, and this attribute needs to be present on every HTML in order to use the application cache. The file extension of your cache can be anything; it doesn't have to conform to the preceding example. The only requirement is the attribute must be named `manifest`.

In addition, it's important to add a mime-type of `text/cache-manifest`. This ensures that the server reads the manifest file properly, based on your file type extension. For the preceding example, you need to add the code to your `.htaccess` file in the root directory of your application:

```
Addtype text/cache-manifest.cache
```

The cache manifest file contains three sections, which are all optional. At a basic level, a manifest cache is written like this:

```
CACHE MANIFEST
index.html
style.css
img/myLogo.png
js/main.js
```

All cache manifest files must begin with the `CACHE MANIFEST` and then list, with a separate line item for each, the files that need to be cached. In the preceding code, all the listed files are stored in an application cache and used in the future, without having to reload the information. It's also important to note that the store limit on application cache is 5MB.

It is possible to expand the use of the manifest file into the three sections described here:

- CACHE: This is the default section that is implied if there are no other sections defined in the document. All files listed under this section are to be cached no matter what network condition is present.
- NETWORK: This section defines elements that are not to be cached and requires network connection to load. These files would be any scripting files that require server-side rendering or API-facing URLs.
- FALLBACK: This section defines fallback files in case a certain resource is not available. You can use this in cases where a network connection is not present; a backup file can be used to indicate the network connection to the user.

If you want to use all three sections to produce a manifest file, the code looks like this:

```
CACHE MANIFEST
CACHE:
index.html
style.css
img/myLogo.png
js/main.js

NETWORK:
script.php
login.php
/script/*

FALLBACK:
main.php simple.html
*.html offline.html
```

In the example file, you see the same CACHE section defined earlier. The NETWORK section defines some scripting files that require a network connection to run. These files will not be cached. Finally, the FALLBACK defines some offline elements that should be used if the first file is not available. For example, in the first line under FALLBACK, if main.php is not available or is unreachable, so simple.html will be displayed. You can also define wildcards such as * that apply to all contents of that folder structure.

Updating Cache

As you make changes to your cache files because of updates, constantly check and tell the user to reload the cache in case a new version available is available. Once data is cached, it isn't removed until one of the following occurs:

- The user clears the browser cache
- The manifest file is edited or removed
- The cache is removed via a script

To check if one of the files in the cache has been updated, you can use the following script after the DOM has loaded successfully:

```
window.addEventListener('load', function(e) {
        window.applicationCache.addEventListener("updateready", function(e){
                if (window.applicationCache.status ==
window.applicationCache.UPDATEREADY) {
                        window.applicationCache.swapCache();
                        if (confirm("We have detected a new version of the
website.
                        Do you want to load it?")
                        {
                                window.location.reload();
                        }
                }
                else
                {
                    // nothing has changed, do nothing!
                }
        });
});
```

Here, when the application is first loaded, UPDATEREADY listens for the application cache status to change to update ready. If this occurs, the script downloads the new cache and swaps the cache to the new version. It then asks the user to load the new version, which loads the new script.

It's important to note that cache manifest file is cached at the bit level, meaning that if you change anything in the manifest (even adding a comment) that the browser will recache everything.

CSS3

CSS stands for Cascading Style Sheets, which define properties and attributes that HTML elements use in order to be displayed on a page. CSS3 is a new version of the syntax that helps designers and developers create rich elements without having to use complex JavaScript, Images, or Flash to display content the users.

It's important to note that CSS3 is not consistent across all browsers. Table 2-4 shows three types of browser frameworks that are used across all browsers.

When building web apps, you should always know your target device. If you want to target Windows Mobile (which runs IE7 Mobile), you need to know what CSS3 functions it supports. Many tools can detect the type of operating system and features that are available. These tools, which I discuss later in this chapter, can help with your development process.

Table 2-4   Browser Frameworks

Browser Framework	Example of Browsers	CSS3 Support?
Gecko	Mozilla Firefox, Mozilla Firefox Mobile (Fennac)	CSS3 support is fully supported as of version 4.0 and higher. All CSS properties must be prefixed with -moz.
Webkit	Apple Safari, Apple Safari Mobile, Google Chrome	CSS3 support is partially supported, depending on the browser version. The latest versions of all browsers should support all CSS3 features. All properties must be prefixed with -webkit.
Mosaic	Internet Explorer, IE Mobile	Most CSS3 functionality is not available via Internet Explorer. Internet Explorer 9 and higher does have support for most CSS3 features; however IE9 is not available on a mobile browser at the time the writing.

KEY CSS3 FEATURES

CSS3 comes with a wide array of features to help you design a faster and better looking website. The goal of CSS3 is to enable developers to design their websites using HTML elements rather than relying on JavaScript libraries and images. Let's take a look at some of the key features of CSS3 that you can start using right away in your web apps.

Box Shadow

The CSS3 attribute `box-shadow` enables you to create a drop shadow effect around a box, to make it appear like it's hovering over elements. (See Figure 2-1.)

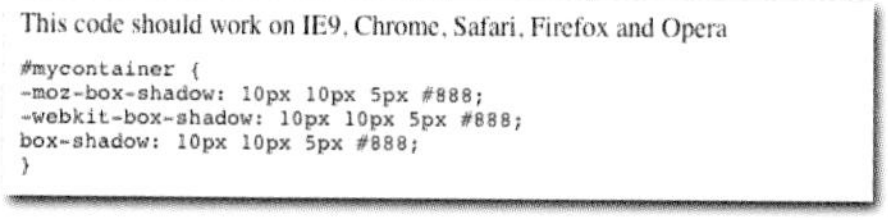

```
This code should work on IE9, Chrome, Safari, Firefox and Opera

#mycontainer {
-moz-box-shadow: 10px 10px 5px #888;
-webkit-box-shadow: 10px 10px 5px #888;
box-shadow: 10px 10px 5px #888;
}
```

Figure 2-1: Create a drop shadow with the CSS3 box-shadow attribute.

To enable box shadow on your elements, you need to add the following syntax:

```
box-shadow: none | <shadow> [ , <shadow> ]*
```

This can be applied using the following code:

```
box-shadow: 10px 10px
box-shadow: 10px 10px 5px #C1C1C1
box-shadow: inset 5px 5px 5px 5px #C1C1C1
box-shadow: 0px 0px 5px 5px #C1C1C1, 0px 0px 5px 5px #C1C1C1, 0px 0px 5px 5px
   #C1C1C1;
```

Although this may seem complicated, if you break down the requirements it becomes very simple. The first step is to define the shape of the shadow that you want on top of your element. You can do this by specifying two to four length values.

1. The first value defines the horizontal offset of the box shadow. The number can be negative or positive, depending on your need to offset the shadow.

2. The second value is the same as the first, but on the vertical axis. If the number is negative, it's offset from the top of the element, and vice versa for a positive number.

3. The third value is optional and defines the blur distance of the shadow. You can't add a negative number for this value, but the larger the value that you enter, the more the shadow's edge will be blurred. There is no default, so if this value is not set, no blur will be set for your box shadow.

4. The fourth value, again optional, defines the spread distance of the shadow. This value can be negative or positive, with a larger value causing the shadow to expand in all directions while a negative value impacts the contrast.

After you set the two to four length values, you can supply an optional color to the shadow. The default is #000, or black.

Depending on your need, you can always play around with the length requirements. For example, if you are attempting to create top header bar on your mobile web app and you want to have a box shadow below it, use the following code on your header element. The output is shown in Figure 2-2.

```
#myheader {
        -moz-box-shadow: 2px 2px 2px 2px #888;
        -webkit-box-shadow:  2px 2px 2px 2px #888;
        box-shadow:  2px 2px 2px 2px #888;
}
```

Figure 2-2: The results of applying box-shadow on the header box in the preceding code are shown here.

This code applies a 2px shadow with a 2px blur and 2px spread shadow. It gives you a header that appears to be hovering over the content below it.

A great website to define the different browser extensions is `http://css3please.com`. The website allows you to create cross-browser CSS3 rules, without having to type all different extensions for each browser, such as webkit, moz, and so on.

Rounded Corners

In the days before CSS3, most rounded corners within boxes on websites were created by using a combination of JavaScript and background images. With CSS3, making rounded corners is easier than ever. To make a box with rounded corners, add the following syntax:

```
border-*-*-radius: [ <length> | <%> ] [ <length> | <%> ]?
```

Here are some examples:

```
border-radius: 10px;
border-top-left-radius: 10px;
border-bottom-left-radius: 75%;
```

Notice that `border-radius` can be defined using percentage or pixels, depending on your need. You can also specify the top, left, or bottom variables using the preceding examples.

You can supply up to four values to each property, similar to `box-shadow`. When you specify the border you want to round, such as `border-top-left-radius`, the four values are defined as the horizontal, vertical, quarter ellipse, and the curvature of the corner. When using the generic `border-radius` property, the four values define the horizontal radii for all four corners. If you only use one value, it is applied to all four corners.

It's easy to make rounded corners for a gray box for your mobile web app like the one shown in Figure 2-3. Just apply this property to the element you want to round:

```
#rounded-box {
        width: 250px;
        margin: 50px auto;
        text-align: center;
        padding: 25px;
        background-color: #c1c1c1;
        border-radius: 10px;
}
```

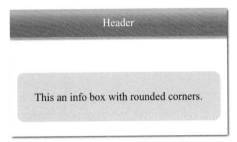

Figure 2-3: Rounding corners give your web app an updated look.

You can also define rounded corners using shorthand, by just defining all the attributes in a single line. To remember which variable corresponds to which, you can use the "trouble" order, or top right, bottom, and left. Here is a good example:

```
border-radius: 10px 10px 10px 10px;
```

Gradients

Before you dive into the syntax used with gradients, consider what gradients look like on mobile apps. As you can see from the example in Figure 2-3, a gradient is defined as a mixture of colors that blend, creating a "glossy" effect on an element. Prior to CSS3, this had to be created via a background image, which took a while to load. Since there is no image load, CSS3 gradients are great for spicing up your web app to make it appear more modern.

The syntax for gradients is a little confusing. This example looks at only the linear version of gradients that is used most in mobile applications. The syntax slightly differs for Firefox, Safari, and Chrome.

- **Firefox:** -moz-linear-gradient(<point> || <angle>, color-stops)
- **Safari/Chrome:** -webkit-linear-gradient(<point>, color-stops)

For example, using the following code snippet, you can set the background gradient differently with Firefox and Safari/Chrome browsers:

- **background:** -moz-linear-gradient(top, #00abeb, #fff);
- **background:** -webkit-linear-gradient(top, 00abeb, fff);

A linear gradient enables you to specify colors to blend together. Creating color palettes is a little tricky when it comes to gradients. Following are tools that easily generate gradients for you:

- **CSS3 Gradient Generator:** `http://gradients.glrzad.com/`
- **ColorZills Ultimate CSS Gradient Generator:** `http://gradients.glrzad.com/`
- **Microsoft CSS Gradient Background Maker:** `http://ie.microsoft.com/ testdrive/graphics/cssgradientbackgroundmaker/`

It's important to note that when you define gradients, you need to account for browsers that can't support them on your mobile device. To do this, you need to set a default color for your background, such as one of the ones shown here:

- **background:** `-moz-linear-gradient(top, #00abeb, #fff);`
- **background:** `-webkit-linear-gradient(top, 00abeb, #fff);`
- **background-color:** `#c1c1c1`

If you structure the code as shown here, and your web-app loads on a browser without gradient support, the browser will load the background color a light grey, instead of showing nothing at all. This can help with usability with buttons on older browsers.

CSS3 Selectors

With CSS, you can select element and their attributes to define styles. With CSS3, the framework introduces new selectors to help you provide a greater deal of granularity when selecting elements. The majority of the new selectors allow you to target specific elements or classes within your structure. For example, you can target all the odd children in a row in a table, like so:

```
tr:nth-child(odd) td {
background-color: #c1c1c1;
}
```

This code finds every odd row and applies the background color to each item in that row. This is a much easier syntax to use than the one provided in previous version of CSS.

There are a lot more selectors that you can use to help create cleaner code. You can find all the valid CSS3 selectors at the W3C website (`http://www.w3.org/TR/selectors/`).

Transformations

Previously, transitions in your browser could only be called with heavy JavaScript methods. With CSS3, you can transform, shade, and translate elements with ease. One of the important methods is *key-frames*. Key-frames allow you to create animations by gradually changing from one class to the other. In a mobile web application, you can use this affect to help with the transition from one page to the other. To use key-frames, you first define the usage:

```
@-webkit-keyframes mymove /* Safari and Chrome*/
{
from {top:0px;}
to {top:200px;}
}
@-moz-keyframes mymove /* Mozilla*/
{
```

```
from {top:0px;}
to {top:200px;}
}
```

In this code, you are just setting the direction of this transition so that it moves from the top of the page (0px), to 200px down the page. While this code creates the transitions require-ments, you need to initialize the requirement for it to take place in your browser. To do that, you need to apply the transition to the element.

```
#myBox {
-moz-animation:mymove 5s infinite; /* Firefox */
-webkit-animation:mymove 5s infinite; /* Safari and Chrome */
}
```

This code starts the transition by assigning the `mymove` property to the element. The attrib-utes that follow specify the duration of the transition (5 seconds) and when to stop (in this case it will go on forever since it's infinite).

An important thing to note about CSS3 translation properties is their effect on mobile browsers. On a desktop, the browser has access to more CPU and RAM, while using many 3D elements on a page can cause slow performance on a mobile browser. Use only the methods that you need to make your application function, because overusing the properties may cause your web application to slow down or even crash.

JAVASCRIPT

JavaScript was around prior to HTML5; however, the elements that can be triggered using JavaScript have improved greatly due to the new properties within CSS3. Numerous JavaS-cript libraries or frameworks help you program faster and easier. Most JavaScript libraries are not formatted for mobile, meaning that they have tons of code for cross-browser capability, such as IE6, that won't be necessary when developing for mobile. The larger a file size, the slower your application will load. It is best to use a library that fits your needs but doesn't come with a lot of extra overhead.

JQUERY

jQuery is one of the most popular JavaScript frameworks on the web. It contains simple methods that help you implement complicated CSS3 functions, such as `CSS3-Rotate`, `CSS3-Animations`, and more. The downside to this library is that it is 31KB. Although that may appear small, there are a lot of references to IE6 code in this script that you never use for mobile development. This can create slower load times when loading the application for the first time.

XUI

XUI is an up and coming JavaScript framework, built by Brian Leroux (a member of the development team for PhoneGap). The goal of this project is create a simple-to-use framework that has syntax similar to jQuery's, but has a smaller footprint for mobile devices. Compared to the 31KB file size of jQuery, XUI is 4.2KB and contains most of the same features of jQuery. If you are looking for similar syntax and a smaller set of features with a small footprint, XUI will fill that void.

ZEPTO

Zepto is another XUI-like framework that focuses on providing a syntax similar to jQuery's, but it is targeted for WebKit browsers only. Although the script file is around 5 to 10KB, depending on your use of its plug-ins, it contains most of the important mobile methods that are contained in jQuery. The downside is that the scripting language is targeted to only WebKit browsers, so Windows Phone 7, Mozilla Firefox Mobile, or other non-WebKit browsers do not have support from this framework.

JQTOUCH

jQTouch is a plug-in for either the Zepto or jQuery framework that enables you to create UI elements and JavaScript functions in your web app. Just like Zepto, this is targeted to only WebKit browsers. This framework requires you to use jQuery or Zepto plus this library, so depending on your needs, it may be too much. The upside is that it has tons of great CSS3 animations built in so you can make your application feel more native with page transition, full-app mode, and more.

UI FRAMEWORKS/UTILITES

When you are building mobile web apps, you have tons of frameworks to help you build the UI without having to hire a designer. These UI frameworks help make your application look and feel native using cross browser technologies and CSS3 properties. For older browsers that may not support these features, there are utilities libraries that help you determine if certain JavaScript or CSS3 functions are available to the user.

SENCHA TOUCH

Sencha Touch has touted itself as the best HTML5 Mobile Web App framework. It has built-in support for many browsers; it supports iOS, Android, and BlackBerry 6+, meaning that it has support for non-WebKit browsers. Most developers consider Sencha Touch to be the kitchen sink of JavaScript frameworks. It contains both UI and JavaScript methods, but unlike other frameworks that I mention, it doesn't have the same syntax and may be confusing to a first-time developer not well versed in object-oriented JavaScript programming.

JQUERY MOBILE

Released in late 2011, jQuery Mobile is a plug-in for jQuery that enables developers to make rich web apps without having to touch a line of CSS. The framework brings the power of jQuery to mobile with specific methods and functions that are formatted for mobile use. jQuery Mobile includes easier ways to detect screen orientation, and provides swipe events and full navigation using the jQuery History plug-in. The downside to this framework is that it requires jQuery (31KB) and weighs in at an additional 24KB. Although this is a powerful framework, be careful about bandwidth and load times with larger frameworks.

MODERNIZR

Modernizr takes the pain out of cross browser development for mobile or the desktop experience. Detecting if a browser has certain HTML5 or CSS3 functionality can be difficult, but Modernizr makes it easy. The tool enables you to build basic if...then statements to determine whether certain features are available for use. Once the JavaScript utility is initialized, it scans through all the HTML5 and CSS3 features of the browser and adds them as a class to the BODY element, as you see in Figure 2-4. Once this is applied, detecting CSS3 and HTML5 functionality is as easy as writing the following code:

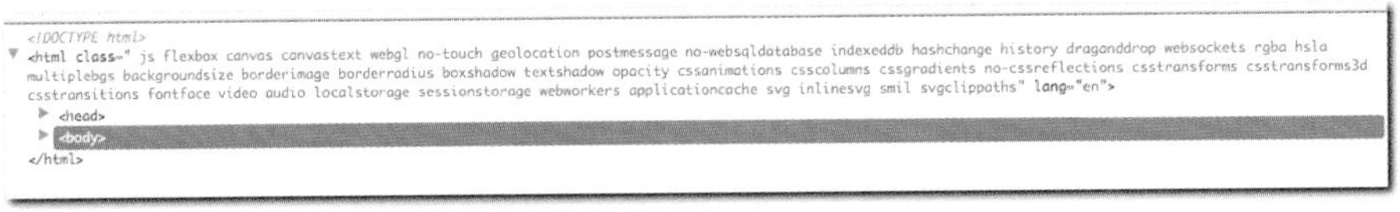

Figure 2-4: Using Modernizr to detect HTML5 compatibility

```
if (Modernizr.localstorage) {
        // the browser is compatible with local storage!
          return true;
} else {
        // handle backup functions here as localstorage is not supported
          return false;
}
```

ISCROLL

Prior to iOS 5, there was no way to have a bottom and top bar in Safari, because the CSS property overflow: scroll was disabled. As of iOS 5, this CSS feature has been enabled; however, it has a few bugs that Apple needs to sort out. To ensure that users with iOS 4 can use your application, there is a handy JavaScript library called iScroll. When it's enabled, you have a static top bar and bottom bar within your web application. iScroll is not written in jQuery, so you have no dependencies on any frameworks. While nothing is perfect, iScroll provides a great solution for pages with static content and provides easy syntax to give you a native feel within your web app.

If you need you use iScroll, but your content elements are a variable height (meaning that you are dynamically adding content), you can easily use the built in the methods of iScroll to refresh the scroll area. For example, if your content looks like this:

```
<div id="scrollarea">
<div id="page1"></div>
<div id="page2"></div>
<div id="page3"></div>
</div>
```

Once content is placed inside of `page1`, you need to refresh `iScroll`'s height to make the entire area scrollable. You can do this like this:

```
function onCompletion () {
        // Here modify the elements inside of page1
        setTimeout(function () {
                myScroll.refresh();
        }, 0);
};
```

Once you have completed this, your content area will be refreshed and you can apply the same logic when performing on other areas of your application.

MUSTACHE/JAVASCRIPT TEMPLATES

Mustache is a JavaScript template library that helps developers work with JSON objects instead of having their data source return HTML. When you make a network call to gather data from mobile devices, it's best to keep the payload, or the return data, as small as possible. JSON, or JavaScript Object Notation, is a string of characters that can be transformed into any array to pull in data. Most of the popular social networks, including Facebook, Twitter, and foursquare, and APIs, use JSON to return data.

With Mustache, you can build simple templates in HTML and then compile them with the data from JSON. For example, say you receive a JSON string with the following elements:

```
data  = {
        first_name: "Greg",
        last_name: "Avola"
}
// you can create a Mustache template with that data, like so:
<div id="mustache_tmp">
        <p class="first">{{first_name}}</p>
        <p class="last">{{last_name}}</p>
</div>
```

When compiling the HTML with Mustache, it replaces the areas inside the double brackets `{{}}` with the property matched to the object inside your data source:

```
<script>
        var content = $("#mustache_tmp").html();
        // data appears in the previous example
        var newTemplate = Mustache.to_html(content, data);
        $("# mustache_tmp").html(newTemplate);
</script>
```

The preceding example uses jQuery to gather the HTML inside the `DIV` of `mustache_tmp`, and then uses Mustache to convert that HTML using the JSON data structure. Once the content has been added, jQuery is used to add that HTML back into the `DIV`.

While it doesn't seem practical in this situation, it can save you from writing out by hand the HTML in JavaScript when obtaining the JSON object. It also saves some time on your server without having to return HTML. Mustache has a lot of other features, including logic and loops that help you easily build out a list of data with a few lines of code.

SUMMARY

This chapter discussed different topics around HTML5 markup, JS and CSS3 that can help developers with their mobile applications. While this chapter provides reference material to be used in your projects, it also discussed the following topics:

- Geolocation
- Cache manifest
- CSS3 selectors
- Rounded corners
- Mobile/UI JS frameworks (such as jQuery, Zepto, and so on)

APPLICATION SETUP AND INFRASTRUCTURE

3

DEVELOPMENT AND PRODUCTION SETUP

FOR EVERY DEVELOPER, having a sufficient development and production environment is the key to success for any project. When you are building a mobile application, having the right tools to test your application can make the difference when it comes to creating a good user experience. You don't have to hire an IT guy to help you set up your environments. You can do it yourself without breaking sweat.

This chapter talks about the differences between development and production environments and discusses the tools you need to manage, develop, and deploy your web app. You get insight into how to create a local development site on your machine so that you can quickly test features as you develop them. It also discusses basic tools that can help you develop and test your application, such as iOS and Android emulators, Firebug, code IDEs, and more.

In addition, the chapter talks about the infrastructure components you need to make sure your web app can scale from 1 user to 10,000 users without skipping a beat.

This chapter will help you accomplish the following goals:

- Learn the difference between production and development environments and understand the need for both.
- Create your own local development environment using tools for Windows and Mac OS X.
- Learn about emulators, IDEs, and browser tools to help you develop your app faster and be more efficient.
- Discover production infrastructure solutions and scaling for your mobile web app.

DEVELOPMENT SETUP

In the old days, the idea of setting up an "environment" scared developers because it meant asking IT system administrators to create a new server so the developers could work on it without affecting the live site. Nowadays, developers can use their own machines to develop and test in real-time without any fear of affecting the production application.

Think of coding environments as different geographic areas of the application. They contain the same code base, but the underlining data (from a database) is static. The goal of separating these environments is to allow code development and testing to take place without affecting your live version of the site. Table 3-1 compares the pros and cons of segregating your environments.

Table 3-1   Pros and Con for Segregated Environments

Pros	Cons
Allows development in a secure area without fear of breaking existing features	Multiple code repositories require tools to keep each environment in sync
Local development is an easy and cheap solution to get started	Local machines have a hard time simulating scale or "live" experience
Wide range of free tools to help you get started quickly	

When dealing with two different environments, it's essential to make sure code is up to date. Nothing is worse than having more than one environment out of sync with the rest of the codebase. You can use tools to help manage iterations of code, called repositories. The most popular repositories are SVN, or Subversion, and GIT. Both provide different feature sets that can help when it comes to keeping everything organized.

While GIT and SVN maybe appear to do the same task, there are fundamental differences between the two. The main difference is that GIT offers distributed version control, while in SVN it is centralized. While GIT and SVN both have a centralized repository or server, GIT is intended to run in distributed mode which allows developers to each have their own working copy of the code. On the flip side, SVN is intended to be a centralized code based on a server and not on the user's local machine. Having a distributed version control environment can very helpful especially when users have no network connection, they can still commit code. The distributed environment is also great for open-source projects, as it allows everyone to work simultaneously and send a pull request to the whole team, without the code getting lost in transport.

IMPLEMENTING LOCAL HOSTING

Because most modern computers give you the capability to host your own website locally for testing, doing so is the easiest and cheapest solution for your mobile web app. Many free tools that are available for Macs and PCs provide out-of-box installation of your local server. The goal of local hosting is to install a web server on your local machine so you can listen to an HTTP port on your local machine to serve HTML files.

Most of the tools discussed in this chapter revolve around the Linux, Apache, MySQL, and PHP (LAMP) stack, which is one of the popular stacks for web apps. Although you will not be using the database and PHP scripting language for the application you build in this book, the tools install the Apache web server that you can use to help load your website on a mobile device.

SETTING UP MAMP (FOR MAC OS X)

Mac, Apache, MySQL, and PHP (MAMP) is a Mac OS X application that enables you to quickly fire up the needed clients to help you start developing.

To set up MAMP on your Mac, follow these steps:

1. **Open your web browser and navigate to** `http://mamp.info` **and download MAMP.** For this demonstration and your purposes, download the free version. As of Version 2.0.5, the Professional and Free are bundled together.
2. **After you install the application, navigate to your Applications folder in Finder, and locate and open the MAMP folder.** (See Figure 3-1.)

Figure 3-1: Locate MAMP in your Applications folder.

3. **In the folder, you should see the MAMP application icon. Click to open it.** The MAMP User Interface for MAMP gives you some controls that help you start and stop the services that are included with the build. (See Figure 3-2.)

Figure 3-2: From the MAMP user interface you can work with the services you need to include in your application.

MAMP also should open a Start page that provides more details about your installation. This information is important, but if you want to use MAMP for server-side languages such as PHP, the most important is the URL in the address bar. It should look like Figure 3-3.

Figure 3-3: The URL in the address bar

The term *localhost* refers the local IP address of the machine, while the number after the colon refers to the port on which the web server is listening. In this case, the web server is listening on port 8888.

4. **Go back to your MAMP folder in your Applications in Finder and open the** `htdocs` **folder.** This is the root directory of your web server, so create an `index.html` file, as shown in Figure 3-4, and start testing. After you create the file, open it in your favorite text editor (which I discuss later in this chapter), and type following code:

```
<html>
     <h2>Hello World!</h2>
</html>
```

Figure 3-4: The index.html file of your
MAMP web server instance

5. **Save the file and reopen it in your web browser and point to your browser to** `http://localhost:8888.` You should see Hello World.

You now can do all your code editing in this directory and then obtain your IP address to do testing on your mobile phone. To access the site on the phone, type the IP address of the machine that you installed MAMP on and include the port 8888 after that. You should be able to view the `index.html` page on your mobile device.

XAMPP FOR WINDOWS

Windows users have a similar tool, XAMPP. This tool is available for all operating systems, but it is the best solution for Windows environments. Just like MAMP, XAMPP installs the LAMP stack on your computer so you can run a local server to perform development. Follow these steps:

1. **Go to** `www.apachefriends.org/en/xampp.html` **and click the link to download XAMPP for Windows.** (See Figure 3-5.) As of the writing this book, the most current release is 1.7.7.

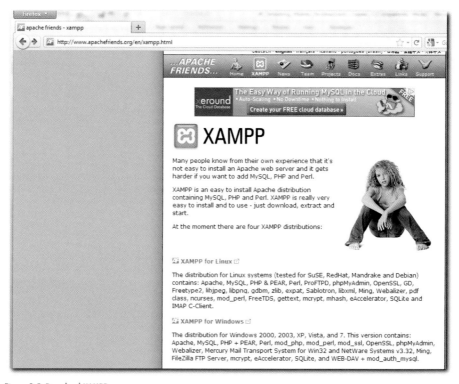

Figure 3-5: Download XAMPP.

© 2002-2012 Apache Friends, Imprint

2. **After you download the Installer, begin the installation process for XAMPP.** As shown in Figure 3-6, you are asked if you would like to run some of the applications as a service. This means that these processes will automatically start up when the computer is running. This is a good way to use the web server without having to remember to run commands to start it every time you power off your machine. However, for this book, select Install Apache as Service. After installation, you see a XAMPP Admin Control box on the bottom-right corner. It indicates the services that are turned on as well as their status.

3. **Click the Admin button next to Apache to get started.** (See Figure 3-7.)

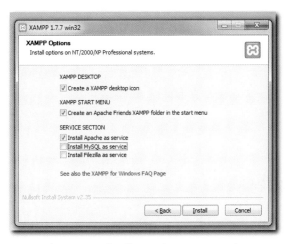

Figure 3-6: The XAMPP Installer offers you the option to run applications as services.

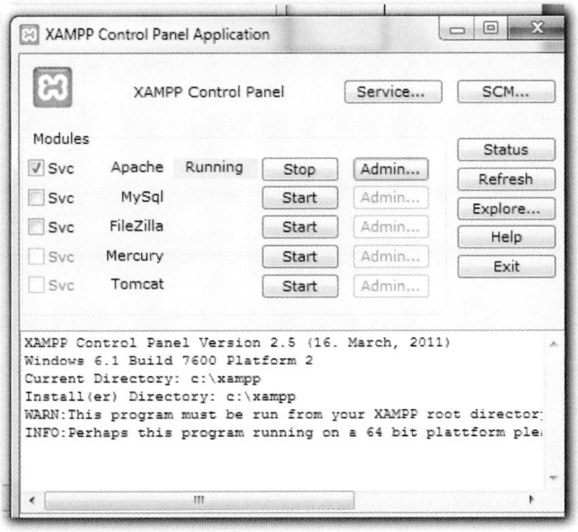

Figure 3-7: Launching Apache's help files

This launches the Help files and provides you with the URL. By default, XAMPP installs listening on port 8080.

4. **To start adding your own files to your web server, open up My Computer, navigate to the installation directory (by default,** c:\xampp), **and open the** htdocs **folder. Then open** xampp, **and in that folder, create a new folder called** mysite. (See Figure 3-8.)

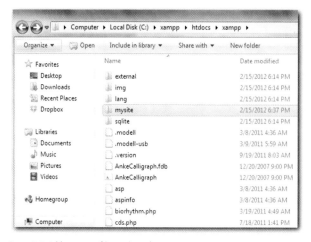

Figure 3-8: Add your own files to the web server.

5. **After creating the folder, create a new file called** `index.html` **and add the following code in your favorite text editor:**

```
<html>
     <h2>Hello World</h2>
</html>
```

6. **Go back to your web browser and navigate to** `http://localhost/xampp/` `mysite.` You should see the HTML code you entered. (See Figure 3-9.)

Figure 3-9: Hello world in your browser

USING IDES TO WRITE YOUR WEB APP

With HTML/CSS/JS, you don't need to use a fancy code editor to write your mobile web app. All you need to do is use your local text editor on your computer to start writing code. WordPad, Notepad, and TextEdit for Mac all work perfectly fine for writing code. However, using IDEs or code editors can help you breeze through the development process. Take a look at some for each operation system.

TextMate (Mac OS X)

TextMate is one the best text editors for Mac OS X. It includes many features: code completion, syntax highlighting, and bundles, for instance. Bundles are third-party snippets of code that you can use when developing your application. They help you quickly write code that you reuse through the application, such as `IF/THEN` blocks and standard HTML templates.

TextMate has bundles for HTML/CSS/JS so you will never be left in the dark when developing your web app.

One important feature in TextMate is the auto-complete option for basic HTML syntax. Within TextMate, a setting at the bottom of the window enables you to set the syntax depending on the document type. It auto detects the language based on what you type, which is even better. After HTML is selected, you can type *style* and TextMate will automatically spit out the relevant HTML syntax, as shown in Figure 3-10.

Figure 3-10: TextMate generates your HTML syntax.

Coda (Mac OS X)

For Mac users, Coda is often considered the Godfather of all text editors. It has everything from coding documentation to a built-in FTP client. Coda, shown in Figure 3-11, has all the features mentioned previously.

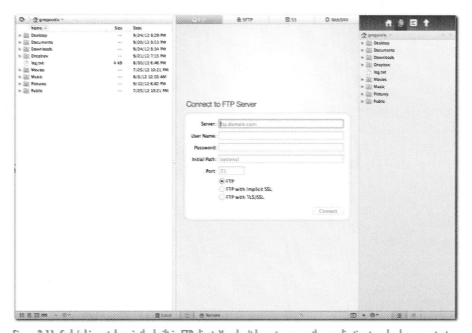

Figure 3-11: Coda's biggest draw is the built-in FTP client. You don't have to use another application to upload your content.

Coda also has "books," which contain documentation depending on the language that you are using. This is helpful when coding certain JavaScript or HTML5 elements without having to refer to search engines like Google for questions on syntax. In addition, Coda also has a built-in code version system that enables you to post your code to GIT or SVN, which can be helpful because you don't have to use multiple applications to commit your changes.

Sublime Text (Windows/Mac OS X/Linux)

Sublime Text is another great text editing application that gives you control when developing your code. Sublime Text is available for Windows, Mac, and Linux operating systems. As of the time of writing this book, version 2 is currently in public beta; it has some amazing features that keep your hair on your head when coding. A great feature within Sublime Text is that it has a mini-map, which enables you to see your code from 25,000 feet. (See Figure 3-12.)

With the mini-map, you can quickly scan through your code and make changes. This saves you from doing complex Find and Search functions within the file. It also gives you an idea of how your code looks as though it is printed on pages. Most programmers work with line numbers, but sometimes knowing a file is three pages long can help you find and fix mistakes.

Another great feature of Sublime Text is that it auto saves your files as you are working, so you never have to worry about losing your code. Finally, it has an in-line spell-checker to prevent you from releasing your web app with misspelled words.

Figure 3-12: Sublime Text offers the mini-map feature.

NotePad++ (Windows)

Every Windows user knows about NotePad, the simple Windows text editor. We have all used NotePad to keep notes and even do some coding. NotePad++, shown in Figure 3-12, is an enhanced version of NotePad — upgraded to make it a powerful code editor.

Like other text editors, NotePad++ has syntax highlights, code snippets, and other useful functions. However, NotePad++ remains true to its predecessor and keeps the layout simple and clean. For a developer who prefers having all the features without bells and whistles in a simple user interface, NotePad++ is a perfect client.

TESTING YOUR CODE

Unlike the testing process involved in building sites for desktops, debugging for mobile can be quite complicated. With web browsers, you might be able to view the source code, make some changes with Firebug, and then quickly retest. With mobile development, having the right tools can help you make testing your web app a breeze. Take a look at the following handy tools and programs that will enhance the experience of HTML5 web-app development.

When doing testing, you will hear the two terms very often — *simulator* and *emulator*. Although technically they do the same thing, some differences set them apart. A simulator is software that intends to duplicate the experience of a process in all possible ways, while an emulator attempts to duplicate the actual system so it can behave like the actual system. For iOS, the simulator gains the CPU and RAM of the host machines so the results are not going to match what the device intends to produce. On the other hand, Android Emulator has to be set to a certain RAM and CPU so it can act like the actual device. Emulators are typically slower than simulators for this reason.

iOS Simulator

Apple makes the best simulator to use when developing for iOS. As part of XCode, the IDE for iOS (see Figure 3-13), users get a simulator that loads an iOS device on their desktops. With iOS Simulator, developers can view any version of iOS in either iPad or iPhone format. This is helpful for testing your application versus Retina and non-Retina displays.

The downside is that it requires you to have Mac OS. It won't work on Windows or Linux machines. Windows or Linux users can use Apple's Safari browser and change the browser's user agent to act like Safari Mobile. This gets you as close as possible to viewing your application as it would appear on a mobile device. There are other solutions, including Flash emulators; however, the experience degrades and isn't as consistent as Safari for Windows. If you want a better experience without having to purchase a MacBook, you can test your web app using your iPod touch or iPhone.

In addition to simulating an iPhone or iPad experience, the iOS Simulator can also simulate memory and CPU warnings and how they affect your web applications. With desktop machines, a web developer rarely thinks about memory and CPU usage; however, within mobile development, it's important to keep these in the front of your mind. It is certainly possible to crash Mobile Safari by running complex JavaScript functions or CSS3 transitions (or both simultaneously). You can test for this in the iOS Simulator by initiating a memory warning, and then code around those changes. It's a great way to prepare for the worst with your web app.

Figure 3-13: The simulator loads an iOS device right onto your desktop.

Another important feature of the iOS Simulator is that you can enable Debug Console in Safari. You can access this by going to Settings→Safari→Advanced→Debug Console. Using this, you are able to see CSS, HTML, and JavaScript errors as the page loads, as shown in Figure 3-14. Sometimes you get warnings that may not have any effect on your web app; however, this tool is a good way to detect JavaScript errors that will stop your application from fully loading.

If you want a web-based simulator, you can use sites such as Testiphone.com and iPhone4Simulator.com. However the experience degrades significantly from the emulator is packaged with XCode. Most of these websites are written in either Flash or HTML5, and provide you a good example of what your application will look like, but do not give an adequate representation on functionality and performance.

Figure 3-14: The Safari Debug Console lets you see errors as the page loads.

Android Emulator

If you are used to the experience of the iOS Simulator, the Android Emulator experience is very different. Android Emulator, shown in Figure 3-15, can be installed on any operating system, but many tweaks are required to get it running properly. To use the Android Emulator, you must download the Software Development Kit (SDK) for the version you want to work with. (With iOS, the SDK is prebundled with previous versions, while the Android Emulator doesn't include any previous SDKs.) Depending on what version of Android you are targeting for your web app (most standard web apps support 2.1 and higher because of enhanced HTML5 support), you will need to download all active versions of the OS prior to testing. (See Figure 3-15.)

Figure 3-15: Using the Android SDK Manager.

To use the emulator, you must create Android Virtual Devices (AVD) within the Android SDK Control Panel. An AVD is a virtual device that is customizable by the developer. When creating an AVD, you first need to specify the OS version, then the screen size and memory. Once created, that AVD is stored and can be used in the future by selecting it from the Control Panel. For web apps, the main differences between Android OS Version 2.1 and up usually have to do with the screen size. The browser functionality rarely changes. However, for HTML5 features such as Geolocation, every phone is different so it's important to test on all versions that are currently in production.

The process of creating your first AVD is a little confusing, so let's walkthrough the steps of creating your first image.

1. **Locate the SDK extract that you downloaded from Android's website.** If you haven't downloaded the latest SDK, you can do that here: `http://developer.android.com/sdk/index.html`.

2. **Extract the contents, open the Tools folder and then click Android.** The Android SDK and AVD Manager should open.

3. **To create a new AVD, click the New button on the top right.** Give your AVD a unique name and set the target. The target should be the model you are testing for you, such as Android 2.2 or Android 4.0.4. You can always create multiple AVD as needed. You can also add other settings such as SD card, Skin and other hardware components.

4. **Click Create AVD.** Your new AVD should appear in the previous window.

5. **To launch the AVD, just click the AVD you want to launch and click Start.** At this point you should be able to use this Emulator to perform any action you wish to try out.

Safari/Chrome/Firefox

Because you are developing a web app, making it work in a standard browser is your first task. Safari and Chrome are based on the WebKit framework and Firefox on the Mozilla framework. If your application works on these browsers, you will be in good shape when viewing your application from your mobile device.

These browsers have a wide range of developer tools, including the option to change your user agent, which can test your code for different browsers. As discussed next, these browsers also provide you with the capability to change your CSS using their developer tools in real-time. This can help you debug CSS issues or test how an element's gradient or property looks next to your other elements.

Firebug

One of the powerful tools in web development is Firebug — a plug-in for Firefox and Google Chrome. On the surface, it enables you to inspect and change HTML and CSS elements quickly on your page — but it also lets you track AJAX and XHR processes to debug your remote URL calls. (See Figure 3-16.)

Figure 3-16: Inspect HTML elements with Firebug.

With JavaScript, if you miss a semicolon, the whole application will fail to load. Firebug will point out the line and failure, which can help you fix the problem quickly. Other developer tools might have this feature, but Firebug is the most accurate in displaying fatal JavaScript errors. On a mobile device, you can turn on Debug mode to see errors; however, it isn't as easy as viewing it from your browser, where you can click the error and see the entry line that caused the web app to fail to load. (See Figure 3-17.)

Figure 3-17: Click the error to see the point of failure.

Because most web apps use AJAX as their primary way of obtaining remote data, Firebug becomes an essential tool in debugging the response from each call. When developing, it's common to make a mistake when parsing a JSON object from a Twitter or Flickr API. With Firebug, you can inspect the response to determine the properties that you need to incorporate in your code.

In Figure 3-18, taken from foursquare, you see how you are able to drill into the responses of a query that returns venues that are around a user's last check-in to get recommendations. Using this tool is great way to find out values and properties returned from an API or a remote data source.

Figure 3-18: Drilling through query responses in foursquare

In addition to Firebug, both Chrome and Firefox have built-in tools that allow you perform the same functions as mentioned earlier. The native developer tools provide the same results as the Firebug, but display them in a different manner. We encourage you to try them out and find out what works best for you.

Mobile Console Tools

While it's nice to have these tools at your finger tips for desktop browsers, it's a different story on then mobile front. Since you don't have access to write to the console, or install Firebug on your device, you can use other tools to find out what is going on under the hood.

For iOS, you can use a product called Winere, which is a tool that allows you to see real-time XHR and HTML elements on your iPhone. The product was developed for use with PhoneGap Project, but can be used for Mobile Web application as well.

On Android, you can use the console inside Eclipse IDE to help debug common problems. Typically, you can use `console.log` to output variables to determine their values and then view the console to see the results. The console doesn't allow you to see HTML; however, you can use Chrome's developer tools to change your browser's user agent to look and feel like a mobile device.

SETTING UP THE PRODUCTION ENVIRONMENT

Now that you have your development environment set up and have your tools in your back pocket, it's time to discuss what type of infrastructure you need for the production or public version of your web app. Depending on the activity and involvement of your web app, you need to pick the level of server performance that your application needs to run. In this section, I talk about the hosting, infrastructure, and bandwidth solutions you can use to make sure your web app can scale from one user to one million users.

HOSTING

There are few types of hosting for your web app. The following list compares the price, features, and scalability of some popular options.

- **Shared hosting:** Vendors include GoDaddy, BlueHost, and Media Temple — and the price is low. A shared hosting solution means that you are sharing resources with other members on the same server. If another user on the server has a spike in traffic, your application suffers. This is a low-cost solution for users who have very low traffic or activity on their service.

  This hosting is usually offered in service-managed plans, so the user doesn't need to manage the server or make updates. An end user will see a Control Panel user interface and can make any changes without having to log into the server through SSH.

- **Virtual Private Server (VPS):** Offered from Media Temple and Rackspace Medium, VPS solutions range from being medium to high in price depending on the size of the server you purchase. The difference between VPS and Shared is you are now guaranteed a minimum and maximum CPU, hard drive, and memory for your instance. It is still on a shared server, but only in its private instance.

  In this hosting option, the server is self-managed and the user is usually responsible for installing and upgrading new versions and patches. Some companies offer service-managed plans; however, this is usually more expensive.

■ **Cloud:** Offered by companies such as Rackspace and Hosting, these hosting options can range in price from high to low because price is computed on usage instead of a flat rate. Cloud hosting has become a very popular choice for startups because the prices are variable depending on what you use. Unlike the other options, cloud hosting charges only when your servers are on and running. They also allow you to be flexible and scale your servers to new memory and hard drive space as you need it.

With cloud hosting, you manage everything with servers, from what OS to use to applications to install. Unlike VPS, there is no pre-installed software. The end user must do it all.

Depending on your application's need, you can select the solution that works for you. For high activity services that require users to make status like updates, a cloud solution would work well. It gives you the capability to scale up your resources depending on the activity level. In addition, if you don't use all your resources, you pay only for what you use, which helps your bottom line.

INFRASTRUCTURE SETUP

The downside of going the cloud route is the level of skill required to set up the servers. As mentioned previously, most of the infrastructure is self-managed. Self-managed servers mean that you must install your web servers, database, and so on. Some companies offer a managed solution, but this option comes with a significantly higher price.

Table 3-2 lists the common infrastructure setups that you can choose, depending on your application:

Table 3-2   Types of Infrastructure Setup

Infrastructure Setup	Complexity	Description
Single server	Simple	A single server keeps all your apps in one place. If your app requires a database, it lives within the application code. The resources are shared within your web server, database, and application code.
N-tier	Complex	This separates the different parts of the app into their own dedicated resources. For example, you would have all your application code, database, and web server on separate machines. This allows dedicated resources to be reserved and each machine to be scaled depending on usage.

For more basic web apps, a single-server solution provides a solid framework to start. As your app grows, you can always migrate to an n-tier system, depending on your needs. Although an n-tier system gives you flexibility over your environment, it is complex to maintain and manage within a small team. Without proper tools, you will find yourself searching for the problem longer than it takes to solve it.

MANAGING BANDWIDTH

Every web app has static files that need to be served every time the app is launched. When this occurs, your server processes these files and sends them to the client, which incurs bandwidth charges on most hosting providers. These bandwidth costs grow over time, depending on the usage. When serving static content, such as images and CSS files, it's a good practice to allow services called Content Delivery Network (CDN) to deliver the content to lower your bandwidth and load times.

These CDNs cache the files on the web browser, which enables users to load the content faster. Amazon Simple Storage Service (S3) provides solutions for storing your images and CSS without affecting your hosting bandwidth or your hard-drive space. Big social network websites such as foursquare and Untappd use Amazon S3 to store the profile avatars, logos, CSS, and other images. The prices for storage and bandwidth are usually much lower for your hosting solution.

Of course, you can always use the Manifest Cache to cache your static images, JavaScript, and CSS. It won't affect your bandwidth on your server and offers great performance before the files load off the local device. This may be the better option, depending on your needs, especially if your app doesn't need to regularly be checked for an updated image or CSS. Just remember that a Manifest Cache requires the users to allow content to be stored on their devices and it has a limit.

SUMMARY

In this chapter, you learned about setting up your environment to start building your mobile web application. In addition this chapter discussed the following topics:

- Debugging tools
- Building your own web server on your local machine
- Hosting and bandwidth solutions for mobile apps
- Software tools for writing code (IDE, text editors, etc.)

4

CREATING THE PROTOTYPE

THE REST OF this book gives you a guided tour of building your own web app based on all the latest HTML5, JS, and CSS3 features. The app that you build in this book is a wine app called Corks. Corks enables you to keep a cellar, or local database of all your wines, share to your social networks, and use geolocation to scan around you for wineries. All these features are built using the HTML5 technologies I discuss in Chapter 2.

This chapter discusses mockups, design, and wire framing for the different pages and navigational elements. It also introduces an HTML5 mobile boilerplate that can help you define the structure of the HTML elements and offer some handy JavaScript functions to get you started very quickly. Finally, it discusses using HTML5 hash change events that can help control the use of a user's Back button on the web browser.

In the demo used in this chapter, you use jQuery Mobile for the CSS3, jQuery as your JavaScript framework, and iOS Simulator as your testing ground. By the end of this chapter, you will be able to:

- Identify the required pages and HTML5 elements
- Design and mock up the user interface for each page
- Understand the navigation using HTML5 hash change events

USING HTML5 TO AID IN STRUCTURE AND DESIGN

One of the hardest things to do when developing your web app is to create a good template and structure that you can replicate throughout the pages. You can save time and be more efficient if you use HTML5 boilerplates that enable you to create HTML5 structures and handy JavaScript functions.

Creating a template or boilerplate can help you build faster and effective code. A lot of times, developers skip this step and end up spending a lot of time backtracking to add new features or increase the scope of a project. Doing it right the first time always saves you from headaches in the future.

USING THE HTML5 MOBILE BOILERPLATE

Using a pre-structured HTML5 template will help you easily start developing and keep your structure clean. Paul Irish, who was involved with the jQuery Project, invented the HTML5 boilerplate framework for desktop browsers, and more recently made this very popular boilerplate available for mobile devices. To obtain the kit, follow these steps:

1. Go to `http://html5boilerplate.com/mobile` and click Download Boilerplate. At the time of writing this book, the current version is 3.0.
2. When you open the zip file, copy the following files as shown in Figure 4-1 to another folder on your computer.
3. Open the project in your favorite software editor, and click the `index.html` file.
4. Lines 79 through 83 hold the JavaScript code for Google Analytics, which you should remove for this example. If you want to reuse it in the future, just change the `UA-XXXX-X` to your correct site from Google.

That's it! Now that you have your structure set up, you code everything in a single HTML file. You just create new HTML sections to represent pages. To provide back button support, you use a method called `onHashChange` to change active status of each `<div>`, which is discussed later in the chapter. All section content is placed within the parent `<div id="container">` area of the script, as shown in Figure 4-2.

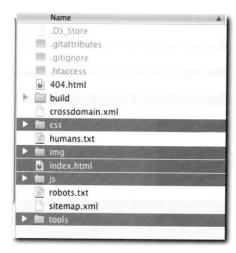

Figure 4-1: Zipped contents in the folder view

```
<div id="container">
    <header>
        Top Header
    </header>
    <div id="main" role="main">
        Content
    </div>

    <footer>
        Footer
    </footer>
</div> <!--! end of #container -->
```

Figure 4-2: The index.html page to use for layout

APPLICATION DESIGN

As discussed in Chapter 1, whether you design a native application or a web application depends on the type of device on which users will view your app. Since the example app is made for mobile only, you use the one-code base methodology to deploy this code to all platforms. This app uses static top navigation and provides the content underneath. As you scroll, the navigation becomes fixed and always remains at the top of the screen. (See Figure 4-3.)

Keeping the top bar fixed enables users to scroll down the page and change to another page without having to scroll back to the top of the page. Additionally, the fixed bar doesn't affect Android menus or back buttons since the main navigation bar is at the top of the page. This is standard design pattern for modern web apps, including Twitter, Facebook, and Untappd.

Figure 4-3: Navigation elements always remain at the top of the screen.

MOCKING UP YOUR PAGES

An important part of the design process is mocking up what the pages will actually look like and how they will function. This process can help you understand which features you need and which features don't make sense. During the course of development, an idea may seem like it can work with your product, but producing mockups can demonstrate that it doesn't fit with your theme. Mocking up your pages can help you develop your app faster and avoid the temptation to put things in that don't fit.

Because you have the basic structure in place, you need to plan the pages that you will be creating to support your application. As discussed at the start of this chapter, Corks has are the following goals:

- Record and save the wines you have in your cellar (using SQL-Lite, local storage)
- Query a wine locator (using geolocation)
- Use social APIs (using AJAX, JSON)
- Create web app settings (local storage)
- Enable searching for and adding wines

Each Page involves a different aspect of HTML5. Because you will be using HTML5 SQL-Lite, you keep all the data for the user in the browser. This will be retained unless the user removes all the data from his or her browser. In the following sections, I discuss each page and introduce a mockup for visual learners.

SETTINGS/ABOUT

On the settings page, you give your users the capability to clear the database in case they want to start over and erase their data. This feature will request that users confirm the changes and then erase any wines that they have currently created.

This page holds static information about the app, its features, and contact information for the app owner. You could also include a help section on features for users learning how to use the application. You use HTML5 input types to enable a user to dial a phone number or send an e-mail from your web app. (See Figure 4-4.)

In this example, you are going to add a simple tool to change your display name within the application. This helps the user define who is using the application and give it a personal touch.

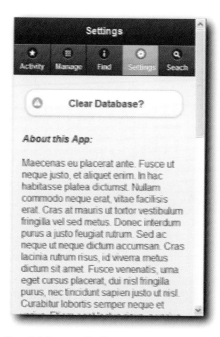

Figure 4-4: Setting up the About page

Because the main point of the application is to add wines to a "virtual cellar," the process of adding, viewing a timeline, and viewing wines will drive users to use your app. The following sections break down each of these sections for a better idea on how they will interact and use features of HTML5 to deliver a solid experience.

Cellaring a Wine

To start, users must be able to add a wine to their cellar. The second tab on the top navigation enables users to add a wine to their cellar through a simple process. The page shows a Search box that enables users to search for a wine. If there is a match, the users can select the wine and enter the quantity they have in their cellar via a pop-up box, with an optional box for a comment about this wine.

Figure 4-5, 4-6, and 4-7 show the example or mock-up of the Manage Wine screen where users can add wines to the database. Subsequently, the user can add a wine to their cellar right away so it appears in their activity.

Figure 4-5: The Manage Wines main screen

Figure 4-6: Additional view of the Manage Wines main screen

Figure 4-7: Add a wine to the cellar.

If no wines are found, the user can use the Search functionality by tapping Add Wine, as shown in Figure 4-8. This enables the user to create a wine using a form. Users enter the name of the wine, winery, alcohol content, and color to quickly add the new wine to their cellar.

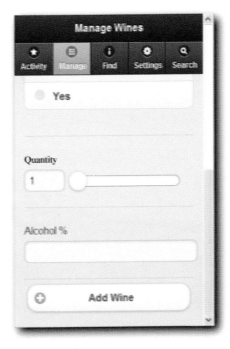

Figure 4-8: Search for wines.

Using the Cellar Timeline

The first tab on the top navigation is the Cellar Timeline. This is a list of all the wines you have added to your cellar, sorted in descending order of being added. You can tap on each item in the list to view the individual wine information page that we discuss later in this chapter. At the top of the feed, a Select button enables users to change the sort of the results based on Name Ascending, Name Descending, and Date Added. (See Figure 4-9.)

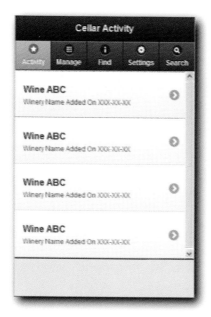

Figure 4-9: Example view of the Activity main page

This project uses SQL-Lite to pull in a query from the local database using the options set by the Select button at the top of page. These settings define the parameters of the query and how to display the results.

Searching for a Wine

The far right button on the top navigation bar enables you to search your wine database. Tapping the search icon displays a search bar below the navigation bar. It will appear superimposed over the content so it will not interrupt your browsing. (See Figure 4-10.) Searching for a wine will take you to the search list page that shows a list of wines that match your results. Tapping the wine will give you the option of adding this wine to your cellar or viewing more information. (See Figure 4-11.)

Figure 4-10: Example view of the Wine Search page

Figure 4-11: Example view of the Wine Search Detail page

Individual Wine Page

On the Cellar Timeline, tapping on any wine displays the individual information on that wine. On the page, you want to show the user the name of the wine, the ABV, color, and winery. When the user adds the wine to his cellar, the page also shows the date it was added along with space for an optional comment. The Cellar Timeline also provides an option for adding a wine to the cellar. (See Figure 4-12.)

In addition, every wine page will have a link to Twitter, which enables the user to scan the social network for tweets and stories about the wine name. The link will open up a new window that will search Twitter using the API and return the results for the selected wine. A back button on the top right enables the user to go back to the preceding page.

Figure 4-12: Example view of the Wine Detail page

Wine Location Search

The goal of the wine location search is to find wine shops within a user-defined radius. This app uses the Google Maps API to gather the data and display the results on a map. The page shows Google Map objects with a GPS Location symbol at the top. (See Figure 4-13.)

When the user navigates to this tab, it gathers the user's location and sends a query to Google to obtain a list of wine shops within a 10-mile radius. The returned results are parsed and added as map markers and scattered along the map. The map is centered on the user's location, and different markers are also placed around it, indicating their proximity to the user's location. (See Figure 4-14.)

Figure 4-13: Example view of the Wine Location page

Figure 4-14: Example view of the Wine Location Detail page

If users leave the Wine Location Search page and return later, the data remains consistent; however, the users can touch the GPS icon to recycle the search to return new results based on their new location.

DEFINING HASH NAVIGATION

It's important to define how the site will navigate. This app uses AJAX to pull data for the database, so you need a way to keep a history of your pages without actually having pages. This enables users to navigate between pages in the app without having to refresh the entire document.

With AJAX and the HTML5 structure, the pages won't actually be pages in the form of separate HTML documents. Each page will live in a `<div>`, which represents a page. All pages are tracked within separate `<div>`, so you use an HTML5 method called `hashChange` to track changes to your navigation. A hash is represented in the URL as shown here:

```
http://example.com/#wine-page
http://example.com/#activity
```

When a user taps a link that triggers the hash change, the script detects there has been a hash change event and fires some custom code. Here is an example of one way to code for detecting page changes:

```
<script type='text/javascript'>
// whenever the onhashchange event is fired, the locationHashChanged function is
executed.
window.onhashchange = locationHashChanged;
function locationHashChanged() {
        // this function passes in the location variable, which contains the hash
(#wine-page)
\var hash = location.hash;
// based on the hash, you can fire particular code
if (hash == "#wine-page")
{
// hides all DIVs with the class of page
$(".page").hide()
$("#wine-page").show();
}
}
</script>
```

The preceding script detects any changes to the hash in URL and then fires the custom function called `locationHashChanged`. This tells the JavaScript to load based on what the hash defined. To make this work, all links will include this hash change in the `href` attribute of your links, as the following code demonstrates:

```
<li>
        <a href="#wine-page">
            ....
        </a>
</li>
```

Every time a user taps the anchor tag, the script detects the change, hides the current page, and makes the `#wine-page` visible. At this point, you run some scripts to pull information in about the wine that you selected.

The power of using the `onHashChange` method is that you have a fully functional back button in your web app without having to code anything special. Once the back button is tapped, the same script runs again and shows the `<div>` that matches the hash name. As long as you give all your `<div>` elements the following structure, the `onHashChange` function you wrote earlier will take care of the rest.

```
<div id="page1" class="page">
        ....
</div>
<div id="page2" class="page">
         ....
</div>

<div id="page3" class="page">
         ....
</div>
```

Hash change events are very popular on both mobile websites and desktop websites. Twitter uses hash change events to direct to the correct page in order to serve the content via AJAX.

Figure 4-15 shows the hash symbol followed by the username. It will serve content based on what follows the hash, which is `gregavola` in this example. Whenever the page is changed, it reloads the content based on the hash. When the user fires the browser back button, the reverse process occurs, as we describe earlier in this chapter.

It's important to note that `onHashChange` isn't supported in all browsers, so it will depend on your target platform. JQuery Mobile supports degradation so it will work with other devices that do not support `onHashChange`. You could always use the following code to detect usage:

```
if ("onhashchange" in window) {
  //...
}
```

Figure 4-15: At Twitter.com, the URL view shows the hash
in the address bar.

PUSHSTATE NAVIGATION

In addition to `onHashChange` events, HTML5 also has a History API that enables
you to change the URL without refreshing the page. It essentially works the same as the
`onHashChange` events; however, the URL actually changes the call you are making.

The method is called `pushState`, and it enables you to push the URL to the address bar, but
load the page without reloading the entire website. This is the default page navigation system
of jQuery Mobile. This method changes your URLs of each page from:

```
http://example.com/#page1
```

to

```
http://example.com/page1.html
```

The benefit is that search engines will be able to read `page1.html` better than `#page1`. For
this sample app, each page is customized to the user so there is no need to use the more
complex `pushState` to handle navigation.

Additionally, the browser has a different implementation, which makes it hard when doing
mobile apps. There are third-party solutions that help you bring the same experience to all
browsers, including History.js (`https://github.com/balupton/History.js`), a
Github project that brings the same methods to all browsers without having to worrying
about cross-browser support.

SUMMARY

This chapter talked about how to mock up an application and included some example screens of the application that you build in this book. As discussed, prototyping helps you define the features of your applications and allows you to set scope. It's much easier to build the application after you define this so you don't lose time developing features after the fact.

In addition to prototyping this chapter also discussed:

- HTML5 boilerplate structure
- Laying out pages in a single HTML design
- Using and detecting onHashChange events for navigation
- PushState navigation

5

MOBILE WEB STRUCTURE

WHEN DEVELOPING FOR mobile web, you must change your whole mindset when you design the structure of your web app. With standard web pages, mouse clicks and keyboard inputs are the mechanisms you program to allow your users to use an app, and therefore are the primary events. With mobile, `click` methods become `touch` events, `onmouseover` events do not exist, and the `CSS:hover` method doesn't work as designed. It's possible in the future that mobile devices will incorporate technology to make use of `:hover` method, however at this time it doesn't provide the desired effects as it does on standard desktop browsers. How a user interacts with your web app is important. You can't design and develop by just testing it on a web browser; testing on a touch device can provide some interesting insights.

In this chapter, you start to build the framework around Corks, which involves setting up some global templates, including the header, footer, and top navigation. We discuss a popular feature on iOS called Full App Mode, which allows a user to create a home screen icon for an app, and remove the bottom and top bars of Safari. These tweaks are very helpful for making your app feel more native.

Android doesn't have a comparable function; however, users can "pin" your web app to their home screen for easy access. Android browsers don't have a bottom navigation bar because the device has an actual back button.

In addition, this chapter discusses `onTouch` events and what makes them different from `onClick` events when dealing with mobile browsers. Because mobile browsers have around a 300m second delay (at certain times) when a button or a link is tapped, known as *touchdelay*, users sometimes tap your link twice without knowing it.

Finally, you revisit ways to adjust content for screen orientation changes, such as when an Android user slides out a keyboard or when the device is rotated. You can handle these events differently depending on your application; however, we discuss the use of media queries to handle these resolution changes and how you can use them to really embrace the one-code multiple platforms by serving your mobile app to desktop browsers.

In this chapter, you continue to develop the sample app Corks. By the end of this chapter, you should be able to:

- Build the basic Corks framework, including navigation elements and the header and footer
- Set up the initial navigation of the mobile app
- Understand the difference between `onClick` and `onTouch` events
- Build methods to detect orientation changes for Corks

ELEMENTS TO BUILD

Having a solid framework and template makes developing for your mobile app a lot easier. Code replication can save hours of work and allow you to focus your attention on content. In this chapter, you build the navigation bar and set up the app's header and footer. After they are built, you can reference these pieces of code every time you start a new physical or virtual (in another `<div>` element) page.

CENTERING YOUR CONTENT WITH VIEWPORTS

Your web app can use viewports to display the content in the center of the screen. Viewpoints are the equivalent of a user pinching and zooming the content for a website that isn't formatted for mobile.

You want the Corks application to be front and center and snap to the width of the screen. To enable this, you want to open the `index.html` file and start editing the content inside the `head` section. Next, add the following code snippet right under the `<html>` opening bracket:

```
<meta name="viewport"
        content="width=device-width; initial-scale=1.0; maximum-scale=1.0;
minimum-scale=1.0; user-scalable=false;"/>
```

This option sets the width of the application to the width of the phone without any scaling. This means no matter how big the screen is, the elements wrap to the edge of the screen.

Finally you set the `user-scalable` option to `false`, which ensures that the user can't resize the content. This is usually set to `false` because all the elements on the screen should be visible and not require the user to pinch and zoom.

USING FULL APP MODE (IOS ONLY)

iOS has a setting for all websites that is called *Full App mode.* Using it enables your application to run in a UIWebView, which gets rid of the address and bottom navigation bar of Safari. Figure 5-1 shows the Untappd website without the Full App mode applied. Contrast that with Figure 5-2. See the difference? Figure 5-1 has the bottom navigation bar, while the other image has a black bar on the top and operates in the full screen.

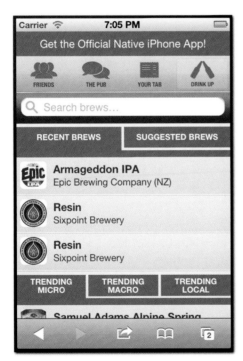

Figure 5-1: Navigation elements take up valuable screen space.

Figure 5-2: With Full App mode, your users get the most out of a small screen.

Although it may seem like Full App mode is the way to go, this isn't always the case. Table 5-1 looks at the pros and cons of using Full App mode.

Table 5-1   Pros and Con Full App Mode

Pros	Cons
Allows your app to feel more native.	Cannot run in the background and requires the web app to be reloaded every launch, without customization.
Allows you set a splash screen that shows on launch.	When users touch links that are inside the web app that are intended to open up the native browser, the web app will immediately close since it cannot run in the background.

Even though you can't retain state after closing, using HTML5 Cache Manifest you can load static files from the manifest and quickly process the user's request. Keeping the page state is another challenge, especially if your app has sub pages. A common problem would be when your user went through three pages to sign up for an account, and then after getting to the last page, tapped a link to read your terms of service, thus losing all information he entered during the registration process. Problem planning and design can eliminate this situation, but using Full App mode can make you think differently about your application.

To enable Full App mode, add the following snippet of code in the <head> section of your index.html page. To start, remove all the text in between the <head> and </head> tags of the HTML5 mobile boilerplate template that you are using for your Corks development. Then add the following:

```
<meta name="apple-mobile-web-app-capable" content="yes">
  <meta name="apple-mobile-web-app-status-bar-style" content="black">
```

The first line enables the web page to add in Full App mode by setting the content to yes. The second line allows you to set the color of the status bar (the bar that contains the clock, battery, and signal information). This is usually set to black, but you can change it to gray depending on the color schemas of your application by setting the content to default. You can also set the content to black-translucent, which makes the status bar black and translucent. This means the content will flow under the status bar. An example of this is in the Photos application on iOS. As you scroll, the content flows below the status bar. Figures 5-3 through 5-5 show these status bar enhancements.

Figure 5-3: Status bar on iOS when using black

Figure 5-4: Status bar on iOS when using default

Figure 5-5: Status bar on iOS when using black-translucent

Even though this enables the use of the Full App for your web app, you need to add an icon for the home screen and splash screen. Since the app launches in UIWebView on iOS, while it loads you need a screen to display. In addition, when users add the app to their home screen, an icon is needed to represent it.

To add an icon, place the following snippet of code in the <head> section either above or below the code regarding the Full App mode:

```
<link rel="apple-touch-icon-precomposed" sizes="114x114" href="location_of_image_
here ">
 <link rel="apple-touch-icon-precomposed" sizes="72x72" href="location_of_image_
here ">
 <link rel="apple-touch-icon-precomposed" href=" location_of_image_here ">
```

Each `link` tag represents an `apple-touch-icon-precomposed` element that tells the operating system which icon to assign as the icon link. Depending on the user's OS, a different line is used. The important part is assigning a different icon for users with high-resolution screens. For iPhone 4 and higher, the 114 x 114 size image is read; iPad 1 or lower adds your web app to the user's home screen using 72 x 72 images. The last option covers non-Retina iPhones, iPad 2, and Android 2.1+ devices. No size is provided, enabling the `link` element to cover the wide range of these devices. Once you add these lines to your document, your icon will display on a user's home screen after your app is added. As we noted previously, although the name of the `rel` attribute contains `apple`, it will be picked up on Android 2.1+ devices. Once the user adds the bookmark to their home screen, Android OS uses this image as an icon.

Another important point is the aspect of `apple-touch-icon-precomposed` and `apple-touch-icon`. When on an iOS device, using `precomposed` allows the operating system to add a glossy effect on your icon when added to the home screen. (See Figure 5-6.) To enable this, just remove the `precomposed` piece from the attribute.

Figure 5-6: Examples of glossy and nonglossy icons

To use Full App mode correctly, users must add the application to their home screen. Here are the steps for users to follow:

1. **Navigate to the web app that you added to your home screen and tap the middle Share button on the bottom of screen.** (See Figure 5-7.) The icon may look different depending on what version of iOS you currently have installed. The following screenshots are from iOS 5.

2. **After the action sheet pops up from the bottom, select Add To Home Screen, as shown in Figure 5-8.**

Figure 5-7: A web application in Mobile Safari with the options shown at the bottom.

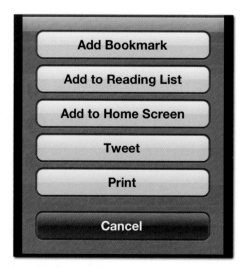

Figure 5-8: The options shown in iOS when you attempt to add the mobile web application to your home screen

3. **Choose the application name to see how the icon will appear on your home screen.** (See Figure 5-9.) This is automatically pulled from the title of the HTML document.

Figure 5-9: The final screen before the web application is added to the home screen

You are all set! The icon should now appear on the home screen with the name that you entered. When you tap that icon, the web app operates in Full App mode. (See Figure 5-10.)

Figure 5-10: Home screen with the new icon for your web app.

You can add tools to make the previous process easier. Italian developer, Matteo Spinelli, created a simple tool for developers to encourage users to add their Full Mode iOS apps to their home screens. The script is called add2home.js and can be easily added to any mobile web app to create an overlay pop-up to tell users to add the web app to their home screens, which is shown in Figure 5-11:

Figure 5-11: Using add2home.js to encourage readers to use Full App mode.

To add `add2home.js`, follow these steps:

1. **Download the** `add2home` **package file from** `http://cubiq.org/add-to-home-screen`.

2. **Include the following snippet of code in the** `head` **section of your HTML document:**

```
<link rel="stylesheet" href="path/to/add2home.css">
<script type="application/javascript" src="path/to/add2home.js"></script>
```

It's that simple. This code fires when the application is first launched and displays the bubble on your user's home screen.

Finally, it's a good practice to add splash screens so users know your application is loading. This is similar to the launch screen that you see when opening native applications. It's very easy to set up, but the image sizes are the complicated piece. For higher resolution devices, use a 960 x 640 image, which will scale down to smaller resolutions. The good thing about iOS devices is that the screen size is either 460 x 320 or 960 x 640, unlike Android, which has multiple screen resolutions. To add the splash screen on iOS, add the following code in the <head> section after you have enabled Full App mode:

```
<link rel="apple-touch-startup-image" href="image_link_here " />
```

It's important to note that while a splash screen is a great way to indicate to your users that your application is loading, it can also slow down the load time. Even if your application is already loaded (with use of cache), the splash screen will display. Some developers use custom loading panels to better indicate to the user that the application is loading.

To close out the changes in the <head> section, add a style sheet that controls all the CSS elements on the HTML page. You are going to use jQuery Mobile to handle your style sheets and JavaScript. jQuery Mobile has a CDN-hosted CSS that can save you bandwidth, so you reference their link in your `link` attribute. To add the CSS file for jQuery Mobile, place the following code after the `apple-touch-start-up-image` element:

```
<link rel="stylesheet"
href="http://code.jquery.com/mobile/1.0.1/jquery.mobile-1.0.1.min.css" />
```

It's also important to note that in Mobile Safari the address bar is automatically shown to users when the web page is shown. To increase your screen real estate you can add some JavaScript that fires when the page is loaded to automatically scroll the window up to hide the address bar. You add this at the bottom of the `index.html` page, right before the </body> tag:

```
window.addEventListener('load', function() {
    setTimeout(function() {
        window.scrollTo(0,1);
    }, 0);
});
</script>
```

This script fires after the page is completely loaded and makes the window scroll to (0,1), which is the first pixel in the Y position. This forces the browser window to scroll down, which hides the address bar.

After you add that to your <head> tag, you should have following code:

```
<head>
<title>Corks - Cellar your Wine</title>
<meta name="description" content="Corks a simple application that keeps track of
 your wines in your cellar.">

<meta name="viewport" content="width=device-width; initial-scale=1.0;
maximum-scale=1.0; minimum-scale=1.0; user-scalable=false;"/>

<meta name="apple-mobile-web-app-capable" content="yes" />
<meta name="apple-mobile-web-app-status-bar-style" content="black" />

<link rel="apple-touch-icon-precomposed" sizes="114x114"
href="start_location_here">
<!-- For first-generation iPad: -->

<link rel="apple-touch-icon-precomposed" sizes="72x72" href="start_location_hereg">

<!-- For non-Retina iPhone, iPod Touch, and Android 2.1+ devices: -->
<link rel="apple-touch-icon-precomposed" href="start_location_here">
<link rel="apple-touch-startup-image" href="start_location_here" />

<!-- CSS File -->
<link rel="stylesheet" href="http://code.jquery.com/mobile/1.0.1/jquery.mobile-
1.0.1.min.css" />
</head>
```

> *Notice the* <title> *and* <meta name="description"> *elements in the* <head> *sections. These are standard elements that you need to add when you write an HTML document. The* <title> *elements are shown when users attempt to add the web app to their home screen. The* meta *tag for description enables search engines to crawl your website and show it in their search results. This is an optional field; use it if you want your site to show up on search engine results.*

In most desktop applications, the development pattern is placed in the JavaScript files in the <head> section; however, research suggests that the page will not load fully until all the JavaScript files are loaded. If a poor connection exists, the page content loads first, followed by the JavaScript. This can lead to shorter load times. Later in this chapter, I discuss the JavaScript files that you are going to use. At this point, you can close the </head> element. It's important to note that placing the Javascript files at the bottom of the document is a lot more effective when loading an HTML document. It is highly recommended that you place all JavaScript files right before the ending <body> tag.

ADDING HEADER AND NAVIGATION ELEMENTS

Now that you have the CSS linked up, you can start with the content of the application. First, take a look at the structure of jQuery Mobile CSS pages. For each page, you must follow this format:

```
<div id="activity" data-role="page">
div data-role="header">
<h1>Page Title</h1>
</div><!-- /header -->

<div data-role="content">
<p>Page content goes here.</p>
</div><!-- /content -->

<div data-role="footer">
<h4>Page Footer</h4>
</div><!-- /footer -->
</div>
```

jQuery Mobile introduces new HTML5 attributes that help the JavaScript define how the element are used. For example, `data-role` defines what type of data is being listed in that element. If you render this page using just this code, you get the content shown in Figure 5-12.

Figure 5-12: The Corks home page

In the `header` data, add the page title, Corks. Since you want to have a tab bar interface, you can add both the header (page title) and the navigational bar with the following code:

```
<h1>Your Activity</h1>
<div data-role="navbar" data-iconpos="bottom">
<ul>
        <li><a data-icon="star" class="ui-btn-active"
href="#activity">Activity</a></li>
 <li><a data-icon="grid" href="#manage">Manage</a></li>
 <li><a data-icon="info" href="#find">Find</a></li>
 <li><a data-icon="gear" href="#settings">Settings</a></li>
```

```
<li><a data-icon="search" href="#search">Search</a></li>
</ul>
</div>
```

From the top, the `h1` tag is the title that displays on each page. The next block of code includes the data for the tab bar. Using the `data-role` of `navbar` tells jQuery Mobile to format all the elements inside `<div>` to conform to the `navbar` CSS styles. Since you plan to use icons on the top of each page, you set the `data-iconpos` element to `top`. You could set it `bottom` if you wanted the icons at the bottom of each button. If you don't want to include icons in your tab bar, you can remove this attribute all together; it just adds a little more UI to your tab bar to define each button.

Next, you create each tab you want in to the form of a `li` element inside a `ul`. To add or remove tabs, add or remove the `li` elements. To pick which icon gets assigned to each tab, use `data-icon` to display the icon. The names of the icons refer to the CSS class name and can be customized. You can even use third-party icon sets with a bit of customization.

The app opens to the Activity page, so you need to add the `ui-btn-active` class to the `li` to make this opening page active. You can apply this same logic to any nav bar items and as you build out the navigation on other pages.

After saving and displaying this on the iPhone, you get the page shown in Figure 5-13.

Figure 5-13: Displaying the Manage page in active state

ADDING HASH CHANGE EVENTS

In a web browser when a user clicks a link, the page usually changes the URL schema. This happens when you navigate from `http://example.com/index.html` to `http://example.com/index2.html`. However with most AJAX-driven mobile applications, you have only one physical page, but need a way to track navigation between virtual "pages."

One way of doing this is through hash change events, which track when the hash (or the URL after the # symbol) has changed. Whenever you click on a link, instead of redirecting to a physical page address, the *hash* is appended to the URL. The `href` attribute holds the hash ID of the page you want to link to. Each `data-role` page element must have an ID attribute that defines that page. For example, the Activity page is the page the user sees when the app is launched, which means the first `<div class="data-role">` element should have an ID of `activity`. This will help the jQuery Mobile handle the `onHashChange` event.

To test this, create a page structure for the Manage tab. After the closing `</div>` from the main page, add this right below your `<div id="activity">` section:

```
<div id="manage" data-role="page">
<div data-role="header">
<h1>Manage</h1>
<div data-role="navbar" data-iconpos="bottom">
<ul>
<li><a data-icon="star" href="#activity">Activity</a></li>
<li><a data-icon="grid" class="ui-btn-active" href="#manage">Manage</a></li>
<li><a data-icon="info" href="#find">Find</a></li>
<li><a data-icon="gear" href="#settings">Settings</a></li>
<li><a data-icon="search" href="#search">Search</a></li>
</ul>
</div><!-- /navbar -->
</div><!-- /footer -->
<div data-role="content">
<p>Manage!</p>
</div><!-- /content -->
<div data-role="footer">
<h4>Page Footer</h4>
</div><!-- /footer -->
</div>
```

This keeps the header, but changes the active tab (using the `ui-btn-active` class) to Manage. After saving the page and launching the web page on your iOS emulator, the first page that loads is the Activity feed. After you tap the Manage tab at the top of the page, a quick fade-in and -out of the content occurs, and the Activity page is replaced by the Manage page. You can even use the back button to return to the Activity feed.

jQuery Mobile provides all the methods to help you get this running without much effort. When the document is loaded for the first time, the script looks for the element with the `data-role` of `page`. The first element on the page that matches this criteria is shown; the rest of it is hidden. Through inspection with any DOM section tool (such as Firebug or Webkit Inspector), you can see that jQuery Mobile by default sets the CSS property of `display: none` and then applies the class of `ui-page-active` to the first element—in this case, `activity`. (See Figure 5-14.)

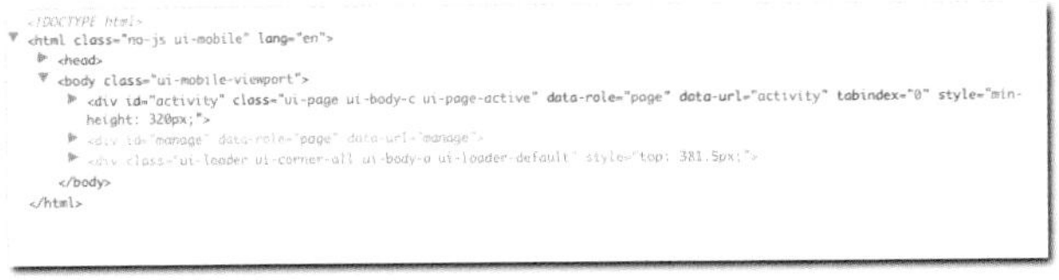

Figure 5-14: The Web Inspector showing the ui-page-active HTML

TRANSITIONS

CSS3 enables you to apply some amazing transitions to animate the change from page to page. These can help your app feel native and enhance the user experience. jQuery Mobile takes away the difficulty of CSS3 transitions by enabling you to set the type in the `data-transition` attribute in each link. For example, when you want to navigate to the Manage page in Corks, you want the transitions to slide to the right. This can be accomplished by adding the new attribute to the anchor tag:

```
<li><a data-icon="grid" data-transition="slide" href="#manage">Manage</a></li>
```

jQuery Mobile has tons of animations to choose from, including the following popular options:

- **Fade**: This is the default transition that is applied for every `hashChange` event.
- **Pop:** The page will pop out as if it is coming from the screen's center and heading toward you.
- **Flip:** This is a common transition on the iPhone and is used to flip the current page 180 degrees to the opposite side.
- **Turn:** This animation acts like page turn in a book.
- **Flow:** The page slides to the back, and the new page is pushed forward.
- **Slide:** Standard slide right and slide left are common in native applications.
- **Slideup and slidedown:** Allow the new page to appear as if it's coming from the bottom or top of the page.

While jQuery Mobile makes transitions easier to implement, it's important to understand how these transitions work so you can correctly apply them to the project you are working on. Transitions are based on CSS3 methods that create animation-like sequences that appear as though an element is moving across the screen. Basically, animation works the same way that a flip book does: When frames containing a static object are shown in rapid succession, the object appears to be moving. Here's a look at how the common slide transitions work. Currently, the page structure code looks like this:

```
<div id="activity" class="page" data-role="page">
....
</div>
<div id="manage" class="page page-right" data-role="page">
....
</div>
```

Add some classes (page, page-right) that you use to show the direction of the slide. This is handled automatically via JavaScript within jQuery Mobile. Next, you assign some CSS values to the page:

```
.page {
  position: absolute;
  width: 100%;
  height: 100%;
  -webkit-transform: translate3d(0, 0, 0);
}
```

Each page element needs to be 100% width and height to prevent the content from spreading from edge to edge of the browser. Finally the -webkit-transform element is very important; it activates GPU acceleration in the browser for each page. If you didn't use this method, WebKit browsers would not turn on the GPU accelerations that allow CSS3 to use the graphics chip to help with the translation. If you see your browser flickering or loading elements in patches, it's most likely due to the fact that this element is not called.

The -webkit-transform feature of CSS is very important for handling complex transitions or heavy CSS functions within your document. Failure to add this around the content you are changing might result in slow scroll or the section of the page appearing to be loading in "chunks." If you are struggling with performance of certain pages, I recommend adding this method to the parent element. It's important to note that on Android 2.3.x, any 3D translate function causes problems with input elements, so be careful to apply this method only when you need it. Overusing it could cause the browser to crash or memory issues.

After you have set the initial CSS, you can look into applying the transitions via JavaScript. Here is the full script, which can be placed inside the script tag at the bottom of the page:

```
function slideLoc(from, to)
{
        var myClasses = document.getElementByID(from").className.split(' ');
        if (myClasses.indexOf(page-left') > 0)
        {
                document.getElementByID(from").className = "page trans page-right";
        }
        else
        {
                document.getElementByID(from").className = "page trans page-left";
        }
        document.getElementByID("to").addClass("page trans page-center");
}
```

Whenever a link is tapped, the script will track the to and from page transitions. In this case, from would be the Activity page and to would be the Manage page. The next step is to take the class name from the activity (from) element and split it. If that element contains a page-left, make the transition begin from the right side. If the element has a page-right, apply the same logic but begin the transition from the left. Finally, set the manage (to) page to be front and center after the transition has taken place.

In the preceding script, applying the trans class creates the transition effect. To make the script complete, add the CSS needed to make the transition occur:

```
.trans {
    -moz-transition-duration: .5s;
    -webkit-transition-duration: .5s;
    -o-transition-duration: .5s;
}
```

So now, you just need to call the slideLoc element whenever you want to apply this transition to your pages. This keeps the app clean and improves functionality. With modern browsers, there should be no reason to reload an entire page to show another element. Using page transitions enables you to mask the fact that you are still loading content in the background.

LETTING USERS SCROLL THROUGH APP PAGES

New events that help users interact with mobile browsers have been developed. The most notable were "touch" events. Touch is a major part of any touch-based mobile phone. Users navigate with their finger, not a mouse, so there is a big difference in the way you program for mobile apps.

onTouch Events

As a mobile web developer, you want to transition away from using onClick and use onTouch events to handle actions. The browser has a 300 to 500ms delay when you use onClick instead of onTouch because the browser is expecting the user to perform another action, such as drag or scroll. When it determines the user is not making a follow-up action, the onClick event fires.

On desktop web browsers, the delay is not noticeable; however, with mobile apps it is very evident. A common place where you might want to use onTouch instead of onClick is when submitting form data. Due to the delay, the form data may be submitted twice, which can cause issues with databases or API functions. Once a web app switches from onClick to onTouch, the delay is removed and the UI appears to be much snappier.

However, when using onTouch you must account for the time it takes for users to lift their finger off the screen. The problem is when the user touches the screen, he or she may not be tapping a link, but rather scrolling, and you don't want your event to fire when the user touches your screen to scroll. This is why you use the `onTouchStart` and `onTouchEnd` events.

This is already implemented in jQuery Mobile; however, if you wanted to look for your own implementation, check out a great article from Google that discusses how to use event listeners to accomplish this task: `http://code.google.com/mobile/articles/fast_buttons.html`.

In the article, Google explains how setting multiple listeners around the touch events can help you get a better idea if a person actual is tapping, scrolling, or doing something else. If you set your `viewport` correctly, all browsers running Gingerman (Android version 3), their default browser, remove the delay.

You can also use libraries like Zepto, which have a `.tap` method that you can use to target clicks. It's really important to use `tap` over `onclick` for methods that create data on your backend, because then your application could create duplicate information.

> *If you want to create own your functions to track taps, measure the time between the* `onTouchStart` *and* `onTouchEnd` *elements. Some developers use only the* `onTouchEnd` *element. However that doesn't work if the user is scrolling. It's best to determine the difference between the two to determine if the user is scrolling or just tapping.*

For best usage, we recommend using jQuery Mobile or Zepto to determine the user interaction. Here is a sample code snippet that you can use in any situation to replace `onclick` methods:

```
<a href="#" class="fireGo">Go </a>
<script>
$(document).ready(function(){
$(".fireGo").live("tap", function() {
// do something here;
});
});
```

This code makes sure the user isn't going to receive multiple actions as a result of a tap and works because of the `onclick` delay.

iOS Scrolling

Prior to version 5 of the iOS for iPhone, the CSS property that allowed it to have fixed footers and headers was disabled. With the introduction of the new operating system, this method has been enabled with a special CSS prefix that allows for native scrolling within web apps. The property is called `-webkit-overflow-scrolling`. The property has multiple values you can use:

- `-webkit-overflow-scrolling: auto` applies the scroll but not the bounce.
- `-webkit-overflow-scrolling: touch` applies a scroll and an elastic bounce back when the user reaches the page's threshold.

It's highly recommended that you use *touch option* scrolling to get the most native look and feel from your web app. With transitions, it is very important to apply the `translate3D` attribute so that the scrolling does not appear jumpy. Since this is the CSS3 function, it works better when GPU is activated via CSS3. In Google Chrome, you can even enable an option to highlight items that are using GPU acceleration. This can be very useful for debugging. To do this, follow these steps:

1. **Open Google Chrome and type** about:flags **in the address bar.**
2. **Search for *GPU Accelerated Compositing*, and then click the Enable link.**
3. **Next, search for *GPU Accelerated Canvas 2D* and click the Enable link.**
4. **Restart the web browser.**

The downside to this is that older iPhone devices running iOS4 and below do not have access to this particular method. This becomes hard to detect because you need to write custom JavaScript functions to parse the version number of the OS. However, once you're able to detect the version number and determine that it is below 5, you can use a third-party solution that mimics the experience of native scrolling without this particular CSS function.

One third-party solution is called iScroll (`http://cubiq.org/iscroll-4`). It can be set up pretty easily. The best part is that it is not dependent upon any JavaScript language; so based on whatever your technology stack is, this can easily be plug-and-play for your project. All you need to do is create an additional `<div>` element called a *wrapper* outside the scrolling area (the main content). The setup should look similar to this:

```
<div id="wrapper">
      <div id="scroller">
          ...
      </div>
</div>
```

Now, in your `<head>` section, add the following code making sure you reference the correct loading of the `iscroll.js` file:

```
<script src="iscroll.js"/></script>
<script>
function loaded() {
      myScroll = new iScroll('wrapper');
}
document.addEventListener('DOMContentLoaded', loaded, false);
</script>
```

The preceding script loads the JavaScript class for `iScroll` so that it sets up the global variables to be used throughout the document. Once that's complete, you add an event listener to detect when the DOM is fully loaded. Once loaded, it calls a new function that creates an instance of the `iScroll` class and applies it to the `wrapper` element. From there, `iScroll` does the rest and automatically computes the inner content height, so the scroll area is appropriate. This solution is not perfect, but it does provide you the opportunity support a wide range of operating systems.

ALLOWING YOUR APPLICATION TO ADAPT TO ORIENTATION CHANGES

The beauty of most mobile phones and tablets these days is there's no wrong way to hold them. Modern apps automatically adjust size and width based on the device orientation. The iOS takes care of moving the actual browser; however, your code needs to adapt to the device's orientation. You can accomplish this in a couple of ways, either through the use of JavaScript or a CSS function called media queries.

Using Media Queries

Media queries or CSS elements can be applied based on any number of elements within a device. A common-use case for media queries is to have one code base that functions as your full desktop browser and the same code base for mobile devices. The way that this works is that it reads the screen resolution when rendering CSS. Media queries are prefixed with a conditional statement that defines certain elements and their sizes based on the screen size of the actual device. Media queries can be tagged on the CSS level or at the initialization of the CSS file. Here is an example of using media queries to set the width based on the resolution or orientation of the device that is displaying the document:

```
@media screen and (max-device-width: 480px) and (orientation:landscape) {
      .page { width: 350px; }
}
.page {width 500px;}
```

In the previous snippet, all media queries are prefixed with an @ symbol. You can set the max device width, orientation, or other elements that define the condition. In this example, you set the body element of the page class to a width of 350 pixels when the max width of the device on which it is being viewed is 480 pixels and the orientation is landscape. This CSS renders only if this condition is met; otherwise, the page renders in normal 500-pixel width.

This is a basic example of what you do with media queries. The goal, however, is to have one code base that serves as your main website and also as your mobile website. Media queries help you bridge the gap and manage one code base. Many sites out there use media queries to serve content to their customers. An easy way to find out if your favorite website is using a media query is to visit the sites on your mobile device and check to see if the address bar has changed URLs. Typically, most mobile websites change their URL structure to `mdomain-name.com` or `domain name.com/mobile` for mobile devices; however, the URL structure does not change from the regular desktop version if the company is using media queries to serve the content.

Using JavaScript to Implement Orientation Changes

There are ways to detect orientation changes via JavaScript. jQuery Mobile provides a function that is built into the library that you use for Corks. As you can see in Figures 5-15 and 5-16, rotating the device to a landscape position extends the inner content based on the width of the screen.

Figure 5-15: jQuery Mobile Home with standard orientation

2012 The jQuery Foundation

Figure 5-16: jQuery Mobile Home with landscape orientation

2012 The jQuery Foundation

If a website doesn't track the differences between the orientation, the web page renders differently. Figure 5-17 shows an example in which a website doesn't account for the orientation change. Figure 5-18 shows the blank space on the right side that isn't adjusted based on the screen size change.

Figure 5-17: A website that isn't optimized for mobile in standard orientation

Figure 5-18: A website that isn't optimized for mobile in landscape orientation

Use this simple script (discussed in Chapter 1) to detect when the device orientation has changed. You can place this at the bottom of the `index.html` document in the `script` tag, however in Corks, jQuery Mobile takes care of this automatically

```
<script type="text/javascript" language="Javascript">
        var supportsOrientationChange = "onorientationchange" in window,
            orientationEvent = supportsOrientationChange ? "orientationchange" :
 "resize";
        window.addEventListener(orientationEvent, function() {
            alert('We just detected a screen resolution change!');
        }, false);
</script>
```

After you've detected an orientation change, the most common practice is to change the `body` class to another class that signifies a different CSS class to represent the wider width. Here's an example of code to do that:

```
<body class="wide">
...
</body>
```

So when writing CSS, you add some additional statements for each class type, such as:

```
body.wide {
        width: 600px;
}

body {
        width: 320px;

}
```

SUMMARY

This chapter covered a wide range of topics that can help you with the HTML structure and JavaScript elements that make up the sample app Corks. In addition, we covered:

- Touch vs onClick events
- Media queries
- Orientation detection
- Hardware acceleration
- CSS3 transitions

CHAPTER

6

CREATING A MOBILE WEB DATABASE

HTML5 DATABASES ENABLE website developers to store rich content within the browser's application cache for fast access. With the introduction of tools like Web SQL, IndexDB, LocalStorage, and other databases, you can store content for reuse after you close the browser. It's a great way of holding information without having to use a backend database such as MySQL for the little tasks.

In addition, we discuss the HTML5 database called Web SQL. You set up the structure and learn how to process and return queries on the database. You use this to generate queries for your pagination and to insert wines into your database via the Manage tab. It's important to note the Web SQL is not supported by Firefox, which supports another non-relational database called IndexDB. Unlike Web SQL, IndexDB is based on objects and isn't relational (there are no schemas). It has limited support, so we don't discuss IndexDB in this book. Firefox Mobile has very small market share, which is why it is not addressed in this book.

In this chapter, you continue to develop the sample app Corks. By the end of this chapter, you should be able to:

- Understand how to implement and use Web SQL
- Discuss the schema for the Web SQL that you will use for Corks
- Build the initial tables needed for Corks using Web SQL

ELEMENTS TO BUILD

You set up your page structure using the jQuery Mobile framework, so you just need to build the content that powers the application for each page. As long as you keep to the standards discussed in the previous chapters, adding pages will be a breeze. It's important to note that the first `<div date-role='page'>` element will be the default start of an application, so you always want that to be the activity feed. We will be building and explaining the following:

- HTML5 databases styles and strategies
- The HTML5 database for Web SQL
- Using transactions to create databases

DATABASES IN HTML5

HTML5 enables you to access permanently and temporarily stored data within the web browser to hold content for cache, queries, and much more. This storage is persistent and remains when the browser is closed or turned off. Table 6-1 compares three different types of databases so you can choose one that best meets your needs:

Table 6-1   Types of Databases

Type of Database	Style	Good Use Cases
LocalStorage	Key-pair database	This is good for storing simple settings in the format of X = Y. For example, you would store `is_logged_in` as `yes`.
Web SQL	Relational	This is good for applications that have multiple tables holding different types of information. Web SQL requires a schema; you need to define the whole structure before using it.
IndexDB	Object-oriented	IndexDB is the new database language based off of object-oriented databases. However, it currently is supported only on Firefox.

For this project you will be using both LocalStorage and Web SQL, which is common in many web applications. With LocalStorage, you can quickly save settings and configurations that may not need to be stored in a table format using WebSQL. Remember that for all HTML5 applications, the maximum size is set to 5MB. However, you can request a higher amount when you initialize the Web SQL database. It's important to note that this request is not standard among all browsers. Request the right size of the database during initialization for the best performance.

> *Web SQL databases are compatible only with Chrome, Opera, IE8, Safari, and all WebKit mobile browsers. They currently do not work within Firefox or Firefox Mobile.*

Some web developers might be scratching their heads about why someone would want to use a local database instead of a powerful database server such as MongoDB or MySQL. Although these server-side databases pack power and offer customization options, sometimes Web SQL can provide these attributes more easily. Here are three key benefits of Web SQL:

- **Serverless:** Web SQL doesn't require an expensive hosting server or that you learn how to manage the server.
- **Zero configuration:** Web SQL setup is dead simple. No configuration is required to start using Web SQL; it works right out of the box. This can be helpful for new and seasoned developers. The JavaScript API is also much easier to work with than other backend equivalents.
- **Self-contained:** Web SQL doesn't require another framework to run; it runs on modern browsers without any external dependencies.

Even though Web SQL provides simplicity, it's best to take a look at your application and what you are attempting to do before choosing your database. For applications that need data to be publicly accessible across multiple devices, SQLite will not work because it is local to the device. It's possible to use Web SQL and a database server together to provide caching and reducing the load on the database server.

Creating the Web SQL Database

Although there is no official dialect for HTML5 SQL, Web SQL is used as the standard for learning and structure purposes. It provides the basic SQL language and capability to query a database. The structure of a SQLite database is relational, which means that you need to form the database schema before inserting any data. Before you start the schema, you need to initialize the database. With SQL, one line of code starts your database:

```
var tx = window.openDatabase( DatabaseName, DatabaseVersion, DisplayName,
 EstimatedSize, callback )
```

Table 6-2 breaks down and defines the variables:

Table 6-2   Web SQL HTML5 Database Creation Variables

Variable Name	Required	Description
DatabaseName	Yes	This is the standard database name that you want your application to use. This is important because you reference this when you start building queries.
DatabaseVersion	Yes	This is the version number of your current database in string format, such as 1.0. HTML5 databases enable you to have multiple versions of a database on a local device. For our demo, you use 1.0.
DisplayName	No	This is the database description in string format. It isn't a required field, but it can be useful if you have lots of local databases and need to remember which database stores which information.
EstimatedSize	Yes	This is one of the most important pieces of information for initializing the database. This value sets the size of the database using the following byte format: `50 * 1024 * 1024`. The max size for a database without prompting the user is 5MB. In this example, that is 100MB.
CallBack	No	This is a function that is called when the database has been completed. Normally, you would put all your CREATE TABLE syntax in this function so once the table is opened, you start to create the tables.

The `openDatabase` command opens the existing database if it exists or creates it if it doesn't, so there are no worries about overwriting an existing database with this command.

You will notice that you define the `db` variable outside the script, so you can use it again through your application. If you didn't do this, `db` is local to that function in which it appears.

> It's important to note that this script creates the database only if it doesn't exist. If the database exists, it just opens it and makes it ready to accept transactions.

To execute SQL commands, you need to use the `db.transaction` method to hold your logic. Note that using the `transaction` command locks the database, meaning no other query can run until this transaction is complete. Use this only when you are performing write actions such as CREATE TABLE, INSERT, UPDATE, and so on:

```
db.transaction(function(tx) {
....
});
```

To create a read-only transaction, use the following code:

```
db.readTransaction(function(tx) {
....
});
```

The `readTransaction` method enables your database to be unlocked so you can run multiple transactions simultaneously.

The preceding statements are calling the db variable that was created when a new database was added. After that you can call the `transaction` method. The `tx` variable holds the methods necessary to complete the transaction, such as `executeSql`, which is shown in the following code:

```
db.transaction(function(tx) {
        .executeSql(QUERY, parameters, successResponse, errorResponse);
});
```

In this snippet, the `executeSQL` command is called on the transaction. Four variables can be passed through this method:

- `QUERY`: This is the standard query that you are going to be writing, such as `SELECT *
  from wines` or `INSERT into wines`, and so on.
- `parameters`: If you are applying any filter to your data, this is where it goes. For example, if your query is `SELECT * from wines where wine_abv > ?`, the parameter would be `[6]`. We discuss this a little later in the book, along with the discussion of creating the `select` statements for the Activity page.
- `successResponse`: This function is called when the SQL statement has executed successfully. The function enables two variables, which represent the transaction (first variable) and the result set (second variable). This does not apply for inserts, updates, deletions, or create tables.
- `errorResponse`: This function is called when the SQL statement fails. The function takes two variables, which represent the transaction (first variable) and the error (second variable).

So to query a table and return the results, you would write this function:

```
var status_id = 5
db.transaction(function(tx) {
        tx.executeSql(
        'SELECT * from MyTable WHERE StatusID = ?',
         [status_id],
        function (tx, resultSet) { displayResults(resultSet); },
        function (tx, errorMessage) { displayError(errorMessage); }
});
```

This code enables the user to select all fields from `MyTable` that match the `statusID` of 5. If successful, it calls the `displayResults` function and passes through the result set. It's important to note that transactions occur in real time, so you can either group them together in the success callback, or you can code them individually. If you code them in a group (via the success callback) and one of them fails, all previous queries are rolled back to the original data. This becomes important. Depending on your structure, if you need data to be inserted and then selected again for parsing, you might want to consider performing this function separately because if the `SELECT` query fails, your insert will be rolled back.

Because most of the code is being generated client side, Safari provides some great tools for viewing the data that is being generated in a graphical way. To see an example of this, perform the following steps:

1. **Head over to** `http://html5demos.com/database` **in Safari for PC or Mac.**

   When the tweets are loaded, you should see the message 20 new tweets loaded (highlighted in green, as shown in Figure 6-1).

Figure 6-1: Tweets loading for the HTML5 demos website

2. **If you don't have the Developer tab available on your website, open Safari Preferences.** On the Advanced tab, choose Show Develop Menu in Menu Bar.

3. **After you open the Develop menu, choose Show Error Console.** On a Mac, you should get a screen like the one shown in Figure 6-2.

4. **Click Resources to open a Databases page, where you click through to see the tables and the metadata for all the tweet data that was collected at** `http://html5demos.com/database`. (See Figure 6-3.)

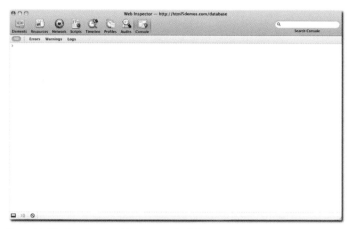

Figure 6-2: The Error Console in Web Inspector for Safari

Figure 6-3: The Web Database Inspector showing the database

Although this is a great tool, you cannot edit the entries or delete old databases; it is a read-only tool.

Setting Up the Tables

Now that you know how to create a database, it's time to build the table that you need to manage Corks. The application is simple, but sometimes it's important to sketch out a database map to see how the tables will interact with each other. (Refer to Figure 6-4.)

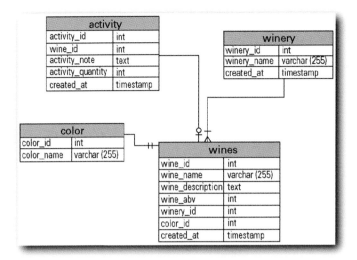

Figure 6-4: HTML5 database schema of tweets from HTML5Demo.com

The schema shown here uses four basic tables: wines, winery, color, and activities. These tables make up the application's database, which enables you to store the relevant data for your queries. Let's dig a little deeper into the relationship among these four tables and how they will be used in Corks.

Creating the wine Table

Use this table to store all the wines that you will use for Corks. Each wine must contain a number of data points, as defined in Table 6-3:

Table 6-3 Table Structure for wine

Field	Data Type	Description
wine_id	`Integer (11) - Auto_Increment`	This is the standard ID for each wine you enter into the database. This will auto-increment on each entry, so you won't have to worry about inserting each row with an ID. The database will take of that function.
wine_name	`VARCHAR (255)`	This is the string wine name that you enter. The default length will be 255 characters or less; if you need more, you can change the data type to **TEXT**. To save data space, you are allowing only 255 characters.

Field	Data Type	Description
wine_description	TEXT	For each wine, the user has the option to enter a description of the wine. This can be a commercial description or just notes about the wine as a whole. This is a free form text entry, so you are making the description limitless in the form of a text data type.
wine_abv	INT (11)	This field represents the alcohol content per volume for each wine item. This is a required field and needs to be entered for each wine item. This can help for future expansion on detailed sorting of your cellar.
winery_id	INT (11)	This is the basic winery ID created for the winery that makes the individual wine. It should be a numeric value and needs to be inserted into each row. This field is a foreign key that links up with the winery table.
color_id	INT (11)	This is the numeric ID that is linked to the color table, which holds all the colors. The reason you use the ID instead of the name White or Red is that the ID enables you to add more styles to the database, which are then shown automatically on the app.
created_at	Timestamp	This is the date/time when the wine was inserted into the table. This is automatically created when the row is inserted.

After you plan the tables and their datatypes, execute the SQLite to create the table:

```
db.transaction(function (tx) {
        tx.executeSql('CREATE TABLE IF NOT EXIST wines(
                wine_id INTEGER PRIMARY KEY,
                wine_name VARCHAR(255),
                wine_description TEXT,
                wine_abv INTEGER,
                winery_id INTEGER,
                color_id INTEGER,
                created_date TIMESTAMP
                );
        );
});
```

Creating the winery Table

The goal of the winery table is to hold all the information for each winery. A single winery can offer multiple wines, while one wine belongs to only one winery. Of course, there can be situations in which multiple wineries may collaborate on a wine, but this example ignores that possibility. It's important to understand the nature of the many-to-one and one-to-one schemas for database, and it helps you determine the direction of the information flow.

The fields you will be using for the winery table are shown in Table 6-4:

Table 6-4   Table Structure for winery

Field	Data Type	Description
winery_id	Integer (11) – Auto_Increment	This is the standard numeric entry for each winery entered in the database. The ID corresponds with the wines tables to identify which winery the wine is a part of.
winery_name	VARCHAR (255)	This is name of the winery in strong format. Similar to the wine_name in the wine table, the maximum number of characters is 255.
created_at	Timestamp	This is the date/time when the winery was inserted into the table. This is automatically created when the row is inserted.

Enter the following code to create this table:

```
db.transaction(function (tx) {
        tx.executeSql('CREATE TABLE IF NOT EXIST winery(
                winery_id INTEGER PRIMARY KEY,
                winery_name VARCHAR(255),
                created_at TIMESTAMP
                );
        );
});
```

Creating the activity Table

The activity table contains all the information about what the user currently has stored in the cellar. This table is dependent on the wines table for the wines, but some other content will be original. The main activity feed will be pulling queries from this table, the structure of which is shown in Table 6-5.

Table 6-5   Table Structure for activity

Field	Data Type	Description
activity_id	Integer (11) – Auto_Increment	This is the standard numeric ID that will be created for each entry.
wine_id	Integer (11)	This field maps back to the wine table, which enables you to pull in information about the wine—such as the color, wine description, and so forth.
activity_note	TEXT	This gives your users the capability to add a note to each cellared wine.

Field	Data Type	Description
activity_quantity	INT (11)	This field represents the numeric value of the total number of wines in your cellar. Your users might have one bottle or they might have a case, so this field helps define that so the user doesn't have to enter a wine multiple times.
created_at	Timestamp	This is the date/time when the wine was added to the cellar. This will be used when looking at the activity feed.

After defining the tables and data types, here is the code for generating the table in Web SQL:

```
db.transaction(function (tx) {
    tx.executeSql('CREATE TABLE IF NOT EXIST activity(
            activity_id INTEGER PRIMARY KEY,
            wine_id INTEGER,
            activity_note VARCHAR(255),
            activity_quantity INTEGER,
            created_at TIMESTAMP
            );
    );
});
```

Creating the color Table

This is a simple color table that holds the ID and the name of the color which is linked to the wine. The wine item can have only one color, so the relationship between this table and the *wines* table is one-to-one. Table 6-6 describes this table.

Table 6-6   Table Structure for color

Field	Data Type	Description
color_id	Integer (11) – Auto_Increment	This is the standard numeric ID that will be created for each color. This ID links back to the wines table.
color_name	VARCHAR(255)	This is the name for the color that will be displayed on the main page.

Finally, here is the code snippet to create the color table. You are going to insert some default values (such as White, Red and Other) for wines in your color table:

```
db.transaction(function (tx) {
    tx. executeSql ('CREATE TABLE IF NOT EXIST color(
            color_id INTEGER PRIMARY KEY,
            color_name VARCHAR(255)
            );
    );
```

```
            tx.executeSql('INSERT INTO color (color_name) VALUES ("Red");
            tx.executeSql('INSERT INTO color (color_name) VALUES ("White");
            tx.executeSql('INSERT INTO color (color_name) VALUES ("Other");
});
```

For this script, it is important to not overwrite data in the database. A good practice is to check to see if the value exists first before inserting White or Red to avoid duplicates. You can do this in a couple of ways:

Set `localStorage` to store a YES or a NO if the values have already been inserted:

```
if (localStorage.getItem("is_inserted") == "NO")
{
        // perform the insert
}
```

Alternatively, perform a Web SQL lookup to determine if that color has been added to the database. If not, insert it:

```
db.transaction(function (tx) {
        tx.executeSql("SELECT * from color where color_name = 'Red',
        function (tx, res) {
                if (res.rows.length == 0)
                {
                        // color "Red" doesn't exist, you should insert it.
                }
        },
        null
        );
}
```

SUMMARY

This chapter touched on the differences between different types of databases as well as what is supported on what browsers. In addition we also discussed:

- Using the Web SQL syntax
- Creating and editing database names and settings
- Implementing read and write transactions
- Working with database schemas

PART

III

DEVELOPMENT

INTERACTING WITH WEB SQL

WHEN DEALING WITH a mobile app, developers have to pay close attention to bandwidth limitations of cellular networks. Being able to cache data and display database-local feeds speeds up your interface. This chapter shows you how to use local storage and Web SQL databases to fuel the sample application. Because these are stored in the browser, it doesn't require any network connection to operate. This can translate into a fast experience for the user, who no longer has to wait for an application to load.

In this chapter, you begin to write queries to load data from the activity feed and set up your local storage configurations. In addition, you set up a Manage Wines section and write the scripts to handle the insertion of new wines into your database.

In this chapter, you continue to develop the sample app Corks. By the end of this chapter, you should be able to:

- Build a basic database and static tables for Corks
- Build a Manage Wines page for Corks

ELEMENTS TO BUILD

In the preceding chapter, you defined the database structure, which is broken into four tables: color, activity, winery, and wines. The first thing you do is run the scripts to create your database so you can start adding elements, such as adding activities and wines.

CREATING THE DATABASE AND ITS TABLES

To follow along, you need to run some code to create the database for Corks. Follow these steps to create your main database.

1. **Open your text editor of choice and start editing in the** `index.html` **file.**
2. **At the bottom of the** `</body>` **tag, add the following snippet of code:**

```
<script type="text/javascript" language="Javascript">
    var db;
    $(document).ready(function(){


        });
</script>
```

This snippet enables you to fire some JavaScript code when the document is fully loaded. The `db` variable is to keep track of your database transactions.

3. **Add the code to create the database for Corks with the following snippet:**

```
var db;
$(document).ready(function(){
    db = openDatabase('myCorks', '1.0', 'My Corks Database', 2 * 1024 * 1024);
});
```

Now the database will be created under the name myCorks. If you save your index file and open your Web Inspector, you should see a page similar to that shown in Figure 7-1.

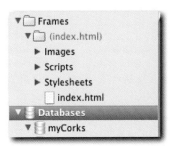

Figure 7-1: Web Inspector open to Databases

Now you start building the tables. Follow these steps:

1. **Open the transaction method of the** `db` **variable and use the** `executeSQL` **command:**

```
db.transaction(function (tx) {
    tx.executeSql("CREATE TABLE
IF NOT EXISTS wines (wine_id INTEGER PRIMARY KEY AUTOINCREMENT, wine_name,
```

```
wine_description, wine_abv, winery_id, color_id, created_at)", null, sR, fR);
        tx.executeSql("CREATE TABLE
IF NOT EXISTS winery (winery_id INTEGER PRIMARY KEY AUTOINCREMENT, winery_name,
created_at)", null, sR, fR);
        tx.executeSql('CREATE TABLE
IF NOT EXISTS color (color_id PRIMARY KEY AUTOINCREMENT, color_name,
 created_at)',
null, sR, fR);
        tx.executeSql('CREATE TABLE
IF NOT EXISTS activity (activity_id PRIMARY KEY AUTOINCREMENT, wine_id,
 activity_note, activity_quantity, created_at)', null, sR, fR);
});
```

Notice that you are setting an `sR` and `fR` callback that will catch errors on creation of the tables. You can define them outside the `document.ready()` function, as shown here:

```
function sR(a,b){
        // The query was successfully!
}

        function fR(a,b){
        // Oops! There was an issue. Let's alert the user.
        alert(b.message);
}
```

In this example, the script will do nothing if the query is successful, but will alert the error (in the form of `b.message`) if there is a problem on creation.

When creating and testing your databases, you will see multiple databases in the Web Inspector, similar to what you see in Figure 7-2.

Figure 7-2: Multiple databases in
the Web Inspector

This is normal behavior, as a new version is created on launch every time. However, if the database table exists, it overwrites the data in the tables. According to the Web SQL specification, there is no way to delete a version of the database. The only way to delete those databases is to clear your web cache and web data from your browser.

Beware! This will clear all active tables as well.

2. **Save this** `index.html` **file and load it in your browser.** Open your last database, myCorks, in the Web Inspector. You should see an image like the one in Figure 7-3:

Figure 7-3: The myCorks database in the
Web Inspector

ADDING VALUES TO THE COLOR TABLE

For you to repopulate the drop-down values during the Add Wine process, you need to add the values to the color name when the application first launches.

To do this, follow these steps:

1. **After you have created the tables, create another transaction to test if there are any values in the color table.** Do this by adding the following code after the `CREATE TABLE` transaction:

```
db.transaction(function (tx) {
      tx.executeSql("SELECT * from color where color_name = ?", ['Red'],
                function(tx, res) {
                    if (res.rows.length == 0) {
                            var start = new Date().getTime();
                    tx.executeSql("INSERT INTO color (color_name, created_at)
VALUES('White', ?)", [start], null, fR);
                        tx.executeSql("INSERT INTO color (color_name, created_at)
VALUES('Red', ?)", [start], null, fR);
                        tx.executeSql("INSERT INTO color (color_name, created_at)
VALUES('Other', ?)", [start], null, fR);
                    }
    else
            {
  // the table already has values - so let's leave it alone.
  }
    },
  fR);
});
```

This script queries the color table to see if there are any values in the database. If there are no rows (the `res.rows.length` variable is 0), you can insert the new data into the database with a d as the variable that indicates the current time of entry. On the other hand, leave everything the way it is if the table already has rows.

2. **Save this file and refresh your browser.** In the Web Inspector, you should be able to see the color table in the myCorks database section. After you click the color table, you should see the image shown in Figure 7-4.

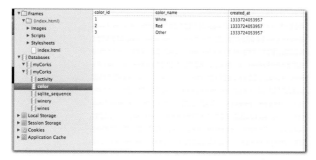

Figure 7-4: The color table and its three results: Red, White, and Other

Since `color_id` is set to an `AUTOINCREMENT` value, it will automatically add the next row with the correct ID.

`AUTOINCREMENT` is an important feature of any database system (not only Web SQL) that allows you to create quickly ID numbers in sequential format. A lot of blog content management systems use this attribute to automatically create a new ID each blog post, so it can always be unique. In most database systems, only the primary key (unique value in the table) can be set to `AUTOINCREMENT`.

BUILDING THE MANAGE WINE PAGE

The Manage Wine page will contain form fields so your users can add wines to the database. It also provides the option to add the wines to the cellar. This section shows how to build the form elements that will power the submission to your database.

1. **Under the navigation for** `Manage`, **in the content area, add a** `form` **element to contain all the input devices:**

```
<h2>Add A Wine</h2>
            <form id="manage-form" data-ajax="false" onsubmit="handleForm();
   return false;">

        </form>
```

You add a simple `h2` tag and then a `form` element. Inside the `form` element, you add a few attributes. In jQuery Mobile, all forms are automatically triggered via AJAX, but in this case, you want to handle the submission via your custom implementation, not by posting to a server file. To do this, add the `data-ajax` attribute, and set it to `false`. By default, jQuery Mobile sets this to `true`. Finally, you add an `onSubmit` and define a JavaScript function that you will write later to add the wine to the database. After the function to call `handleForm`, you do a `return false`, which prevents the form from "submitting" the content. You might notice that when you type a username and password in your favorite website and press Enter, that page refreshes. You want to prevent this action from occurring, so you tell the browser to "quit" after the submit function has been called.

You can also use other methods to control the `onSubmit` element using jQuery, such as intercepting the submit method from the actual form. You can do this by adding the following snippet in the `$(document).ready()` area:

```
$("#manage-form").submit(function() {
        ....
    Return false;
        })
```

2. **Next you add some basic forms, such as Wine Name, Winery Name, and Wine Alcohol Percentage.** With jQuery Mobile, adding fields is easy:

```
<label for="wine_name">Wine Name:</label>
<input type="text" name="wine_name" id="wine_name" data-mini="true" />

<label for="winery_name">Winery Name:</label>
<input type="text" name="winery_name" id="winery_name" data-mini="true" />
```

The `data-mini` attribute enables the field to extend to the width of the screen, no matter the orientation. When rendering the page, you should get something like the screen in Figure 7-5:

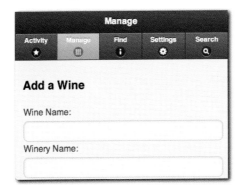

Figure 7-5: The Add a Wine page

3. **Now you add a list to display the colors that you created earlier.** You will use a drop-down list to display the values that you entered in your database in the previous chapter. First, you need to add the code for the drop-down list:

```
<label for="color_id" class="select">Color:</label>
<select name="wine_color" id="color_id" data-mini="true"></select>
```

Notice that you are not setting any values inside the drop-down list. When you render this page in your browser, you get the screen shown in Figure 7-6:

Figure 7-6: The Add a Wine Page with the Color drop-down list

4. **Now add the content inside the drop-down list to show all the colors from the database.** To do that, you will create a new function called `get_color`:

```
function get_color() {
        db.transaction(function (tx) {
        tx.executeSql("SELECT * from color order by color_name", null,
                    function(tx, res) {
                            if (res.rows.length == 0) {
// this shouldn't happen - as we already inserted them.
                            }
                            else
                            {
var len = res.rows.length;
                                    var code = "";
for (var i = 0; i < len; i++) {
                                    code = code + '<option
value="'+res.rows.item(i).color_id+'">'+res.rows.item(i).color_name+'</option>';
                            }
                            $("#color_id").html(code);
                            }
```

```
                                  },
                             fR);
              });
       }
```

Although this may seem complicated, it's pretty easy to understand after you look through the code. This function makes a query to the database to obtain all rows from the color table ordered by `color_name` descending. Once this function obtains those rows, the code checks for the number of rows returned, using the `res.rows.length` propriety. A return of 0 means that no rows were inserted into your table.

5. **If there are rows, loop through those results creating a string of colors to be added to the drop-down list in the form of** *<option value="">text</option>*. The text should be the name of the color (`color_name`), and the value should be the `color_id`, so you have the following code:

```
code = code + '<option
value="'+res.rows.item(i).color_id+'">'+res.rows.item(i).color_name+'</option>';
```

6. **The code is appended every time with the new drop-down value, so by the end of the loop it contains all the values needed to add to the drop-down list.** To add this string of text to the drop-down, use the following code to take the string and add it to the inner HTML of the `color_id` drop-down list:

```
$("#color_id").html(code);
```

7. **To make sure this function is called properly, you add it right after you insert the new rows for the color table or in the** `else` **statement, like this:**

```
db.transaction(function (tx) {
        tx.executeSql("SELECT * from color where color_name = ?", ['Red'],
                function(tx, res) {
                        if (res.rows.length == 0) {
                                // here is where you added the insert statements
previously
                                get_color();
                        }
                        else
                        {
                                get_color();
                        }
                },
        fR);
});
```

Now when you refresh the page on the Manage tab, you can click the drop-down box to see all the values, as shown in Figure 7-7.

Figure 7-7: Your new color drop-down list lets users choose
among wine types.

Wine Description and Cellar Options

Now, you add the other fields required for this page, namely Wine Description and the Add to
Cellar Options. Follow these steps:

1. **First, add a text area to hold a wine description.** It's very simple to do — just like
   adding a text box:

   ```
   <label for="wine_description">Wine Description:</label>
   <textarea name="wine_description" id="wine_description"></textarea>
   ```

2. **Add an option the users can click to add the wine that they are creating in the database to for their cellar.** Remember, you have two tables (one for wine and one for
   activity), enabling users to add a wine to your database, and then choose to cellar it. To
   make it simple for users, combine these activities into one.

   To detect whether users want to add the wine to their cellar, use a check box and then fire
   an onChange event to show or hide a div of other options. First, create the check box
   and hidden div:

   ```
   <label for="is_add">Do you want to add this wine to your cellar?</label>
   <input type="checkbox" name="is_add" onchange="toggleBox(this);" id="is_add"
   class="custom" />

   <div id="cellar_ques" style="display: none;">
   <label for="cellar_qty">Cellar Quantity:</label>
   <input type="text" name="cellar_qty" id="cellar_qty" value=""  />
   ```

```
<label for="cellar_description">Cellar Notes:</label>
<textarea name="cellar_description" id="cellar_description"></textarea>
</div>
```

This code creates a simple check box, which has an onChange attribute that calls the function toggleBox and passes the variable this. The variable this refers to the current element that the user is selecting, so it will pass back the check box element. Below that is the hidden div (set to display: none) that displays or is hidden, depending on the selection from the user. If you add all the previous steps together and render the page in the browser you get the page shown in Figure 7-8:

Figure 7-8: Add Wine page with cellar options and wine description

3. **Now you need to build the function that will support showing or hiding the div.** To do this, call the toggleBox function:

```
function toggleBox(a) {

if ($(a).is(':checked'))
{
        $("#cellar_ques").show();
        $("#cellar_ques input").addClass("required");
}
else
```

```
        {
            $("#cellar_ques").hide();
            $("#cellar_ques input").removeClass("required");
        }
    }
```

This simple function takes the variable a, which is the element of the check box, and runs a quick jQuery command to see if it's checked. If it is, then the script uses the show() function to display the hidden div. On the flip side, if a user changes his or her mind and unchecks the box, the div will disappear. You also should add the required class to handle your validation checker, which we discuss a bit later. Refresh your screen to see it in action. See Figures 7-9 and 7-10.

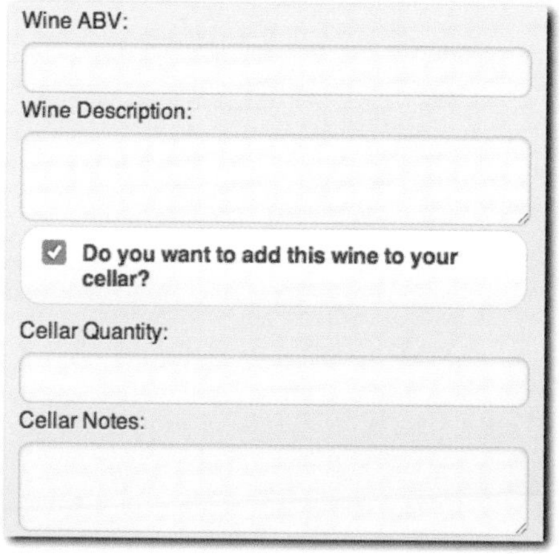

Figure 7-9: When checked, the Cellar field will show more options.

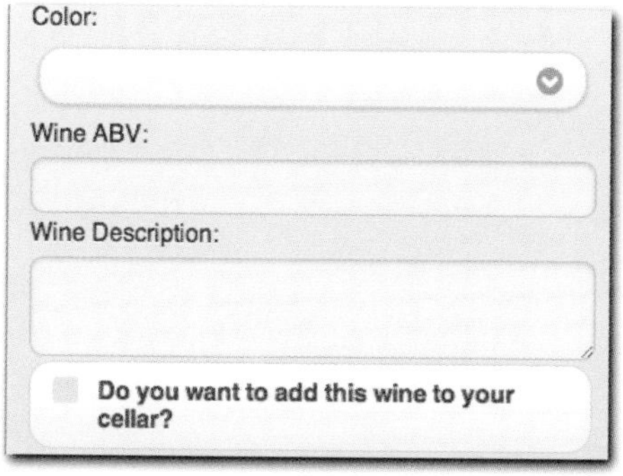

Figure 7-10: When the Cellar field is unchecked the additional options are hidden.

4. **Add the Submit button to the page to allow users to add the wine**. jQuery Mobile makes creating buttons such as this one easy. It automatically makes any button trigger the submission of the form. So you could use:

```
<button>Add Wine</button>
```

or

```
<input type="submit" value="Add Wine" />
```

Either one of these works and will process the `onSubmit` function of the `form` element that you set earlier.

Once rendered, your final page should look something like Figure 7-11.

Figure 7-11: The final Add Wine page

Validation

Now that you have created the contents of the Manage Wine page, you create the script that adds the wine to the database and cellar.

1. **First, create a function of** `handleForm` **in the form on submission.** Let's break down the function into two parts: one collecting the data, and one on parsing the data to be added the database.

Check that the data entered into the form is accurate and all the required fields are entered. To do this, you write a simple validation that checks all the input fields to make sure they contact values. To determine which fields you mark as required, you create a new class in all elements called `required`:

```
<label for="color_id" class="select">Color:</label>
<select class="required" name="wine_color" id="color_id" data-mini="true">
  </select>
```

Note that you don't need to add `required` to any of the fields in the hidden `div` area for the cellar because you have automatically added them within the `toggleBox` function. You also need to add another `div` outside the form that has the error message, so you can tell users when there is a problem. You also add a success `div` to let users know when the wine has been added successfully.

```
<h2>Add A Wine</h2>
<div class="success" id="success-msg" style="display: none;">
Awesome, your wine is created!
</div>
<div class="error" id="error-msg" style="display: none;">
You have errors in your form, please check the data.
</div>
<form id="manage-form" data-ajax="false" onsubmit="handleForm(); return false;">
...
</form>
```

2. **After adding these classes to the required fields, you need to create the function to check:**

```
function handleForm() {
var is_error = false;
      $("#error-msg").hide();
      $("#manage-form input").each(function() {
            $(this).prev().removeClass("error");
});
$(".required").each(function() {
if ($(this).val() == "")
            {
                  $(this).prev().addClass("error");
                  is_error = true;
            }
});
if (is_error) {
      $("#error-msg").show();
}
else {
      ....
}
}
```

The function creates a new variable called `is_error`, which will detect whether there is an error within your form validation. Next, you loop through each input class that is marked `required`.

Finally, you do a loop on each `required` input field and make sure that the `error` class is removed. You do this so you can prepare for the next input. If you didn't perform this cleanse, all your inputs could retain the `required` class prior to resubmitting.

3. **Perform the same loop, but check this time to see if the value is empty.** If so, you make `is_error` true and add the class of `error`. You add some CSS to change the text to be read at the top of the HTML style sheet:

```
<style type="text/css" media="screen">
label.error  {
color:#FF0000;
        font-weight:bold;
}
</style>
```

This allows jQuery to assign `error` as the class for every label that doesn't have any value in its element. If you save this file, refresh your browser on the Manage tab, and press the Add Wine button, you will see the message shown in Figure 7-12:

Figure 7-12: Example of a Wine Name, Winery Name, and Wine ABV error for not being filled out on the Add Wine page

This means that your script worked and now will track all error messages and apply them before submitting the form.

4. **To start collecting data to insert, you add on to the** `handleForm` **function after the** `else` **statement for the** `is_error` **variable:**

```
if (is_error) {

        $("#error-msg").show();
}
else {
        var wine_name = $("#wine_name").val();
        var winery_name = $("#winery_name").val();
        var color_id = $("#wine_color").val();
        var wine_abv = $("#wine_abv").val();
        var wine_description = $("#wine_description").val();

        var qty = $("#cellar_qty").val();
        var note = $("#cellar_description").val();
addWineActivity(wine_name, winery_id, wine_abv, color_id,
$("#is_add").is(':checked'), wine_description, qty, note);
}
return false;
```

Inserting into the Database

Notice that you call `return false` to stop the page from refreshing, which is standard process for an HTML form. This code goes through each piece of input, grabs the value, and stores it into a variable for later use. You also call the `addWineActivity` function, which we discuss later in this chapter.

Now that you have all the required information, you can begin to write the code to insert the row into the database. Since you store all the wineries in another table, you need to check to see if the winery was entered already and grab its `winery_id`.

1. **To accomplish this, you need to understand the use of the** `insertID` **attribute when making inserts:**

```
db.transaction(function (tx) {
        tx.executeSql("INSERT Into test_table (test_var) values(?)",
   ['test'],
        function(tx, res) {
                // you can get the ID of the insert if you are using
auto-increment fields by using res.insertId
                var new_id = res.res.insertId
        },
        fR);
});
```

This method enables you to retrieve the last ID of any insert, which is similar to the way other databases' languages, such as MySQL or Oracle, work.

2. **Now that you know how to grab the last ID of the database insert, you need to start building the massive function,** addWineActivity**.** It takes all the variables that you previously stated, including the check box to determine if the user's intent is to add it to his or her cellar.

Here is the code for this function. You want to place the outside the $(document). ready function in the script tag

```
function addWineActivity(wine_name, winery_name, wine_abv, color_id, is_act,
wine_description, qty, note) {
        db.transaction(function (tx) {

                tx.executeSql("SELECT winery_id from winery where winery_name =
  ?",
[winery_name],
                function(tx, res) {
                        if (res.rows.length == 0) {
                                var start = new Date().getTime();
                                tx.executeSql("INSERT INTO winery (winery_name,
created_at) VALUES(?, ?)", [winery_name, start],
                                function(trx,response) {
                                        var a = response.insertId;
                                        addWine(wine_name, a, wine_abv, color_id,
wine_description, is_act, qty, note);
                                }
                                , fR);
                        }
                        else
                        {
                                var a = res.rows.item(0).winery_id;
                                addWine(wine_name, a, wine_abv, color_id,
wine_description, is_act, qty, note);
                        }
                },
                fR);
        });
}
```

The script first takes the winery_name and checks to see if it's the database. Because you don't want duplicate entries, you search and attempt to find a match. If a match is found, grab the winery_id and pass it along to the addWine function. If not, create the winery in the database, then use the insertId method to grab the winery_id and pass it to the addWine function.

The addWine function is only called on the completion of the SQL query to check the winery, which is why this function is nested in the success callback in the transaction method. This function adds the wine to our database for reuse.

3. **You need to add the code for the** addWine **and** addActivity **functions.** First, here's the code for the addWine function:

```
function addWine(wine_name, winery_id, wine_abv, color_id, wine_description,
    is_act, qty, note) {
        db.transaction(function (tx) {
            var start = new Date().getTime();
            tx.executeSql("INSERT into wines (wine_name, wine_description,
    wine_abv, winery_id, color_id, created_at) values (?,?,?,?,?)", [wine_name,
    wine_description, wine_abv, winery_id, color_id, start],
                function(tx, res) {
                    var a = res.insertId;
                    if (is_act) {
                        addActivity(a, qty, note);
                    }

                    $("#success-msg").show();
                    $("#manage-form input").val('');
                    $("#manage-form textarea").val('');

                },
                fR);
        });
    }
```

This code is straightforward and is similar to what you have done in the past to facilitate data insertion. Here we break it down to make it clear what functions you are performing:

1. You open the transaction on the database that you created earlier.

2. You open a standard transaction to the databases and prepare it to add data. Since the function accepts all the variables, you just create a standard insert statement and pass all the variables. You will notice that you don't pass the time it was created, so you create a standard JavaScript timestamp called start and add that query.

3. Once the query is successfully, you want to obtain the last insert ID, and you do that by grabbing the res.insertID. You need this to add into the activity table if the user decides to the add the wine to their cellar.

4. If the user wants to add the wine to his cellar, the variable is_act is set to true, which tells the addActivity function to fire and adds the newly created wine to the activity table.

That's it for the addWine function, but to complete the process, you need to add the addActivity function. Place this below the addWine function in the script tag:

```
function addActivity(wine_id, activity_qty, activity_note) {
        db.transaction(function (tx) {
            var start = new Date().getTime();
            tx.executeSql("INSERT into activity (wine_id, activity_quantity,
    activity_not, created_at) values (?,?,?)", [wine_id, activity_qty,
    activity_note,
```

```
        start],
                        null,
                        fR);
            });
    }
```

This code is similar to the `addWine` function, but it inserts the data into activity table and doesn't return when it is completed. The `addWine` function assumes the data has been inserted and continue to process the submission.

Both functions contain similar structures, where the data is passed to the function and then inserted into the appropriate tables. The key in the `addWine` function is that it checks to see if the `is_act` variable is `true`, which means the wine should be added to the activity table once the wine has been created.

It's important to note that after the wine has been created, you show the success message `div` and clear the form input values.

Now that you have taken care of adding the wine and winery, it's time to put everything together and finish the Add Wine page. Your whole `handleForm` function should look like the one shown here, and if not, make adjustments to your code to match it. You can enter this code outside the `$(document.)ready()` function:

```
function handleForm() {

        var is_error = false;

        $("#error-msg").hide();

        $("#manage-form input").each(function() {

                $(this).prev().removeClass("error");

        });

        $(".required").each(function() {

                if ($(this).val() == "")
                {
                        $(this).prev().addClass("error");
                        is_error = true;

                }
        });

        if (is_error) {
```

```
                         $("#error-msg").show();

                         return false;
                   }
             else {
                         var wine_name = $("#wine_name").val();
                         var winery_name = $("#winery_name").val();
                         var color_id = $("#wine_color").val();
                         var wine_abv = $("#wine_abv").val();
                         var wine_description = $("#wine_description").val();

                         var qty = $("#cellar_qty").val();
                         var note = $("#cellar_description").val();
            addWineActivity(wine_name, winery_id, wine_abv, color_id,
$("#is_add").is(':checked'), wine_description, qty, note);
return false;
}
}
```

If you enter everything correctly, you see the success message shown in Figure 7-13.

Figure 7-13: Your wine has been added.

In addition, you can view your databases in the browser and you can see the wine and winery were created, as shown in Figures 7-14 and 7-15.

winery_id	winery_name	created_at
1	Test Winery	1333769669607

Figure 7-14: Your winery information is now in the database.

wine_id	wine_name	wine_description	wine_abv	winery_id	color_id	created_at
1	Test Wine	This is a test description.	10.2	1	2	1333769...

Figure 7-15: Your wine is entered in the database.

SUMMARY

This chapter focuses on building the main interaction queries and setting up the Manage page. Here is a summary of some of the topics covered:

- You built the basic database for Corks and added the example color table using Web SQL.
- You built the Manage Page for Corks, including the Web SQL queries for adding wines and wineries.
- You built queries to add new wines to you Cellar activities.

8

GEOLOCATION AND AJAX

ONE OF THE BENEFITS OF using HTML5 on mobile devices is that it provides you with the capability to use the geolocation feature to deliver local content to your users. This can range from showing a list of nearby restaurants, or specials, or even friends. Geolocation lets you find the user's physical location, which you can then use to find local information or deliver content based on location. The introduction of this new technology in HTML5 opens up numerous ideas to web developers. Before HTML5, location information couldn't be accessed in the browser, but only by building a native app. Most mobile apps use geolocation, and desktop browsers supporting HTML5 features can also access this feature.

Once an app has accessed the user's location information, most of the time it will want to make an external call to a service to return some data. For example, you could use an API such as Instagram to scan for pictures around the current location. The method of making an external HTTP call asynchronously (meaning without having to reload the web page) is called AJAX, which stands for Asynchronous JavaScript and XML. AJAX enables you to use the coordinates that come from geolocation to provide rich, local content to your users.

In this chapter, you finish the Find tab and write some AJAX and geolocation functions using the foursquare API. This will enable you to quickly scan around the user's current location for wine shops. You also use the Google Maps API to display these results on an interactive map that gives your users the capability to touch on the custom markers to display more details.

In this chapter you continue to develop our sample app Corks. By the end of this chapter you should be able to:

- Build the Find tab for Corks.
- Build in geolocation functionality to grab the user's location.
- Use AJAX to submit the query to the foursquare API to obtain relevant venues around the user's current location.
- Use the Google Maps API to plot the spots on the map using an info box to provide more information.

ELEMENTS TO BUILD

In the previous chapter, you built the database structure that holds the wines and wineries in the system. In this chapter, you build the Find tab, the geolocation, and AJAX elements that will enable you to interact with the user's location and surrounding venues.

CREATING THE FIND TAB

Since you already defined the top navigation structure with the Find tab, you just need to build the page containing the map and other geolocation elements. Start with the following steps:

1. **Open your text editor of choice and start editing in the** `index.html` **file.**
2. **In** `index.html`**, after the close of the** `<div>` **for the Manage tab, add the following structure for the Find tab.** The markup for this tab is the same as for the Activity tab, but with `ID="find"` which allows the page transitions to work properly.

```html
<div id="find" data-role="page">
    <div data-role="header">
      <h1>Find</h1>
      <div data-role="navbar" data-iconpos="bottom">
        <ul>
            <li><a data-icon="star href="#activity">Activity</a></li>
              <li><a data-icon="grid" href="#manage">Manage</a></li>
                <li><a data-icon="info" " class="ui-btn-active"
href="#find">Find</a></li>
            <li><a data-icon="gear" href="#settings">Settings</a></li>
            <li><a data-icon="search" href="#search">Search</a></li>
    </ul>
        </div><!-- /navbar -->
        </div><!-- /header -->

        <div data-role="content">
```

```
<p>Find</p>
        </div><!-- /content -->
</div><!--/find
```

3. When using Google Maps in elements that are set to be hidden or not viewable, sometimes you deal with issues in which the map is loaded perfectly but is cut off, as shown in Figure 8-1.

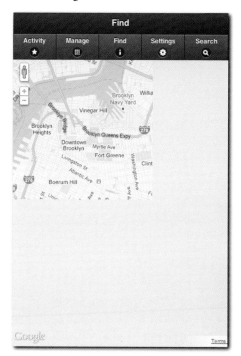

Figure 8-1: The map can sometimes be partially hidden.

map data 2012 © Google

To prevent this from happening, write a custom script that handles the map being created and destroyed. In `global.js`, before the `$(document).ready()` function, add the following code:

```
$(window).bind('hashchange', function(e){
e.preventDefault();
newHash = window.location.hash.substring(1);
if (newHash == "find") {
    if ($("#map").html() == "") {
            navigator.geolocation.getCurrentPosition(successPosition,
errorPosition);
    }
}
```

```
    });
$(window).trigger('hashchange');
```

This script checks to see when the `hashchange` (or the page navigation) changes, and then checks to see which page is set to load. If it's the Find tab (`if (newHash == "find")`), the code checks to see if there is anything in the `map` element. If there isn't, the geolocation call is made and grabs the user's location. This prevents you from reloading the map every time the tab is tapped.

In addition, you are calling the `getCurrentPosition` method to get a onetime location of the user. You are starting two callback functions here, `successPosition` and `errorPosition`. In each of these functions, you will write some code to use the location and store it for later use.

This app uses the `getCurrentPosition` method to obtain the user's location. An alternative would be to use the `watchPosition` method, which starts off with a less accurate location and then focuses in until a more accurate location is determined. This can save on battery life. For more information on both, see `https://developer.mozilla.org/en-US/docs/Using_geolocation`.

The first time you request access to a user's location, you get a warning on most devices that will ask for the user's location. On iOS, it looks like the message shown in Figure 8-2.

Figure 8-2: This warning asks for the user's location.

It's important to note that the website's URL (`http://m.untappd.com` in the example) is what will show up on the alert to the user. If you are running this off your localhost, the IP address may appear instead of the URL, depending on your virtual host configuration.

You have just a couple of more steps to finalize the capability to use Google Maps:

1. **Add some global variables, `lat` and `lng`, which will store the variables for latitude and longitude that you use in the application.** Add the following code to `global.js`, above the script you've just written, and below the line `var db; //`:

```
    var lat;
  var lng;
  $(document).ready(function(){
  ..
    // database initialization is here
      });
```

2. **Add some JavaScript to the top of the page.** Simply add the following `script` tag in the `head` section of `index.html`:

```
<script type="text/javascript"
src="http://maps.google.com/maps/api/js?sensor=false"></script>
```

This code enables the `google.maps` object that you use later in this chapter to map the points returned from the Google Places API.

CREATING THE CALLBACK

When interacting with geolocation, the developer needs to set the callback functions that process based on the success or failure of the geolocation implementation. Let's start with the success function. Here are the steps:

1. **The `success` function takes in the `position` variable and then stores the latitude and longitude of the user's location to a global variable that you defined earlier in this chapter.** Open `geo.js` and add the following code at the end of the file.

```
function successPosition(position) {
    lat = position.coords.latitude;
    lng = position.coords.longitude;     }
```

2. **Next, below this function, add the `errorPosition` callback, which will take an object called `error`.**

```
function errorPosition(error) {
switch (error.code) {
    case 0:
        message = "Something went wrong: " + error.message;
        break;
    case 1:
        message = "You denied permission to this page to retrieve a
location.";
        break;
    case 2:
        message = "The browser was unable to determine a location: "
+ error.message;
        break;
    case 3:
    message = "The browser timed out before retrieving the location.";
```

```
        break;
    }

    alert(message);}
```

This function takes the `error` object and executes a `switch` command on the `error.code` attribute. Depending on the code that is returned, it then assigns a `message` to the value. At the end of the function, you use the JavaScript `Alert` function to alert the user about the issue. This lets the user know whether the app has been able to access location data from the device.

HANDLING LOCATION WITH GOOGLE MAPS

Your app now gets the user's location on loading. The next step is to create a map of the current location:

1. **Set the height and width of the element you want to place on the map.** Because of limitations of the Google Maps API, you must set this attribute or the map will not display. To do this, add the following code just before the close of `<div ID="find">` in `index.html`.

   ```
   <div id="find" date-role="page">
         .      ....

   <div id="map" data-role="content" style="height: 100%; width: 100%">
   </div>
   ....
   </div>
   ```

   This code sets the content area at 100% height and width, which is best for large devices and high-resolution screens. If you set height and width to be small (or just the standard width of the phone, 320px), the map will look pixilated on high-resolution screens. Note that you must give the new element an `ID` of map, so you can reference it later in your code.

2. **Globally declare the `map` variable, which you will use to interact with the map objects.** Add the following code right before you declare the `db` variable that you use for the database activity. You are also going to declare an `infowindow` variable that you use later for a pop-up window for the marker.

   In `global.js`, right at the beginning of the file and before the line `var db`, add the following:

   ```
   var map;
   var infowindow = new google.maps.InfoWindow();
   ```

3. **Now it's time to actually generate the map.** To test to see if everything is working, create a map and place a marker on the map where the user is located. In `geo.js`, add the following code within the `successPosition` function:

```
var latlng = new google.maps.LatLng(lat, lng);
var myOptions = {
  zoom: 13,
  center: latlng,
  mapTypeControl: false,
  mapTypeId: google.maps.MapTypeId.ROADMAP
};
map = new google.maps.Map(document.getElementById("map"), myOptions);
```

This code creates a new Google Latitude and Longitude object called `latlng`, which is needed to center the map and to place markers on top of it. In addition, you create some default values for your map in the `myOptions` array, such as zoom, the map center (which refers back to `latlng`), and others. For more information on what options you can set on your map, check out Google Maps API (`https://developers.google.com/maps/documentation/javascript/`).

Finally, create the new `map` object by referring to the `myOptions` array and the `map` div that you added earlier. After you save the `index.html`, you can load up the website. You should see a map, similar to the one in Figure 8-3, once you navigate to the Find tab.

Figure 8-3: Obviously, the location will vary depending on your physical location; however, you should see a rough estimate of your current location on the map.

map data 2012 © Google

4. **Now that you have the map working, add a marker with your current location so you can get an idea of how markers work.** To add a marker of your current location, add the following code after the map initialization (the line containing `var latlng` in `geo.js`).

```
var marker = new google.maps.Marker({
        position: latlng,
        map: map,
});
```

Notice that you use the two variables you defined earlier, `map` and `latlng`, to define where the marker is placed and which "map" it gets plotted on. After saving and reloading your page, you should see something similar to Figure 8-4.

Figure 8-4: The map image with your current location plotted with a red marker.

map data 2012 © Google

5. **Code an info window that displays text relating to the marker when the user taps it.** It's simple to include this window using the Google Maps API. Just add the following code in geo.js, after the marker code you just added:

```
google.maps.event.addListener(marker, 'click', function() {
    getInfoWindowEvent(marker,"Hello!");
});
```

```
function getInfoWindowEvent(marker, text) {
    infowindow.close()
    infowindow.setContent(text);
    infowindow.open(map, marker);
}
```

This code assigns a `listener` function to the marker that activates when the user taps on a marker. When the marker is touched, a pop-box will show with the word "Hello!" Save the page, refresh, and tap the marker to see the pop-up, as shown in Figure 8-5.

Figure 8-5: Users can see more information by tapping on a marker.

map data 2012 © Google

USING THE FOURSQUARE API TO FIND VENUES

Now that you have the user's location and you have created the example map, you use AJAX to query the foursquare API and gather venues around the user's location matching the criteria of "wine." Foursquare is a location-based app that enables users to check into venues all over the world. It has one of the largest databases of locations with an open API. You use its places database to get a list of venues close by that match a certain term. Follow these steps to use the foursquare API:

1. **You need to obtain an API key from foursquare.** To do this, head over to `https://foursquare.com/oauth/`. After logging in, click Register a New Consumer, as shown in Figure 8-6.

Figure 8-6: Click the Register a New Consumer button in foursquare.

2. **Fill out all of the fields, as shown in Figure 8-7, and click Register Application.**

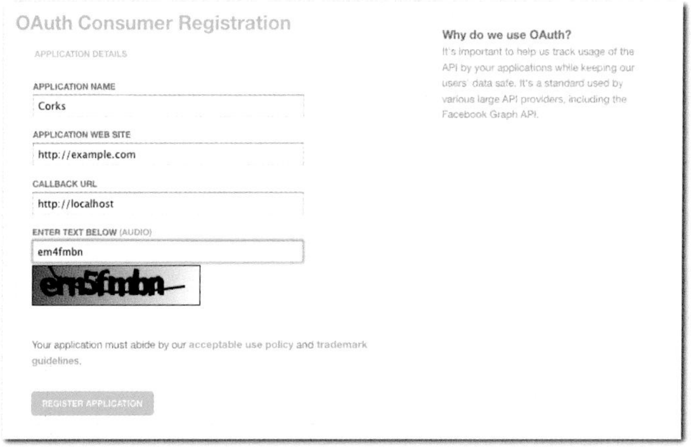

Figure 8-7: Complete these fields to register your application.

After you click Register, you are returned to your applications list and you should see a new entry with your client secret and ID. (See Figure 8-8.)

Figure 8-8: Your Client ID and Client secret will be displayed here.

3. **After obtaining your key, you can start building the AJAX structure. Start by creating a new function called** `findPlaces`**. Add this code to** `social.js`**:**

```
function findPlaces() {
        $.getJSON("https://api.foursquare.com/v2/venues/search?client_id=CLIENT_KEY
client_secret=CLIENT_SECRET&ll="+lat+","+lng+"&query=wine store&limit=25",
  function(data) {
                      console.log(data)
                  })
}
```

This function finds locations which correspond to the search term — in this case, the 25 venues closest to the user's current latitude and longitude matching the criteria of "wine."

When you run this code, you should see the code shown in Figure 8-9 in your Web Inspector.

The function you've just written uses the `console.log` function to write the contents of the JSON results to the console so you can inspect them. In this case, 25 venues came up via foursquare. It's time to parse those results onto your map.

```
▼ Object
  ▼ meta: Object
      code: 200
      errorDetail: "This endpoint will stop returning groups in the future. Please use a curr
      errorType: "deprecated"
    ▶ __proto__: Object
  ▼ response: Object
    ▼ groups: Array[1]
      ▼ 0: Object
        ▼ items: Array[25]
          ▼ 0: Object
            ▶ categories: Array[0]
            ▶ contact: Object
            ▶ hereNow: Object
              id: "4b3d501ff964a5202e9225e3"
            ▶ location: Object
              name: "Penn wine & spirits"
            ▶ specials: Array[0]
            ▶ stats: Object
              verified: false
            ▶ __proto__: Object
          ▶ 1: Object
          ▶ 2: Object
          ▶ 3: Object
          ▶ 4: Object
          ▶ 5: Object
          ▶ 6: Object
          ▶ 7: Object
          ▶ 8: Object
          ▶ 9: Object
          ▶ 10: Object
          ▶ 11: Object
          ▶ 12: Object
          ▶ 13: Object
```

Figure 8-9: Code for a venue returned from the foursquare API, as seen in the Web Inspector

4. **Now that you have your results, you can continue to build the function to parse the foursquare API and place the markers on the map.** Here is the full code to add the markers to the map based off of foursquare's API:

```
function findPlaces() {
$.getJSON("https://api.foursquare.com/v2/venues/search?client_id=CLIENT_ID
   &client_secret=CLIENT_SECRET&ll="+lat+","+lng+"&query=wine store&limit=25",

         function(data) {
                if (data.meta.code == 200) {
                var venues = data.response;

                $(venues.groups).each(function(i, group_items) {

                       $(group_items.items).each(function(q, venue_items) {
                                var latlng = new
                                google.maps.LatLng
                                (venue_items.location.lat,
                                venue_items.location.lng);
                                var marker = new google.maps.Marker({
                                position: latlng,
                                map: map,
});
                       });
               });
  }
     })
   }
```

This script requests data from the foursquare API for venues matching wine stores and then returns the result in the variable `data`. Foursquare returns all its data in JSON format, so you start to parse through the data to get the desired venue attributes.

Once you've fetched the venue attributes (which are all stored in groups), you grab the latitude and longitude of the venue and add it your map.

5. **Save your work and refresh the page.** You will see 25 red markers on the map. (See Figure 8-10.)

Figure 8-10: Your map with 25 markers now displayed.

map data 2012 © Google

CREATING THE INFO WINDOW

Now that you have all of your markers in place, you create an info window for each one to contain information about that particular venue.

1. **Showing all the markers on the map is nice, but it would be better to show more detail about them.** You can add an info window to each listing. It's pretty easy; just add this code inside the $(venues.groups) loop in geo.js. In Step 5, you added an info window to display the text "Hello!". You now edit that code to add new variables to display information about the venues. After the line beginning $(venues.groups), add the following:

```
$(group_items.items).each(function(q, venue_items) {
        var venue_name = venue_items.venue_name;
        var latlng = new google.maps.LatLng(venue_items.location.lat,
venue_items.location.lng);
       var marker = new google.maps.Marker({
              position: latlng,
              map: map,
       });
       google.maps.event.addListener(marker, 'click', function() {
          getInfoWindowEvent(marker, venue_items.name);
        });
});
```

This code defines a new variable that fetches the name of the venue and displays it in an info window when the user taps on a venue's marker, by using the `infowindow` listener you added earlier. After applying that change, you can click on the markers to show the pop-up box. (See Figure 8-11.)

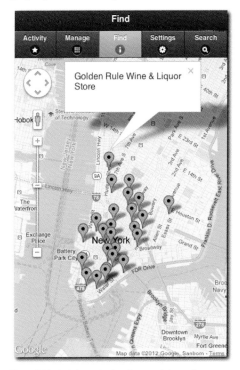

Figure 8-11: An information box for one of the markers on your map

map data 2012 © Google

2. **Showing the name is nice, but what if you want to style the box a bit?** Say, for example, that you want to display an appropriate icon for each venue. Here's the snippet of code to add to the end of the `$(venues.groups)` loop:

```
...

if (venue_items.categories.length == 0) {
      venue_image = "http://foursquare.com/img/categories/none_64.png"
}
else {

      $(venue_items.categories).each(function(o, cats) {
            if (cats.primary) {
                  venue_image = cats.icon;
                  return false;
            }
      })
}
```

This code takes the data points of the JSON object returned from foursquare and formats them based on their attributes. First, it checks to see if the `categories` element is empty, which signifies that a category hasn't been assigned to the venue. If that element is empty, it assigns a generic icon. If `categories` is not empty, it loops through the entries, looking to find the `primary` attribute. When it finds this attribute, it obtains the `icon` data attribute to display the correct icon and exits the loop.

3. **It's also going to be helpful to display the venue's name and address.** Below the code you just added, insert the following:

```
if (venue_items.location.address && venue_items.location.city) {
      venue_info_city = '<div style="font-size:
12px;">'+venue_items.location.address+'</div><div style="font-size:
12px;">'+venue_items.location.city+", "+venue_items.location.state+"</div>";
}
else {
      venue_info_city = "";
}

var html = "<span class='venue_image' style='float: left; margin-right:
10px;'><img
src='"+venue_image+"'></span><div>"+venue_items.name+"</div>"+venue_info_city;
   google.maps.event.addListener(marker, 'click', function() {
      getInfoWindowEvent(marker, html);
   });
```

This code checks to see if the address and city are stored for the venue and creates HTML strings in case they exist. It puts all of this together into a variable HTML and sends that over to the `getInfoWindowEvent`. The result should look something like Figure 8-12.

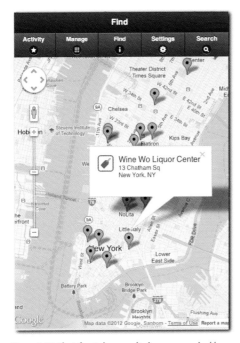

Figure 8-12: The info window now displays name and address information for a venue.

map data 2012 © Google

BUILDING THE REFRESH BUTTON

Because you obtain the user's location when the application loads, it's important to add a function that refreshes the location to obtain a new latitude and longitude if a user moves locations. Follow these steps:

1. **In index.html, inside** `<div ID="find">` **and before the navigation** `<div>`, **add the following code:**

   ```
   <div data-role="header" data-position="inline">
   <h1>Find</h1>
   <a href="javascript:void(0);" data-role="button" onclick="refreshLocation();"
    class="ui-btn-right" data-icon="refresh">Refresh</a>
   ...
   ```

   This code basically adds a new element, with an `onclick` method called `refreshLocation`. After you render this in the browser, the button is automatically styled and placed to the right, as shown in Figure 8-13.

Figure 8-13: The Refresh button is now displayed at the top right of the window.

map data 2012 © Google

2. **Now you add the function** refreshLocation **at the very beginning of** geo.js, **which just re-uses code that you previously wrote:**

```
function refreshLocation() {
    navigator.geolocation.getCurrentPosition(successPosition, errorPosition);
}
```

This code is called when the user touches the Refresh button. It recycles the location and recreates the map object based on the new location. In addition, it repopulates all the markers on the map.

SUMMARY

This chapter focused on building the Find tab and adding the geolocation and AJAX elements with Google Maps and the foursquare API. In addition, it also discussed:

- Creating markers on Google Maps for mobile
- Customizing pop-up windows within Google Maps
- Interacting with the foursquare API to customize info windows
- Handling geolocation changes

Now that you've added geolocation, the next step is to connect with feed, search, and external social media services, which is the subject of the next chapter.

CHAPTER

RUNNING QUERIES AND CONNECTING WITH SOCIAL MEDIA

WITH MOBILE PHONES, the capability to share information across the Internet becomes an important part of any application. Social networks, like Twitter and Facebook, have been at the forefront of this on mobile devices. Thankfully, they both have APIs that can easily be used on mobile devices using AJAX and JSON. When dealing with mobile devices, bandwidth reduction is always important, and JSON objects usually are smaller in size and easy to transform with JavaScript.

Having access to Twitter and Facebook APIs means you can do interesting things with your mobile application. Obviously, you can let users share content with their friends and followers, but it's also possible to scan Twitter and return data relating to the app's content, such as individual wines. In Chapter 8 you used the foursquare API to find venues around the user. In a similar way you can use APIs of social networks to pull in data that people have shared using those services.

In this chapter, you build your Activity tab and Wine Detail pages, where you write social functions to share wines on Twitter and Facebook and use their Search APIs to find out more information about what people are saying about the wine. This can provide you with a better outlook on the wine that you have added to your cellar.

In this chapter, you continue to develop the sample app, Corks. You build the functionality enabling users to search for wines, view detailed information on those wines, and see what other people have been saying about the wines on Twitter.

By the end of the chapter, you should be able to:

- Build the Activity tab with queries from the cellar
- Build the Search tab with wine results
- Enable the user to add wine found via Search to his or her cellar
- Build a Wine Detail page with more information on the selected wine
- Use Twitter to find more information and share the selected wine

ELEMENTS TO BUILD

Because you have already created your database, you have what you need to build the Activity tab, which includes all the wines the user has cellared, ordered by the dates they were added. Once you get the feed working, you can start building the Wine Detail page that lists information about the wine and the options to share to Twitter.

CREATING THE ACTIVITY TAB

Before you can add any social functionality, you need to create the tab in the app from which people will access Twitter, which is also where they will see information about wines added to the cellar.

WRITING THE QUERY

The Activity tab is where everything begins for the user. It displays all the recent wines added to the cellar. Because jQuery Mobile handles page navigations via hashChange events, you create a small function to handle the generation of Google Maps for the Find tab. You expand that build in some queries that will be fired when the Activity tab is active. To start, follow these steps:

1. **In global.js, after the existing variables (i.e. after the line beginning var infowindow), add the following code:**

```
$(window).bind('hashchange', function(e){
        e.preventDefault();
        newHash = window.location.hash.substring(1);
        if (newHash == "find") {
                if ($.trim($("#map").html()) == "") {
                 navigator.geolocation.getCurrentPosition(successPosition,
errorPosition);
                }
        }
});
```

2. **Because you need to capture when the app first loads (which is an automatic indication that the Activity is active since that is the opening view), you need to add some code to the script to handle that situation.** To do this, change the if statement to the following:

```
        if (newHash) {
                if (newHash == "find") {
                        if ($.trim($("#map").html()) == "") {

        navigator.geolocation.getCurrentPosition(successPosition,
errorPosition);
                        }
                }
                else if (newHash == "activity") {
                        grabActivity();
                }
        }
        }
        else {
                // the app just loaded, activity
                grabActivity();
        }
```

This script checks to see if the URL has a hash. If so, it runs through the same loop you used for the Find tab. However, this time you are checking to see if the newHash variable matches the activity, which indicates that the user is on the Activity tab. If this occurs, you want to fire a new function called grabActivity, for which you write scripts to pull from your database of Wine Cellar Activity.

3. **Next, you build the grabActivity function that connects the database to pull in the activity:**

```
function grabActivity () {
        db.transaction(function (tx) {
                tx.executeSql("SELECT wine_name, wine_description, activity_note,
  activity_quantity, activity_id from activity INNER JOIN wines on activity.
  wine_id = wine.wine_id order by created_at desc LIMIT 25", null,
                function(tx, res) {
                        if (res.rows.length == 0) {
                                // there are no results

                        }
                        else
                        {
                                //results go here

                        }
                })
        });
}
```

This code runs a query to extract the following data from the Activity table, sorted in descending order based on the Created At field:

- Name of the wine (`wine_name`)
- Description (`wine_description`)
- Notes on activity relating to the wine (`activity_note`)
- Quality of wine in the cellar (`activity_quantity`)
- The ID of any activities relating to the wine (`activity_id`). This lets you join the wines to activities that relate to each wine and to grab some of the wine detail. This join enables you to pull everything that has been added and in the correct order.

WORKING WITH TEMPLATES

Now that you have written the query, you can start playing with the results. Similar to the way you dealt with data coming out of the Color table, you tackle the same thing with your Activity feed.

Before you start collecting and manipulating data for the activity feed, you need to understand some additional ways to create HTML with data that is returned via your HTML database. As discussed previously, you can simply create a JavaScript string variable and append data to the end of it like so:

```
var code = "";
for (var i = 0; i < 10; i++){
        code += "<p>Hi!</p>"
}
```

Although this works, it's not the best practice for outputting complex HTML markup. It also can be very hard to update and make changes, because making a small mistake can mess up your HTML structure. An alternative solution is called templating. Using a template can help you reuse HTML structures very easily throughout your projects.

There are several template libraries that can be used in JavaScript. However, the one that we recommend is called HandlebarsJS. Handlebars uses regular HTML, but with special Handlebars expressions that are embedded and that return values from Handlebars templates which you write. To find out more about Handlebars and how to use it, see `http://handlebarsjs.com`.

To use Handlebars, you must add the library in the `<head>` section. Follow these steps:

1. **Add the following code to the end of the `<head>` section in `index.html`:**

   ```
   <script src="http://cloud.github.com/downloads/wycats/handlebars.js/handlebars-
   1.0.0.beta.6.js"></script>
   ```

   For this example, use the content delivery network (CDN) from GitHub to obtain the cached JavaScript file. For a production-ready application, you might want to copy the source locally to increase performance.

2. **Define your template structure.** To use Handlebars, you must create a template in a `script` tag with the desired HTML. Add this code before the closing `</body>` tag in `index.html`:

   ```
   <script id="activity-template" type="text/x-handlebars-template">
   ....
   </script>
   ```

This allows you to create a re-usable template that you can reference in future versions of the activity feed. If you want to change the structure of the feed, you just edit the contents.

Handlebars uses `{{ }}` to define areas of the HTML that should be switched with their JSON counterparts. However, it also has built-in functions to help you iterate through loops. For example, if you want to loop through objects, you could do so by using the following code:

```
{{#each object}}
<p>{{object.name}}</p>
{{/each}}
```

In this example, the code loops over entry in the object and outputs the property of name. You open the loop by using #each and close the loop by adding /each. While this may seem confusing, this code is conceptually no different than the simple for loops that you have been working with:

```
for (i = 0; i < object.length; i++) {
        code += '<p>'+object[i].name+'</p>';
}
```

Using this method when writing your Handlebars templates, you should better make use of the #each and /each statements.

ADDITIONAL FUNCTIONALITY OF HANDLEBARSJS

While using templates is a great way to simplify the creation of HTML markup, sometimes you may want to add some logic. For example, you may want to add a new class to an element depending on the contents. While traditional template libraries do not have support for logic, HandlebarsJS has helper files that serve logic functions within your application. To start creating helpers, follow these steps:

1. Create a new file in your `assets/js` directory called `helpers.js` and add it inside your `<head>` area as you have done previously with new JavaScript files.
2. Add the following code, which acts as a boilerplate for creating helper functions.

```
Handlebars.registerHelper(helperName, function(x) {
    ...
});
```

In the previous function, you are registering a new helper with Handlebars called `helper-Name`, which can be changed to anything you want during your creation. The variable *x* is the data passed to the function. Inside the function you can perform any functions that you want based on the logic you need to perform.

On the template side, you only need to add the following code to invoke the helper.

```
{{#each object}}
     {{helperName object}}
{{/each}}
```

This code sends the object data to the `helperName` function to output a result. It's that simple to do!

USING TEMPLATES TO BUILD THE ACTIVITY FEED

Since you have an understanding of templates through Handlebars, you can start to build the template to generate the activity feed.

1. First, you need to build the template for your data, which you can place in the `<script id="activity-template" type="text/x-handlebars-template">` element you added earlier:

```
<script id="activity-template" type="text/x-handlebars-template">
<li>
<a href='#wineDetail' onclick='viewWine({{activity_id}})'>
<h2>{{wine_name}}<h2>
<p>Added {{activity_quantity}} to My Cellar</p>
<p class="pad">{{timeDiffActivity created_at}}</p>
      </a>
</li>
</script>
```

2. **After you have added this code, place the `Handlebars.compile` script in the `grabActivity` function.**

```
var len = res.rows.length;
var code = "";
var obj  = {};
for (var i = 0; i < len; i++) {
var source  = $("#activity-template").html();
var template = Handlebars.compile(source);
code += template(data);
}
$("#my-activity-list").html(code);
$('#my-activity-list').listview('refresh');
```

Several things are happening in this template and code block:

- It calculates the number of rows that are available by using the res.rows.length, which you assign the len variable.

- It creates a variable code that will store the string of the HTML being created from our template.

- It calculates the relative time from when you posted the wine and the current time using the timeDiffActivity function (through the helper function called timeDiffActivity), which is discussed later in this chapter.

- It assigns an onclick method called viewWine. (Later in this chapter, you define methods to interact with an individual activity item.)

- You use the Handlebars function to compile the data based on the template that you created and passed the variable of res.rows.item(i). This passes the row of data to your template. Once you get that HTML back from the template, you append the string to the variable code

- It uses the html () function from jQuery to insert the HTML into the my-activity-list element.

3. **You want to be able to attach the code HTML string in the HTML elements inside the Activity tab, so you need to give the content area of that tab an ID to reference.** You also want to add a Refresh button to the feed to enable the user to refresh the feed. Do that by adding a couple of lines of code to the activity tab in index.html.

First, after the `<h1>`, you add:

```
<a href="javascript:void(0);" data-role="button" onclick="grabActivities();"
class="ui-btn-right" data-icon="refresh">Refresh</a>
```

4. **Next, inside `<div id="my-activity">` add:**

```
<ul data-role="list-view id="my-activity-list"></ul>
```

This code adds the Refresh button, which fires the `grabActivities` function on click and creates a new jQuery Mobile List View, where you will place the elements for your feed. A List View is a special data role from jQuery that enables you to create lists that display dynamic and static data and is commonly used in web and native applications.

5. **The next step is to write a helper function called `timeDiffActivity`.** This will take the current timestamp and subtract it for the timestamp of the post, to generate something to the effect of *X minutes ago*. This is a very common pattern in activity-based applications because it provides more insight than just saying *June 5, 2012* does. It helps users see how recently a wine was added and makes the experience of using the app feel more immediate and immersive. You are probably familiar with this way of displaying time from Twitter.

You add it to the file `helpers.js`.

```
Handlebars.registerHelper('timeDiffActivity', function(string) {
    var system_date = string;
    var user_date = new Date().getTime();
    var diff = Math.floor((user_date - system_date) / 1000);
    if (diff <= 1) {return "just now";}
    if (diff < 20) {return diff + " seconds ago";}
    if (diff < 40) {return "half a minute ago";}
    if (diff < 60) {return "less than a minute ago";}
    if (diff <= 90) {return "one minute ago";}
    if (diff <= 3540) {return Math.round(diff / 60) + " minutes ago";}
    if (diff <= 5400) {return "1 hour ago";}
    if (diff <= 86400) {return Math.round(diff / 3600) + " hours ago";}
    if (diff <= 129600) {return "1 day ago";}
    if (diff < 604800) {return Math.round(diff / 86400) + " days ago";}
    if (diff <= 777600) {return "1 week ago";}
    return "on " + system_date;

});
```

The script takes in two timestamps and then calculates the number of seconds, minutes, and so on in milliseconds. Then after subtracting the start and end values, it performs `if/then` statements to determine the bucket that best defines the situation. These `if/then` statements enable you to define the timestamp as *X minutes ago*. When it's larger than the `diff` variable, it moves up 2 hours.

RUNNING YOUR SCRIPT AND DISPLAYING THE RESULTS CORRECTLY

Now that you have your structure, logic, and templates, you can start to run your script:

1. **Save the `index.html` file and refresh the page.** You won't see anything at first load because you have not added anything to your cellar yet.

2. **Click the Manage tab and add a couple of wines to your cellar, and then head back over to the Activity tab.** Click the Refresh button, and you will see a screen like the one in Figure 9-1.

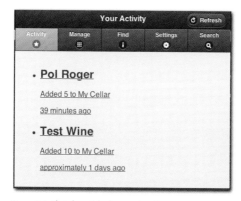

Figure 9-1: That doesn't look very sharp!

At the moment, the CSS isn't being applied to the content. Your lists are supposed to look like the one in Figure 9-2, but don't. You fix this by telling jQuery Mobile that this element should be displayed as a list.

Figure 9-2: Your lists should look like this.

3. **So how can you fix your lists?** jQuery Mobile has a special method for defining dynamic content that is added to List Views after the initial DOM is loaded. To change this, you need to allow jQuery Mobile to know that you want to use this element as a list view. To enable the list view, add the following code in the `grabActivity` function:

```
$('#my-activity-list').listview();
var len = res.rows.length;
...
```

This tells jQuery Mobile to add special classes to the elements to make sure that they are affected by the CSS. However, because jQuery Mobile adds most of the classes to the elements after the DOM has loaded, you need a way to refresh the list view after the content has been displayed. Do this by adding the following code at the end of the `for` loop:

```
....
$("#my-activity-list").html(code);
}
$('#my-activity-list').listview('refresh');
```

Now after saving and refreshing the page, you should see something like Figure 9-3.

Figure 9-3: Now your lists have a nice clean look.

That's it for the Activity tab. You touch bases with this tab again when you build the Wine Detail page—which you tackle next!

CREATING THE WINE DETAIL PAGE

The Activity tab displays all the wines added to the database. The feed is nice, but what if you wanted to see more information? That's where the Wine Detail page comes into play.

CREATING THE WINE DETAIL PAGE STRUCTURE

The first thing you need to do is create a new page in your structure. Add the following code to a new file called `detail.html`, which will hold the markup for the Wine Detail page.

Copy the `<head>` section from `index.html` and insert the following code into the new file's `<body>`:

```
<div id="wineDetail" data-role="page">
      <div data-role="header" data-position="inline">
      <h1>Wine Detail</h1>
      <div data-role="navbar" data-iconpos="bottom">
            <ul>
                  <li><a data-icon="star" href="#activity">Activity</a></li>
                  <li><a data-icon="grid" href="#manage">Manage</a></li>
                  <li><a data-icon="info" class="ui-btn-active"
href="#find">Find</a></li>
                  <li><a data-icon="gear" href="#settings">Settings</a></li>
                  <li><a data-icon="search" href="#search">Search</a></li>
            </ul>
      </div><!-- /navbar -->
      </div><!-- /header -->
      <div id="detail" data-role="content">

      </div><!-- /content -->
      <div id="social"><p>Loading Social Results...</p></div>
</div>
```

This page, while similar to the Activity tab, has some differences:

- In the content area, you give the `div` an `ID` of `detail`.
- You add a new `<div>` with an `ID` of `social`, which you will use to display data pulled in from social media.

BUILDING THE WINE DETAIL PAGE LOGIC

Now that you have the markup in place, you build the logic to serve the results.

> *Although you could use HandlebarsJS to generate the template, this example creates an HTML string of markup to give you a chance to see both methods.*

1. **Remember that you set the `onclick` method called `viewWine` that takes the `activity_id` variable?** Now it's time you build out that function. In `database.js`, add the following:

```
function viewWine(act_id)
{
db.transaction(function (tx) {
tx.executeSql("SELECT wine_name, wine_description, activity_note,
```

```
activity_quantity, activity_id, activity.wine_id, activity.created_at from
activity INNER JOIN wines on activity.wine_id = wines.wine_id where activity_id
= ?", [act_id],
function(tx, res) {
    if (res.rows.length == 0) {
            // There are no results found for that ID. Perhaps
it was passed incorrectly?
        }
        else
        {
            var code = "";
            var start = new Date().getTime();

            diff = timeDifference(start, res.rows.item(0).created_at)

            code += "<h2>"+res.rows.item(0).wine_name+"</h2>
<p>Added " + res.rows.item(0).activity_quantity + " </p>
<p>You said: "+res.rows.item(0).activity_note+"</p>
<p>Wine Description</p>
<p>"+res.rows.item(0).wine_description+"</p>
<p>You added this wine to your cellar: <strong>"+diff+"</strong>";


            $("#detail").html(code);

        },
        fR);
    });
}}
```

The overall theme of the function is similar to the script that you used to gather the data for the Activity tab, with a few differences:

- Unlike the previous query, you are only querying the activity and wine tables where the `activity_id` equals the number referenced in function. That's why this code doesn't include the `for` loop used to output data to the Activity tab. If you remember, that `for` loop outputs a list of wines currently loaded to the cellar. Instead, you use the first index (0) to gather the data relating to the wine being queried.

- You are displaying the `wine_name`, `activity_quantity`, `wine_description`, and `activity_note` to be displayed in the Details page. You then insert that data into the selected `<div>`.

2. **One thing you must add is an additional function to handle the time difference.** When you were using your templates, you could use the `timeDiff helper`, but you can't use that function here. You need to build our `timeDifference` function, which you can place the following code the `util.js` file.

```
function timeDifference(current, previous) {
    var msPerMinute = 60 * 1000;
    var msPerHour = msPerMinute * 60;
    var msPerDay = msPerHour * 24;
    var msPerMonth = msPerDay * 30;
  var msPerYear = msPerDay * 365;

  var elapsed = current - previous;

        if (elapsed < msPerMinute) {
        return Math.round(elapsed/1000) + ' seconds ago';
        }
        else if (elapsed < msPerHour) {
           return Math.round(elapsed/msPerMinute) + ' minutes ago';
         }
        else if (elapsed < msPerDay ) {
           Math.round(elapsed/msPerHour ) + ' hours ago';
        }
else if (elapsed < msPerMonth) {
  return 'approximately ' + Math.round(elapsed/msPerDay) + ' days ago';
}
else if (elapsed < msPerYear) {
    return 'approximately ' + Math.round(elapsed/msPerMonth) + ' months ago';
}
'approximately ' + Math.round(elapsed/msPerYear ) + ' years ago';
}
}
```

3. **Save your work.** You should see a screen like the one in Figure 9-4.

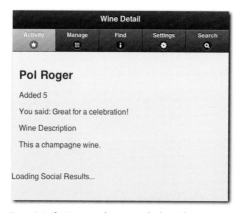

Figure 9-4: The Wine Detail page now displays information about the wine.

SHOWING DETAIL ON THE PAGE

The next step is to display more detail on each wine. You need to change the detail view on the page to display some different materials:

1. **Add some labels to define the content areas of your detail page:**

```
code += "<h2>"+res.rows.item(0).wine_name+"</h2>"
<p>Added " + res.rows.item(0).activity_quantity + " of these wines to your
  cellar. </p>
<label>Your comment was:</label>
<p> "+res.rows.item(0).activity_note+"</p>
<label>Wine Description</label>
<p>"+res.rows.item(0).wine_description+"</p>
<p>You added this wine to your cellar: <strong>"+diff+"</strong>";
```

2. **Save your work. You should see a screen like the one in Figure 9-5.**

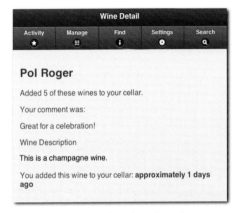

Figure 9-5: Your Wine Detail page has a cleaner layout.

3. **Add some `<h3>` tags to clearly define your sections as shown in Figure 9-6.** You can do so like this:

```
code += "<h2>"+res.rows.item(0).wine_name+"</h2>"
<p>Added <strong>" + res.rows.item(0).activity_quantity + "</strong> of these
  wines to your cellar. </p>
<h3>Your comment was:</h3> <p> "+res.rows.item(0).activity_note+"</p>
<label><strong>Wine Description</strong></label>
<p>"+res.rows.item(0).wine_description+"</p>
<p>You added this wine to your cellar: <strong>"+diff+"</strong>";
```

Figure 9-6: Adding the <strong> tags makes the text cleaner.

That looks good! Now let's move onto adding in the social results in the *social* element.

CONNECTING TO EXTERNAL SITES

When dealing with AJAX in JavaScript, you can connect to a wide range of free APIs to pull in data. In the previous chapter, you used foursquare to connect to local places. In this example, you will use the Twitter API to search for mentions of the wine that you are looking for and display the results below the wine details.

BUILDING THE TEMPLATE

Because Twitter's data is returned in JSON, you can use Handlebars to help build the HTML template that each tweet will display. If you followed the steps previously for the activity feed, you should have added HandlebarsJS to your project already, otherwise you can refer back to get it set up within your project.

1. **Define your template structure.** To use Handlebars, you must create a template in a
   `script` tag with the desired HTML. Add this code before the closing `</body>` tag in
   `index.html`:

   ```
   <script id="social-template" type="text/x-handlebars-template">
   ....
       </script>
   ```

   When you compile your template, Handlebars takes the contents of this script file and combines it with the JSON object to produce the desired result.

2. **Build the script to pull in the tweets based on the wine name.** Add this script right after you insert the wine data into the `detail` element.

```
$("#detail").html(code);
$.getJSON("http://search.twitter.com/search.json?q="+res.rows.item(0).wine_name,
  function(data) {
console.log(data);
});
```

As of March 15, 2013, Twitter will be rolling out a new version of their API that requires all API requests to be authenticated, meaning that you must provide additional parameters to your call. To learn more about these changes, refer to this link: `https://dev.twitter.com/docs/api/1.1/overview`.

What this does is:

- Use the `getJSON` method to query the Twitter API to return search results for the current selected wine.
- Use the `res.rows` object to grab the `wine_name` that the SQL command just generated.

3. Save this file and refresh the page. Then select an item in your Activity tab. Your screen should look like Figure 9-7.

```
▼ Object
    completed_in: 0.157
    max_id: 197850369911570430
    max_id_str: "197850369911570433"
    next_page: "?page=2&max_id=197850369911570433&q=Pol%20Roger"
    page: 1
    query: "Pol+Roger"
    refresh_url: "?since_id=197850369911570433&q=Pol%20Roger"
  ▼ results: Array[15]
    ▼ 0: Object
        created_at: "Thu, 03 May 2012 00:49:38 +0000"
        from_user: "familyfoodie"
        from_user_id: 41268882
        from_user_id_str: "41268882"
        from_user_name: "Family Foodie"
        geo: null
        id: 197850369911570430
        id_str: "197850369911570433"
        iso_language_code: "en"
      ▶ metadata: Object
        profile_image_url: "http://a0.twimg.com/profile_images/1724243069/Screen_shot_2011-12-30_at_1.54.14_PM_
        profile_image_url_https: "https://si0.twimg.com/profile_images/1724243069/Screen_shot_2011-12-30_at_1.54
        source: "&lt;a href=&quot;http://www.familyfoodie.com&quot; rel=&quot;nofollow&quot;&gt;Family Foodie&lt
        text: "Pol Roger 'White Foil' Champagne a Study in Elegance http://t.co/ckuDuDrF via @tampawinewoman"
        to_user: null
        to_user_id: null
        to_user_id_str: null
        to_user_name: null
```

Figure 9-7: The generated code in your Activity tab

This view reveals that you want to pull the following four attributes out of the `results` object:

- `created_at`
- `from_user_name`
- `text`
- `profile_image_url`

Handlebars Functions for Compiling the Template

Now that you know what data you want, you can start to build your Handlebars template. As discussed before, you now can add these elements in the format that is required for Handlebars.

For this situation, you want to do the same thing, but with the `results` object:

```
<script id="social-template" type="text/x-handlebars-template">
{{#each result}}
<p>{{ result.from_user_name}}</p>
{{/each}}
</script>
```

Integrating Functions into Your App

Now back in your `getJSON` function, you want to use Handlebars to compile the template you just created and generate the new template with the data from Twitter. To accomplish this, do the following:

1. **Insert the following code:**

```
$.getJSON("http://search.twitter.com/search.json?q="+res.rows.item(0).wine_name
, function(data) {
        var source    = $("#social-template").html();
        var template = Handlebars.compile(source);
        var html = template(data);
        $("#social").html(html);
});
```

   Using Handlebars, you obtain the inner HTML from your template, then compile the template into a new variable. Once you have completed that, you pass the data from Twitter into a new variable called `html`. At this point, the data has been collected and parsed through so the results should show a paragraph tag for every user who talked about your wine name.

2. **Save the file, reload the page, and navigate to an activity item.** You should see a screen similar to the one in Figure 9-8.

Figure 9-8: All the usernames from Twitter are placed in a paragraph tag.

CREATING THE LIST VIEW

Now that you understand how template engines work, you can build a more functional model of this list so you can see more detail of tweets about the wine — the tweets themselves, the username of people posting them, and their Twitter profile images.

1. **To create a new list view of the content, amend the `social-template` script you added to `index.html`, so it reads:**

```
<script id="social-template" type="text/x-handlebars-template">
    <ul data=role="list-view" id="my-social-list">
    <li data-role="list-divider" role="heading">Twitter Search Results</li>
    {{#each results}}
    <p>{{this. from_user_name}}</p>
    {{/each}}
    </ul>
</script>
```

Adding the UL of the list view enables you to create a list view that you used on the Activity tab. You also added a new UI element called a `list-divider`. This enables you to create a divider for your content.

2. **Save the page and reload the wine detail section.** You should see something like Figure 9-9.

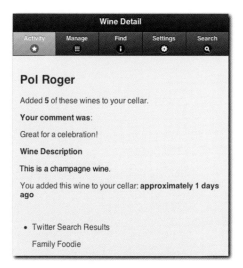

Figure 9-9: Usernames are now displayed within one list item

The usernames are all appearing within a single <li> element, with no <p> tags applied. What did you miss? If you remember what you did when building your Activity tab, you need to create a list view and use the refresh method when new content is added:

1. **Add this simple code to the getJSON function in social.js:**

```
$.getJSON("http://search.twitter.com/search.json?q="+res.rows.item(0).wine_name
, function(data) {
        var source   = $("#social-template-test").html();
        var template = Handlebars.compile(source);
        var html = template(data);

        $("#social").html(html);

        $('#my-social-list').listview();

        $('#my-social-list').listview('refresh');
});
```

   Once you add the HTML to the social element, you grab the ID of the <ul>, create a new instance of a list view and then implement the refresh method to recycle the styles.

2. **Save your work.** You should see a screen like the one in Figure 9-10.

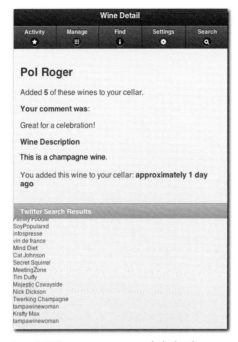

Figure 9-10: Usernames are now correctly displayed in <p> tags.

BUILDING THE TEMPLATE FOR YOUR TWEETS

Now that you have the correct data being pulled in from Twitter, you can move on to build a template for displaying the tweets.

1. **First add a profile picture of the user on the far right.** You can do that by adding the following to your template:

```
<ul data=role="list-view" id="my-social-list">
    <li data-role="list-divider" role="heading">Twitter Search Results</li>
    {{#each results}}
        <li>
            <a href="">
                <img class="ui-li-thumb" src="{{this.
profile_image_url}}">
            </a>
        </li>
    {{/each}}
</ul>
```

2. **Save the file.** You should start seeing some Twitter profile images on the left side of the list view, as shown in Figure 9-11:

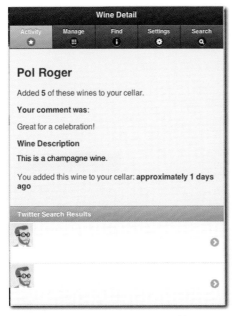

Figure 9-11: Now your page displays Twitter profile images.

3. **Next, add the username, text, and timestamp for the tweet.** If you follow the same schema, you only need to add the following to the inner HTML of the `<li>` element:

```
<li>
        <a href="">
                <img class="ui-li-thumb" src="{{this.profile_image_url}}">
                <h2>{{this.from_user_name}}</h2>
                <p>{{this.text}}</p>
                <p>{{ this.created_at}}</p>
        </a>
</li>
```

4. **Save your work.** You should see a nice clean tweet template like the one in Figure 9-12.

Even though your Twitter stream looks professional, one thing stands out: the timestamp. Although it's readable as is, you can also make it consistent with the other parts of the app with the more user-friendly "X minutes ago."

Figure 9-12: Your users will like this familiar look.

DEFINING A CUSTOM FUNCTION FOR RELATIVE TIMESTAMPS

Since you are using Handlebars to deliver the content in a template, how can you dynamically deliver fields that need to be calculated or changed? Luckily, Handlebars has a built-in function called registerHelper, which enables you to define a custom function to perform on an attribute. The syntax is below:

```
Handlebars. registerHelper('name_of_function', function(variables) {
    // do what you want here!
});
```

To show an example of how to use this function, create a new helper called userFull in helper.js:

1. **Enter this function.** It takes the user's screen name and full name on Twitter and combines them into one result.

```
Handlebars. registerHelper('userFull', function(tweets) {
    return tweets.from_user_name + " ("+tweets.from_user+")";
});
```

This function takes the object tweets and returns the from_user_name and the from_user attributes with a little bit of formatting. Place this JavaScript code before the helper.js file.

2. **To call this function in Handlebars, just use the name you created (userFull) followed by the variable you want to pass through, like this:**

```
<h2>{{userFull this}}</h2>
```

3. **Save the file.** You should see a screen like Figure 9-13.

Figure 9-13: Example of Twitter feed with username and full name

TWEAKING THE TIMESTAMP

Now that you know how to write custom helpers, you can write a function that will handle the timestamp section to turn it into relative time format.

1. **If you remember from before, you created a helper function to handle timestamps in your Handlebars templates.** You reuse that functionality to tweak the timestamps for your Twitter feed. You make one tweak to accept various date input. Create a helper for Handlebars called timeDiff and have it pass a string. In the `helper.js` file, add the following code:

```
Handlebars.registerHelper('timeDiff', function(string) {
    …
});
```

2. **After you have the structure, you need to tweak the functionality of the date input.** You want to copy the `timeDiffActivity` function you created earlier and insert into the newly created `'timeDiff'` function.

```
Handlebars.registerHelper('timeDiff', function(string) {
    var system_date = new Date(Date.parse(string));
    var user_date = new Date();
    var diff = Math.floor((user_date - system_date) / 1000);
    if (diff <= 1) {return "just now";}
    if (diff < 20) {return diff + " seconds ago";}
    if (diff < 40) {return "half a minute ago";}
    if (diff < 60) {return "less than a minute ago";}
    if (diff <= 90) {return "one minute ago";}
    if (diff <= 3540) {return Math.round(diff / 60) + " minutes ago";}
```

```
        if (diff <= 5400) {return "1 hour ago";}
        if (diff <= 86400) {return Math.round(diff / 3600) + " hours ago";}
        if (diff <= 129600) {return "1 day ago";}
        if (diff < 604800) {return Math.round(diff / 86400) + " days ago";}
        if (diff <= 777600) {return "1 week ago";}
        return "on " + system_date;
});
```

Notice that you changed only the first two lines of the function to represent the date input from Twitter. Your function in the activity feed accepts Unix Timestamps (12343225), whereas Twitter accepts a different timestamp, which is the reason for the switch.

Putting the whole template together, including the existing helpers, it looks like this:

```
<script id="social-template-test" type="text/x-handlebars-template">
    <ul data=role="list-view" id="my-social-list">
    <li data-role="list-divider" role="heading">Twitter Search Results</li>
    {{#each results}}
        <li>
    <a href="">
        <img class="ui-li-thumb" src="{{this.profile_image_url}}">
        <h2>{{userFull this}}</h2>
        <p>{{this.text}}</p>
        <p>{{timeDiff this.created_at}}</p>
    </a>
        </li>
    {{/each}}
    </ul>
</script>
```

3. **Save your work.** Refresh your screen and you will see something like Figure 9-14:

Figure 9-14: Your timestamp entry is now in relative time, which is more user-friendly.

CHANGING THE TWEET IN THE LIST VIEW

Finally, it would be great to have the user touch the list element and be directed to Twitter to view the whole tweet because jQuery Mobile cuts off the text if it goes beyond the list view area. Because jQuery Mobile handles every link as if it's a `hashchange` event or tries to perform an AJAX on the `href` attribute, you need to tell jQuery Mobile that each link in this list is external.

1. **Do that by adding a rel attribute to the link:**

```
<a href="#" rel="external">Content</a>
```

This will help jQuery Mobile to redirect the link to another browser window instead of trying to load the content via AJAX.

2. **To send the user the correct page from the tweet, you need to build the link to direct users.** Using the existing data, you can create a new `registerHelper` to help you with the legwork:

```
Handlebars.registerHelper('generateURL', function(tweet) {
    return "http://twitter.com/"+tweet.from_user +"/statuses/"+tweet.id_str;
});
```

3. **Finally, you put the entire template together:**

```
{{#each results}}
     <li>
          <a rel="external" target="_blank" href="{{generateURL
this}}">
               <img class="ui-li-thumb"
src="{{this.profile_image_url}}">
               <h2>{{userFull this}}</h2>
               <p>{{this.text}}</p>
               <p>{{timeDiff this.created_at}}</p>
          </a>
     </li>
  {{/each}}
```

4. **Save and refresh.** You should be able to click through the tweets and get directed to Twitter's mobile website, as shown in the Figures 9-15.

Figure 9-15: The view for an individual tweet

SHARING ON TWITTER AND FACEBOOK

While searching using the Twitter API shows a lot of interesting detail, it would be nice to share content about the wine to Twitter or Facebook. This is easy using the *Intent* functionality of the two social networks. It allows you to create a link with all the relevant information to be included in your post.

1. To get started, create an additional template called `share-template` and place it in the bottom of the `<body>` tag in the `index.html` file:

```
<script id="share-template" type="text/x-handlebars-template">
....
</script>
```

2. Now create the content, which will be a link that the user will click to share to Twitter and Facebook.

   You can find out more about Twitter Intent Links here: `https://dev.twitter.com/docs/intents#tweet-intent`.

```
<script id="share-template" type="text/x-handlebars-template">
<h3><a rel="external-link"
href="https://twitter.com/intent/tweet?text=I+just+added+{{wine_name}}+
  to+my+cellar+using+Corks!">Tweet</a></h3>
<h3><a rel="external-link"
href=http://facebok.com/sharer.php?u=http://example.com&title=I+
  just+added+{{wine_name}}+to+my+cellar+using+Corks!>
Share on Facebook</a></h3>
</script>
```

This script creates two links with the parameters specific from the provider. In the Twitter example, the `text` parameter is where the text of the tweet goes, and in the Facebook example, you use the `u` parameter to specify what link you want to share. You can also add the `title` parameter, which will give your post a title.

1. In your `viewWine` function, add the following code right before `$("#detail").html(code)` section:

```
var source   = $("#share-template").html();
var template = Handlebars.compile(source);
code += template(res.rows.item(0));
```

This code grabs the share template that you created, compiles it using Handlebars, and then passes in the data you received from the database query. That will help you generate the URL to pass to Facebook and Twitter.

2. **Save and reload the application.** After navigating back to your Wine Detail page, you should see a screen like Figure 9-16.

Figure 9-16: Wine Detail page showing Share on Facebook and Tweet links

Once you click on them, you will be directed to Twitter and Facebook to add additional comments to your tweet or share, like in Figure 9-17:

Figure 9-17: Example of sharing on Twitter using the Web Intent Link

SUMMARY

This chapter focused on building the Activity and Wine Detail pages, plus using external services to connect to Twitter to pull additional content. In addition, we discussed:

- Creating templates with Handlebars
- Creating custom helpers with Handlebars
- Parsing the Twitter Search API
- Sharing to Twitter and Facebook
- Handling external links in jQuery Mobile

10

LOCATION STORAGE AND SEARCH

ONE OF THE major reasons native applications tend to "feel faster" is their capability to cache large amounts of data in a phone's memory. With native APIs, developers can store databases and caches of the largest data sets and don't require the application to contact the server every time a person navigates to an existing page.

With Corks, you are not accessing an external server for your data, but you do use foursquare and Twitter to retrieve information regarding venues and tweets. This can be bandwidth intensive, so with Mobile Web, you can use technologies such as local storage to store the results of data in the DOM in order to use that data later.

Local storage provides web-app developers the opportunity to cache large data sets in order to

make them appear rapidly through page transitions. The addition of this in HTML5 prevents having to wait long for a web page to load. Being able to load data using AJAX, coupled with the power of Local Storage, creates a rich experience for users because they can access it without connecting to the Internet.

Local storage allows you to store data only in *key-pair* format, so when storing the data from foursquare or Twitter, you must convert the raw JSON to a string in order to use it again.

In this chapter, you use local storage to cache the foursquare venues and Twitter results. You will also use local storage in the Settings panel to create some customized features to enhance the Corks experience. Finally, you build your final tab, Search, to search for your latest activity.

In this chapter you continue to develop for the sample app Corks. By the end of this chapter you should be able to:

- Cache locations for foursquare using local storage
- Cache tweets from Twitter using local storage
- Build the Settings tab for customized settings using local storage
- Build the Search tab with wine results

If you haven't already worked through them, you may find it helpful to take a quick look at Chapters 8 and 9 as these deal with adding geolocation to your web app and with Twitter and foursquare integration. All of these are necessary before being able to store this data locally.

ELEMENTS TO BUILD

Local storage is the main focal point in this chapter, so start by caching some of the data that you receive from external services. Before you start caching, you need to build a function that you can reference through this exercise to make interacting with local storage easier. Here you'll write a function called `myStorage`, which includes the functionality you need to store data locally. You can then use this function every time you need to do this in your app.

CREATING THE MYSTORAGE FUNCTION

When developing features that you will use all the time, sometimes it helps to write a basic function that you can call and iterate through your code.

1. **In the `index.html` file, create a new variable called `myStorage`, which will contain a few methods:**

```
var myStorage = {
        set: function(a,b) {
        },
        remove: function(a) {
        },
        get: function(a) {
        },
        clear: function() {
        }
}
```

While these functions may mimic the syntax of `localStorage.setItem` and `localStorage.getItem`, it's nice to incorporate these methods in a function that you can change later. Say, for example, that you wanted to perform one action before saving something as a local storage element. You could just edit the code for the set function of myStorage once instead of scanning the whole file looking for instances of local-Storage.setItem().

2. **For the** set **method of** myStorage, **you pass two variables,** a **and** b. In this case, a represents the index, or the *key*, while b represents the value.

```
. .
set: function(a,b) {
        var val = "";
        if (typeof b=="object") {
                val = JSON.stringify(b);
        }
        else {
                val = b;
        }
        localStorage.setItem(a,val);
}
. . .
```

The preceding code uses the typeof method to determine the data type of the variable b. If the variable is an object, which is the type that will be returned from Twitter and foursquare, you want to save the result as a string, to variable val. Remember, local storage cannot save objects or arrays, so you must convert them. JSON.stringify is a function that is built into most modern web browsers; however, to be on the safe side, add the following script tag in your <head> section:

```
<script src=" https://raw.github.com/douglascrockford/JSON-js/master/json2.js"
 /><script>
```

Alternatively, you could always download the JSON.js file separately and apply it locally. Adding this script tag ensures you have support for Windows Phone and other WebKit devices that may not have local support.

3. **Now add the** remove **and** get **methods.** They are similar to the local storage methods:

```
. . .
        remove: function(a) {
        localStorage.setItem(a, "");
        },
        get: function(a,b) {
                if (b == "JSON") {
                        return JSON.parse(localStorage.getItem(a));
                }
                else {
                        return localStorage.getItem(a);
                }
        }
. . .
```

For the `remove` function, you are simply using the local storage method to set the variable a (which is your index or key) to an empty string. On the `get` function, you take in two variables: a, which is your index, and b, which is a string that you use to test if you want to return the results as an object or just plain text. This enables you to define what type of data you want to receive.

Finally, you add the `clear` function, which is the same as `localStorage.clear()`. This wipes out all your local storage elements on this domain. Sometimes it's good for testing or debugging. In a production app, use this only if you want your users to remove all their data. Note that this doesn't affect WebSQL, which you use for your database.

```
. . .
clear: function() {
        locationStorage.clear();
}
. . .
```

That's all there is to the `myStorage` function! You now can use the function within your code to retain and serve data easily whenever you need to.

CACHING GEOLOCATION AND VENUES

One of the problems with caching users' latitude and longitude is that if they physically move their location, you need to update your information. You could use `watchPosition`; however, that quickly drains battery life on a mobile device. The solution is to keep track of the timestamp of the last geolocation success. If a user requests the location again and the difference is minimal, you serve that user the cached latitude and longitude.

1. **Refer to the** `successPosition` **function that you created in Chapter 8, and then add the following line of code:**

```
. . .
var currentTime = new Date().getTime()
myStorage.set("lastGeo", currentTime);
. . .
```

   This piece of code stores the current timestamp into a local storage object called `lastGeo`. You use this later to detect the time difference between the two dates.

2. **In the** `onHashChange` **function where you call the** `getCurrentPosition,` **add some code to detect whether the last known location is old enough to require a refresh:**

```
. . .
if ($("#map").html() == "") {
        var lastTime = myStorage.get("lastGeo")
        if (lastTime) {
```

```
            var currentTime = new Date.getTime();
            var subtract = parseInt(currentTime) - parseInt(lastTime);
            // if difference is greater than 250 seconds or 4 minutes, refresh
   the location
            if (parseInt(subtract) >250) {
                        getCurrentPosition();
            }
            else {
            navigator.geolocation.getCurrentPosition(successPosition,
   errorPosition);
            }
        }
        else {
            navigator.geolocation.getCurrentPosition(successPosition,
   errorPosition);
            }
   }
   ...
```

While the preceding function looks complex, it's actually pretty simple. You are just amending the previous function to first check to see if the `lastGeo` key has been set in local storage. If it is, then you take the current time and subtract it from the last known location. If the difference is greater than 250 seconds, which is around 4 minutes, the user might have moved locations and you should refresh by calling `nagivator.geoloca-tion.getCurrentPosition` again. Otherwise, just call `successPosition`.

3. **Now you are probably wondering how you can get the latitude and longitude, if you don't pass the** `position` **object to the** `successPosition` **function.** The answer is simple: Because you stored the latitude and longitude in variable form, you easily call them within the `successPosition` function, as the following code shows:

```
function successPosition(position) {
        if (position) {
                lat = position.coords.latitude;
                lng = position.coords.longitude;
                var currentTime = new Date().getTime()
                myStorage.set("lastGeo", currentTime);
                drawMap();
        }
        else {
                drawMap();
        }
}
```

The additional methods that you are calling enable you to call the `drawMap` function, recognizing that you already stored the latitude and longitude in variables. Caching the location uses less battery power and provides quicker response time.

4. **Because you now are caching the location, it's time to store the venue objects in your local storage object for lightning fast results.** First, you need to change the way your `findPlaces` function works.

Here is the old function:

```
function findPlaces() {
        $.getJSON("https://api.foursquare.com/v2/venues/search?client_id=
    YOURCLIENTID &client_secret=YOURSECRET&ll="+lat+","+lng+"&query=wine
    store&limit=25", function(data) {
    ...
```

Change it to the following:

```
function findPlaces() {
        var venue_data = myStorage.get("foursquareVenues")
var lastTime = myStorage.get("lastVenuePull")
if (lastTime) {
        var currentTime = new Date.getTime();
        var subtract = parseInt(currentTime) - parseInt(lastTime);
        if (parseInt(subtract) >= 250) {
        $.getJSON("https://api.foursquare.com/v2/venues/search?client_id-CLIENTID
    &client_secret=CLIENTSECRET&ll="+lat+","+lng+"&query=wine store&limit=25",
    function(data) {
                          parseMap(data, "store");
                });
        }
        else {
            parseData(venue_data);
            }
}
else {
        $.getJSON("https://api.foursquare.com/v2/venues/search?client_
    id=CLIENTD&client
    _secret=CLIENTSECRET&ll="+lat+","+lng+"&query=wine store&limit=25",
    function(data) {
                parseMap(data, "store");
        });
}
```

You've done a few things to your existing function, `findPlaces`:

- You've removed the logic that parses the points on the map and will replace it in a new function called `parseMap`.

- You're checking to see if the cached time of the Local Storage object is greater than 5 minutes. If it is, you need to pull fresh data. Otherwise, use the cached information to pass along to the `parseMap` function.

- If everything else pans out, you pass either the cached venue object or the new venue object to the `parseMap` method. In addition, you pass a second variable if the venue needs to be stored.

5. **You are rewriting the logic for placing the markers on the map, so you need to take into account the second parameter of the** `parseMap`, **like so:**

```
function parseMap(data, store) {
        if (data.meta.code == 200) {
                if (store) {
                        myStorage.set("foursquareVenues", data);

                        var currentTime = new Date.getTime();
                        myStorage.set("lastVenuePull", currentTime);
                }
```

While the . . . piece extends the logic that you used to add the markers to the map earlier, the new piece checks to see if you want to store the venue data in local storage. If you are pulling the information from cache (local storage), you don't want to restore and reset the counter. However, if the data is fresh, you want to capture the last timestamp from which you received the information.

6. **Finally, at the end of the loop where you place the marker on the map, you need to add a new Google Map command called** `resize` **to enhance your map.** This command enables the map to resize to fit your page and display all of the content; without it, some of the map might be missing.

```
google.maps.event.trigger(map, 'resize');
```

7. **Now refresh the website and go to the Find tab. You won't find anything new in appearance, but it will be faster on your mobile device.** You added some `console.log` statements to show the caching versus a live pull, as shown in Figure 10-1 and 10-2.

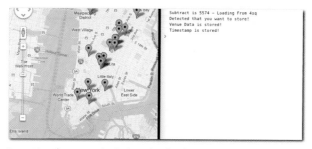

Figure 10-1: The generated code shows that data has been stored locally.

map data 2012 © Google

Figure 10-2: The data is being retrieved from the local cache, not from foursquare.

map data 2012 © Google

CACHING TWEETS

Because you have a great function to use to cache data using local storage, do the same thing for Twitter. Here's how to start:

1. **Just like the foursquare parse function, you will create a new function called** parseTweets, **as shown in the following code example:**

```
function parseTweets(wine_id, data, store) {
        if (store)
        {
                myStorage.set("tweetWine_"+wine_id, data);
                var currentTime = new Date().getTime();
                myStorage.set("lasttwitterPull", currentTime);
        }
        var source    = $("#social-template-test").html();
        var template = Handlebars.compile(source);
        var html = template(data);
        $("#social").html(html);
        $('#my-social-list').listview();
        $('#my-social-list').listview('refresh');
}
```

There are some differences between this function and the previous function that you wrote for parseData for the foursquare venues:

- You are taking three variables, with one being the wine_id.
- You use the wine_id to set the index of the local storage object (for example, naming the index name to tweetWine_1).

2. **You need to change the function that pulls in the wine detail, so add the following code:**

```
....
$("#detail").html(code);
var twitter = myStorage.get("tweetWineName_"+res.rows.item(0).wine_id, "JSON");
var lastTime = myStorage.get("lasttwitterPull");

if (lastTime)
{
        var currentTime = new Date().getTime();
        var subtract = parseInt(currentTime) - parseInt(lastTime);
        if (parseInt(subtract) >= 1500)
        {
        $.getJSON("http://search.twitter.com/search.json?q="+res.rows.item(0).
  wine_id, function(data) {
                        parseTweets(res.rows.item(0).wine_name, data, "store");
                });
        }
        else
```

```
        {
                parseTweets(res.rows.item(0).wine_name, data);
        }
    else
    {
            $.getJSON("http://search.twitter.com/search.json?q="+res.rows.item(0).
    wine_id,
    function(data) {
                parseTweets(res.rows.item(0).wine_name, data, "store");
        });
    }
```

Just like the venue caching, you're setting the time of the most current data pull, checking to see if the time difference is greater than your limiter (in this case, 1,500 ms) and then displaying the cached results. It's that simple!

SAVING DETAILS IN THE SETTINGS TAB

With local storage, you not only can save data from external social services, but you also can save settings and user preferences. In this example, you add another page for the Settings tab, which will save the user's name.

1. **First, build out the Settings tab.** You need to add markup similar to the HTML you have used to build the other pages within jQuery Mobile. Add the following code to index. html, below the rest of the HTML but above the scripts you've added:

```
<div id="settings" data-role="page">
      <div data-role="header" data-position="inline">
      <h1>Settings</h1>
      <div data-role="navbar" data-iconpos="bottom">
            <ul>
                    <li><a data-icon="star" href="#activity">Activity</a></li>
                    <li><a data-icon="grid" href="#manage">Manage</a></li>
                    <li><a data-icon="info" href="#find">Find</a></li>
                    <li><a data-icon="gear" class="ui-btn-active"
  href="#settings">Settings</a></li>
                    <li><a data-icon="search" href="#search">Search</a></li>
            </ul>
      </div><!-- /navbar -->
      </div><!-- /header -->
      <div data-role="content">
            <div class="success" id="success-msg-user" style="display:
  none;">Awesome, your name is saved!</div>
                    <label for="user_name">Your name:</label>
                    <input type="text" class="required" name="user_name"
  id="user_name_save" data-mini="true" />
                    <button onclick="saveUser();">Save User</button>
      </div>
</div>
```

This adds a simple form in your page containing an input box and a submit button. The button, upon click, fires a function called `saveUser`. Notice that you defined the ID as `user_name_save`.

2. **Now build out of the `saveUser` function, which enables you to take the contents of the input box and apply it to a local storage element.**

```
function saveUser() {
        $("#success-msg-user").hide();
        myStorage.set("userName", $("#user_name_save").val());
        $("#success-msg-user").show();
}
```

The function is very simple and just uses the `hide` and `show` methods to toggle the results message from being shown to the user. In between, you are saving the value of the `user_name_save` element to the `userName` local storage index.

3. **One of the most important things is to make sure you set the input box to the correct value from local storage, if it is set.** You need to add the following code to the `$(document).ready` function, like so:

```
$(document).ready(function(){
var user = myStorage.get("userName");
        if (user) {
                $("#user_name_save").val(user);
        }
...
```

This script fires upon load of the application and checks whether there is a value set for the index of `userName`. If so, it grabs the value and inserts it into the `value` attribute of the input box. After you refresh your `index.html` file, navigate to the Settings tab. After entering your name and saving, your screen should look like Figure 10-3:

Figure 10-3: The app tells the user that his or her name has been saved.

After this, close your browser and reopen it. Navigate to the Settings tab. You should see what is shown in Figure 10-4, which confirms that your name has been saved:

Figure 10-4: After entering your name, it will appear when you navigate to the Settings tab.

SEARCHING YOUR HISTORY

After entering several wines in your cellar, the best way to check to see if it contains a specific wine is by searching. With the final tab, Search, you will enable users to search their Activity tab by wine name and display the results. Follow these steps:

1. **As you did with the Settings tab, you need to create a basic template for the page.** Add the following immediately before the markup for the Settings tab that you just added:

```
<div id="search" data-role="page">
        <div data-role="header" data-position="inline">
        <h1>Search</h1>
        <div data-role="navbar" data-iconpos="bottom">
                <ul>
                        <li><a data-icon="star" href="#activity">Activity</a></li>
                        <li><a data-icon="grid" href="#manage">Manage</a></li>
                        <li><a data-icon="info" href="#find">Find</a></li>
                        <li><a data-icon="gear" href="#settings">Settings</a></li>
                        <li><a data-icon="search" class="ui-btn-active"
    href="#search">Search</a></li>
                </ul>
        </div><!-- /navbar -->
        </div><!-- /footer -->
        <div id="my-search" data-role="content">
                <form id="search-form" data-ajax="false" onsubmit="SearchWines();
    return false;">
                        <label for="search-basic">Search Input:</label>
                        <input type="search" name="search" id="search-basic"
    value="" />
                </form>
                <ul data=role="list-view" id="my-search-list"></ul>
        </div>
</div>
```

Although this is a standard page implementation, note that you added a new input value called `search`, which will give you a standard search bar in which users can enter text. It's already themed and looks like Figure 10-5 when you refresh your `index.html` file:

Figure 10-5: You now have an input box for searching.

2. Now that you have the structure laid out, it's time to build the function that enables you to search your wines from your activity list. As you can see from the content of the `<form>` element, in the HTML you've just added, you will name your function `SearchWines`:

```
function SearchWines() {
        var search_term = $("#search-basic").val();
        db.transaction(function (tx) {
                tx.executeSql("SELECT wine_name, wine_description, activity_note,
  activity_quantity, activity_id, activity.wine_id, activity.created_at from
  activity INNER JOIN wines on activity.wine_id = wines.wine_id where wine_name
  LIKE ?", ["%"+search_term+"%"],
                function(tx, res) {
                        if (res.rows.length == 0)
                        {
                                console.log("seriously");
                        }
                        else
                        {
                        var len = res.rows.length;
                                var code = "";
                                for (var i = 0; i < len; i++){
                                var start = new Date().getTime();
                                diff = timeDifference(start,
  res.rows.item(i).created_at)
                                        code += "<li>
<a href='#wineDetail'
onclick='grabActivity("+res.rows.item(i).activity_id+");'>
<h2>"+res.rows.item(i).wine_name+"</h2>
<p>Added " + res.rows.item(i).activity_quantity + " to My Cellar</p>
```

```
                <p style='margin-top: 10px;'>" + diff + "</p>
            </li>";

                                            }
                                $("#my-search-list").html(code);
                                $('#my-search-list').listview();
                                $('#my-search-list').listview('refresh');

                                        }
                                },
                                    );
                            });
                }
```

This function is similar to the `grabActivity` function; however, because you want this to be a search query, you are using the DB query type as a LIKE, which will match all cases of the word that you search. After you grab the results, you format them in a similar way to the Activity tab, inject them into the `<ul>`, and then refresh the list view.

After saving the page, use your Search tab to look for a specific wine. Upon searching, you see something interesting, as shown in Figure 10-6:

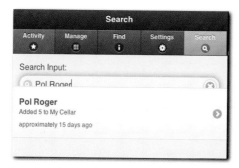

Figure 10-6: The app is finding the wine you're searching for, but it doesn't quite look right

This is strange! It appears that when the List View is rendered, it pushes the `<ul>` up and overlaps the form. This problem can be solved in a couple of ways, but the easiest solution is to add some padding to the `<form>` element by creating a new class called `pad`:

In your `<head>` tags add the following script:

```
...
<style type="css/text">
.pad {
padding-bottom: 25px;
}
</style>
...
```

Then add the following class to the `<form>` element:

```
...
<form id="search-form" data-ajax="false" onsubmit="SearchWines(); return false;"
 class="pad">
...
```

Of course you could always add the `.pad` class to a new style sheet file, however we just added this for our demonstration. It's best practice to include all your styles in a separate file to allow for updating and maintenance easier.

Upon saving and refreshing, the screen shot looks much better, as shown in Figure 10-7:

Figure 10-7: That looks better!

You can always tweak the query to select any field you would like to search. For example, say you want to search only the `activity_note` field. In that case, you would just make the change shown here:

```
...
tx.executeSql("SELECT wine_name, wine_description, activity_note,
activity_quantity, activity_id, activity.wine_id, activity.created_at from
activity INNER JOIN wines on activity.wine_id = wines.wine_id where
activity_note LIKE ?", ["%"+search_term+"%"],
...
```

In the previous query, you use a SQL technique called `INNER JOIN`, which allows you to take two tables in your database schema and join them on a common field. In this case, the common field `wine_id` joins both the wines and activity tables. By doing this, you now can get information about both the activity and the wine with having too many separate queries.

Great! You now have added an Activity search to the application!

SUMMARY

This chapter focused on building the Settings and Search pages, plus using Local Storage to cache and save external feeds from foursquare and Twitter. In addition, we discussed:

- Building a custom local storage helper file for JSON
- Parsing strings and objects via JavaScript
- Making Web SQL queries with the `LIKE` operator

IV

PERFORMANCE AND PRODUCTION

11

TESTING AND ORGANIZING YOUR CODE

NOW THAT YOU have finished the development of Corks, you are ready to perform some testing to get Corks ready for deployment to our web servers for use. To prepare for deployment and for easy maintenance, you need to organize your files. At the end of the project development, it's also a good practice to refactor your code to place each JavaScript function into its own file. When dealing with mobile bandwidth, loading multiple small files is better than loading one large JavaScript file. You can accomplish this by removing the white spaces between each line in your JavaScript to decrease the size.

This chapter discusses refactoring your code by looking for improvements and moving each section into its own separate JavaScript and caching via manifest cache. Then you look into using optimization plug-ins such as head.js to deliver the contents of your JavaScript files asynchronously as the page loads. Finally, you determine your app's compatibility with multiple browsers.

In this chapter, you test, clean up, and refactor your code on Corks. By the end of this chapter, you should have accomplished the following:

- Organize your JavaScript code
- Know how to use `head.js` and the manifest cache
- Learn some testing techniques for mobile apps

ORGANIZING YOUR JAVASCRIPT FILES

Until now, you have been keeping all your JavaScript files in the bottom of the `index.html`. This is good for a development build, but you also want to organize these files better based on their purpose. A good practice is to create a new JavaScript file defined by the type of actions the script will perform. For this scenario, you can order the structure as defined here:

```
assets
  js
    global.js
    database.js
    util.js
    social.js
    geo.js
    helper.js
```

This structure enables you to quickly find the action you want to edit and organize your JavaScript files. You also will be able to separate the files so they download faster upon first load. Table 11-1 breaks down the files and their usage:

Table 11-1   Explanation of JavaScript Files

File Name	File Explanation
Global.js	This contains global variables, the `document.ready()` function, and any setup functions.
Database.js	As the name implies, this holds database connections, queries, and any other function interacting with the database.
Util.js	This file contains utility functions such as those that determine the time between two entries and other basic functions that get reused throughout the application, such as `myStorage`.
Social.js	This contains any social interaction between Corks and external sources, such as foursquare and Twitter.
Geo.js	This file contains all elements relating to maps or geolocation.
Helper.js	This file contains the `HandlebarsJS` helpers for your template library for tweets.

SETTING UP GLOBAL.JS

`Global.js` is the first file that will load in your HTML document. That said, you must make sure it contains all the variables and content that need to be in the web app when it starts up.

Focus on adding the following items to your global section:

- Functions, or elements, that are required to run when the application starts
- Global variables that are used throughout the application

Here is the process:

1. **Add the global variables to the top of** `global.js`. **These variables are used throughout the application:**

```
/* System Variables */
var map;
var db;
var lat;
var lng;
var infowindow = new google.maps.InfoWindow();
```

2. **Add the code regarding the** `hashchange` **event below the global variables:**

```
/* Hash Change */
$(window).bind('hashchange', function(e){
      newHash = window.location.hash.substring(1);
...
});
```

Remember, `hashchange` *events were used earlier to track the page navigation of the Corks application. This allows you track which pages users have navigated to, so that they can use their back button to navigate through the stack of pages.*

3. **Add the** `document.ready()` **function that contains all the initialization scripts of your database and some setup functions:**

```
/* Document Load */
$(document).ready(function(){
    var user = myStorage.get("userName");
    if (user) {
      $("#user_name_save").val(user);
      }
      db = openDatabase('myCorks', '1.0', 'My Corks Database', 2 * 1024 *
  1024);
        ...
});
```

That should round out the `global.js`, which contains everything you need to start the application.

CREATING DATABASE.JS

This file contains all the queries and interactions with the database, besides the initialization of the table:

1. **Extract all functions that relate specifically to database calls.** They should include the following:
   - `grabActivities()`
   - `viewDetails()`
   - `searchWines()`
   - `get_color()`
   - `addWineActivity()`
   - `addWine()`
   - `addActivity()`

2. **Once you have extracted these functions from the** `index.html` **file, copy and paste them in** `database.js` **based on the structure defined previously.**

3. **Add your success and failure callbacks for your DB queries, as shown here:**

```
/* Callbacks */
function sR(a,b) {
        // The query was successfully!
}


function fR(a,b){
        // Oops! There was an issue. let's alert the user.
        alert(b.message);
}
```

4. **After you add all the relevant content, save the** `database.js` **file.**

CREATING UTIL.JS

Separate all functions that can be repeatable and add them to the `Util.js` file.

To start, grab the following functions:

- `last_id()`
- `handleForm()`
- `toggleBox()`
- `timeDifference()`
- `myStorage`
- `saveUser()`

Copy all these functions over to `Util.js` so you can access them through the web app. If you wanted, you also could easily add on utility functions to this file.

CREATING SOCIAL.JS

Whenever you make an API call to foursquare or Twitter, you need to extract those related functions and place them in the `Social.js` file.

Extract the following functions:

- `parseTweets()`
- `findPlaces()`

Remember that you are looking only for instances in which you call the respective APIs. Do not add to this JavaScript file any functionality that contains template helpers, which you will place in the `helpers.js` file.

CREATING GEO.JS

Writing the code for maps and geolocation was tough, but organizing them for further edits shouldn't be difficult. In this file, you will add the initialization and the updating of geolocation and map settings.

Following are the six functions to extract:

- `refreshLocation()`
- `drawMap()`
- `parseMap()`
- `getInfoWindowEvent()`
- `successPosition()`
- `errorPosition()`

CREATING HELPER.JS

The goal of the `helper.js` file is provide additional methods to help HandlebarsJS compile your templates. You already have done this previously; however, the code is included here as a reminder:

```
/* HandlebarsJS Helpers */

Handlebars. registerHelper('userFull', function(tweets) {
      return tweets.from_user_name + " ("+tweets.from_user+")";
});

….
```

PUTTING IT ALL TOGETHER

Now that you have put everything in separate JavaScript files, you need to declare them in the `head` section of your HTML file. Note that some browser tests have shown that putting all JavaScript files at the bottom of your HTML will improve performance, because the contents of the HTML load first, then the script. HTML documents load from top to bottom. In this case, the performance isn't a big issue; however, depending on your application, you might want to see the difference. The Corks example contains very little markup in the actual HTML file, which just is filled by your JavaScript. It's also important to note that you can add all the JavaScript files at the end of HTML file for better performance. This forces the main HTML text to load, followed by the JavaScript.

To add the JavaScript files, simply type the following snippet after the `script` tag for the `HandlebarsJS`:

```
    <script src="http://cloud.github.com/downloads/wycats/handlebars.js/handle-
  bars-1.0.0.beta.6.js"></script>

    <script src="assets/js/global.js" type="text/javascript"
charset="utf-8"></script>
    <script src="assets/js/database.js" type="text/javascript"
charset="utf-8"></script>
    <script src="assets/js/geo.js" type="text/javascript"
charset="utf-8"></script>
    <script src="assets/js/helper.js" type="text/javascript"
charset="utf-8"></script>
    <script src="assets/js/util.js" type="text/javascript"
charset="utf-8"></script>
    <script src="assets/js/social.js" type="text/javascript"

charset="utf-8"></script>
```

That's it! Now all your files are centrally located, and you can easily detect which function each JavaScript file contains. This can help with updating and troubleshooting, plus allows for easy downloading. It's also important to note that sometimes, adding all these JavaScript files together can reduce the number of HTTP requests, however if you keep your JavaScript files light (meaning fewer files), the performance will not be detrimental to your application.

LOADING YOUR JAVASCRIPT FILES

Loading JavaScript files can be time intensive, depending on the size of the file. Remember, HTML loads from the top down. Web developers can use a couple of tools to help speed up the process on mobile devices.

It's good to note that JavaScript always loads synchronously, which means that nothing can load while the JavaScript loads. This is why it might be important—depending on your application—to place the JavaScript files at the bottom of the HTML document. However, we will discuss an alternative that loads JavaScript files asynchronously, using a service called `head.js`.

HEAD.JS

`head.js (http://headjs.com/)` is a JavaScript library that enables you to load the `head` section asynchronously along with the rest of the HTML. This speeds page load times for your script and CSS files.

To add it your page, follow these steps:

1. **Head over to the** `headjs.com` **page and click the Download link.** You can copy and paste the URL to the latest version of `headjs` (`https://raw.github.com/headjs/headjs/v0.96/dist/head.min.js`).

2. **Add the following snippet below the** `handlebarsJS` **script tag in the** `head` **section of the** `index.html`:

```
<script type="text/javascript" language="Javascript"
src="https://raw.github.com/headjs/headjs/v0.96/dist/head.min.js"></script>
```

3. **Remember all those** `script` **tags that you added earlier?** You're now going to remove them and write one script to take care of them loading:

```
<script type="text/javascript" language="Javascript">
      head.js("assets/js/global.js", "assets/js/database.js", "assets/js/geo.
 js",
"assets/js/helper.js", "assets/js/util.js",  "assets/js/social.js");
</script>
```

It's that simple! Now all your JavaScript files will load faster when the page loads. Although you may not see a big improvement in Corks, you might see a big improvement with other JavaScript-heavy applications.

MANIFEST CACHE

Manifest Cache provides you with an easy way to provide browser storage for static files loaded on a mobile device. Basic setup is easy. However, you must write code to check if the files have been updated. It's important to note that you don't use `head.js` and Manifest Cache together; they provide different caching solutions that can' t be combined.

1. **Add the following code to the HTML tag of the document:**

```
<html manifest="manifest.appcache">
```
   If you are working with multiple pages, you must include this on every page to use the cache.

2. **Create a new file called** `manifest.appcache` **and place it in the root directory of your project.** The file needs to have the same name as the one in the `html` tag.

3. **Finally, in that file, add the following code:**

```
CACHE MANIFEST
index.html
assets/js/*
```

This enables the application to cache every file in the `assets/js` directory, which includes all your JavaScript files. You can expand this to cache more items; just follow the examples in Chapter 2.

An important part of the `.appcache` file is that it must be served with the correct MIME file type. This can be accomplished in many ways; however, the most common approach is to set the type via the `.htaccess` file (if you are using Apache as your Web Server). Simply create a new file in the root directory of your web app called `.htaccess` and then add the following code:

```
AddType text/cache-manifest .appcache
```

Once this is completed, you will be able to use the Manifest Cache feature. An important note is that when the user first views your website and you have enabled this feature, all files will download for offline use. This may decrease the performance of your website because more bandwidth is required; however, once the files are downloaded the application will start responding at a much faster rate since the files are cached.

> *The file is cached at the bit level, which means that if one file is changed, then the whole manifest will be reloaded and re-cached, so be careful how frequently you update your app cache.*

DECREASE YOUR JAVASCRIPT FOOTPRINT

When building mobile applications, the goal is to create small JavaScript files so the browser can quickly read them and compile them to run in the browser. One method of decreasing the size of your JavaScript footprint is to use a process called *minifying*.

This process removes all the "white space" (such as new lines and spaces between variables) and turns a long JavaScript into a single string. This can easily be read by the browser and decreases the overall size of the file. In addition to removing the white space, some services that offer a tool can rewrite your variables to a single letter, which decreases file size.

You can use the tools listed here to minify your JavaScript:

- `http://www.minifyjs.com/javascript-compressor/`
- `http://jscompress.com/`
- `http://refresh-sf.com/yui/`

It's important to note that you can minify your CSS and HTML files to decrease the overall footprint of your files. The downside to minifying everything is that the files become hard to edit and update. You always want to have a minified version of your JS and a full version.

> *You can always use tools like JS Beautifier (* `http://jsbeautifier.org/` *) to reverse the minification by expanding your JavaScript to make it easier to read.*

MOBILE TESTING TECHNIQUES

Most programmers tend to write once and never revisit their code to improve the syntax. With programming, there are many ways to perform the same action; however, not all ways provide the best performance. Refactoring is the method in which you revisit your code and tweak certain aspects for better performance.

Most of the time, developers tend to refactor their code based on browser testing. This is the result of seeing the web page rendering on older browsers, which may have performance issues with CSS3. The Corks application is targeted toward mobile devices. Here are some tips to keep in mind during your testing approaches:

- **Device and emulator tests are completely different:** Make sure you test your app on the actual device to see if memory usage comes into play. For example, some apps run smoothly in Safari for a desktop computer, but don't render very well on a mobile device. As a developer, sometimes it's easy to forget the CPU and RAM power of a mobile device.
- **Use HTML5 features and functionality that will support your users:** When building your app, make sure you use features in HTML5 that your primary device supports. For example, because you use Web SQL in Corks, your application will not work in non-WebKit browsers, such Mozilla Firefox. Perhaps you knew this going into the build, but did not discover this during your testing phase. Using HTML5 features that your primary device supports makes your life a lot easier when choosing what tools to use.
- **There is no mouse:** A common issue when testing web apps on desktops is that you interact with a mouse, not a finger. Make sure you use functions like `ontouchstart` and `onclick` interchangeably, depending on what you need to do. `hover` attributes will not work correctly on mobile devices.

TESTING FOR CORKS

So you probably are wondering how to test and ensure that Corks operates on other browsers. Because you used jQuery Mobile, you can feel confident that the appearance testing is successful, because it includes everything in the compatibility chart shown in Table 11-2.

Table 11-2   jQuery Mobile Support

Operating System / Version	Approved Devices
Apple iOS 3.2-5.0	Tested on the original iPad (4.3 / 5.0), iPad 2 (4.3), original iPhone (3.1), iPhone 3 (3.2), 3GS (4.3), 4 (4.3 / 5.0), and 4S (5.0)
Android 2.1-2.3	Tested on the HTC Incredible (2.2), original Droid (2.2), HTC Aria (2.1), Google Nexus S (2.3). Functional on 1.5 & 1.6 but performance may be sluggish, tested on Google G1 (1.5)
Android 3.1 (Honeycomb)	Tested on the Samsung Galaxy Tab 10.1 and Motorola XOOM
Android 4.0 (ICS)	Tested on a Galaxy Nexus S. Note: transition performance can be poor on upgraded devices
Windows Phone 7-7.5	Tested on the HTC Surround (7.0) HTC Trophy (7.5), LG-E900 (7.5), Nokia Lumia 800
Blackberry 6.0	Tested on the Torch 9800 and Style 9670.
Blackberry 7	Tested on BlackBerry® Torch 9810
Blackberry Playbook (1.0-2.0)	Tested on PlayBook
Palm WebOS (1.4-2.0) / Palm WebOS 3.0	Tested on the Palm Pixi (1.4), Pre (1.4), Pre 2 (2.0) / Tested on HP TouchPad
Firebox Mobile (10 Beta)	Tested on Android 2.3 device
Chrome for Android (Beta)	Tested on Android 4.0 device
Skyfire 4.1	Tested on Android 2.3 device
Opera Mobile 11.5	Tested on Android 2.3
Meego 1.2	Tested on Nokia 950 and N9
Samsung bada 2.0	Tested on a Samsung Wave 3, Dolphin browser
UC Browser	Tested on Android 2.3 device
Kindle 3 and Fire	Tested on the built-in WebKit browser for each
Nook Color 1.4.1	Tested on original Nook Color, not Nook Tablet

The biggest requirement for testing your application is testing your support database. Web-SQL is not supported by Firefox or Opera, so your application will not work with those browsers. In such cases, you need to let your users know that their browsers are not supported. Achieve this by providing an informational message.

To do this, go to your `assets/js/global.js` and add the following code at the start of the `document.ready()` function:

```
if($.browser.msie || $.browser.firefox) {
        alert("This browser is not supported.")
        window.location.href = "http://google.com";
}
```

In this case, you are using the special `browser` function of jQuery to determine whether the browser is Internal Explorer or Firefox. If the browser matches, the user is given an alert and is then redirected away from the page. For a production application, a more graceful exit would be required, but this example provides you with the backbone for a more eloquent solution.

To support these other browsers, you need to drop the WebSQL database and use something that isn't held within HTML5—such as an actual database server. You can use `$.get` and `$.post` methods to communicate with the server and save your content. Although the content is not local on the device, it allows for greater expansion of mobile browser platforms.

In addition, you could use `IndexDB`, which a Web HTML5 database that we discussed earlier as a fallback. The methods are similar, but `IndexDB` requires additional code to get started. To learn more about `IndexDB` check out this link: `https://developer.mozilla.org/en-US/docs/IndexedDB/Using_IndexedDB`.

While we have discussed some testing approaches and strategies, in the next chapter, we discuss testing in more detail, covering the simulators and emulators you can to use to make sure your app is functioning well on your target device.

SUMMARY

This chapter showed you how to organize your JavaScript files and revealed testing techniques for a web app. In addition, you learned how to

- Use Manifest Cache to store JavaScript files
- Load script files asynchronously using `head.js`
- Detect browser types using `$.browser` from jQuery

12

PREPARING FOR LAUNCH

IN THIS CHAPTER, you take the final steps and launch your application. By the end of the chapter, you will be able to:

- Set up debugging tools to iron out any hanging issues in the Corks app
- Switch gracefully between click and touch handlers

- Reduce demands on mobile bandwidth
- Improve JavaScript and animation performance
- Optimize CSS

DEBUGGING TIPS

When it comes to debugging, mobile apps can be much more difficult than their desktop counterparts:

- Desktop browsers offer comprehensive debugging tools such as Firebug and Chrome's Developer Tools. Although some mobile browsers provide a certain amount of debugging information, it pales in comparison to what is available in non-mobile browsers.
- Mobile applications typically require a larger number of test cases, due to the wide variety of mobile devices on the market.

In this section, you learn how to set up different mobile testing environments, using both real devices and emulators. You also learn how to set up development tools to get useful debugging information on the fly. Finally, you learn miscellaneous debugging tips that will make your mobile development smoother.

TESTING ENVIRONMENTS

Most bugs can be recreated in your standard development browser. However, there will inevitably be some bugs that are specific to a certain browser or operating system. In these cases, you need to set up a test environment that closely matches that of the user who filed the bug.

To comprehensively test a desktop app, you typically need two operating systems (Windows and Mac), a handful of browsers in each (IE, Firefox, Chrome, Safari), and a couple versions of each of those (perhaps the two most recent). While testing 10 or so desktop browsers may seem like a pain, it is a walk in the park compared to responsible mobile testing.

With mobile, you not only need to test a variety of different operating systems, browsers, and versions, but you also need to test across an even wider variety of devices. To make matters worse, the capability differences across different devices is staggering.

Not to mention the fact that many device manufacturers fork the codebase of their mobile browser. The Android Browser on an HTC device may not be the same on a Samsung, even if both have the same version of Android installed.

Creating a Support List

Before setting up your testing environment, it is important to first accept that your tests will never be 100% complete. There are just too many devices, browsers, versions, and even user configurations out there. But this is not to say that you cannot still test thoroughly to cover the vast majority of environments.

The best way to figure out which environments to support is to look at your app's analytics. Determine a benchmark percentage that you want to reach (somewhere between 95% and 99%), and then figure out which devices you'll need to support that many users. These devices will make up your support list.

> *If you're making a new app, you can use overall market share data to determine your support list.*

Emulators and Simulators

Testing on a wide variety of real devices is rarely cost effective. That said, you will probably need to turn to emulators and simulators to approximate the experience of the devices you don't own. But always make sure to test on at least a couple actual mobile devices, even if you have to borrow your friend's phone. Bear in mind: Even a 100% perfect emulator cannot give you an idea of the true user experience.

Before getting started, it is important to understand how emulation differs from simulation:

- Emulators run the native device operating system (OS) on your desktop machine with only minimal changes to accommodate the different interface (for example, fake on-screen buttons to mirror hardware buttons).
- Simulators, on the other hand, try to simulate the native experience as closely as possible. They do, however, use a different core.
- Emulators are, in general, more accurate than simulators.

Although less accurate than actual physical device testing, emulators and simulators can be easier to use. That's because you can use the hardware keyboard of your desktop machine.

iOS Simulator

For iOS devices such as iPhone and iPad, the best testing option is the official iOS Simulator released by Apple.

> *Unfortunately, the iOS Simulator only runs on Mac OS X. If you are not a Mac user, you will have to use an alternative, such as* www.iphone4simulator.com.

To use the simulator, first download Xcode from the Mac App Store (it's free). After installing Xcode, the simulator will be buried within Applications→Xcode→Contents→Developer→ Platforms→iPhoneSimulator.platform→Developer→Applications→iOS Simulator. Or you can create an empty iOS project and run a test from within Xcode.

Figure 12-1 shows that the simulator works pretty much identically to an iOS device; you can use iOS Safari and even install native apps. You can switch between testing iPhone and iPad, so fire up Safari in whichever device you want to target, and begin testing the *Corks* app.

Figure 12-1: The iOS Simulator in action.

> *Pro-tip: Drag HTML files from Finder and drop them in the Simulator to pull them up in iOS Safari.*

Android Emulator

The best option for Android testing is the official Android Emulator, which can be downloaded for free as part of the Android Software Development Kit (SDK): `http://developer.android.com/tools/help/emulator.html`.

Unlike the iOS Simulator, the Android Emulator requires that you manually create a testing environment for each device you want to test.

So the first step is to open the SDK and create an Android Virtual Device (AVD). Here you can adjust a variety of settings, such as the screen dimensions, pixel density, and size of the SD card. For a list of common device settings, see `http://mobile.tutsplus.com/tutorials/android/common-android-virtual-device-configurations/`.

After setting up your AVD, testing in the emulator is pretty much the same as in the iOS Simulator: Simply fire up the Android browser and start debugging.

> *You may also want to test alternative browsers in both Android and iOS. To do so, simply install these browsers within the emulator or simulator.*

Other Emulators and Simulators

Beyond iOS and Android, you can use additional emulators and simulators to test your app in any environment you want to support.

First, for Nokia devices, you can use Nokia Remote Device Access, which allows you to test all Symbian and Nokia devices for up to 8 hours a day for free: `http://www.developer.nokia.com/Devices/Remote_device_access`.

Next, Samsung provides a similar service called Samsung Lab.Dev. Here you can test Samsung Android devices for free: `http://innovator.samsungmobile.com/bbs/lab/view.do?platformId=1`.

Additionally, BlackBerry provides a number of free simulators for its smartphones and Playbook tablet: `http://us.blackberry.com/sites/developers/resources/simulators.html`.

Finally, if you want to test simultaneously across a wide range of different devices, consider using a paid service such as `www.deviceanywhere.com`. Although somewhat costly, this service provides an unparalleled amount of native device testing capabilities.

DEVELOPMENT TOOLS

After setting up a variety of testing environments, you should be able to re-create any bugs that users report. But finding the bug is only half the battle—you also need to fix it.

That's where JavaScript consoles and developer tools come in. These tools enable you to:

- Track down JavaScript errors
- Output debugging information from your app
- Profile performance (of both JavaScript and HTTP requests)
- Adjust CSS styles on the fly

Dev Tools in Desktop Browsers

You're probably already familiar with using a console in desktop browsers, such as Firebug or Chrome's Developer Tools. But even if you haven't used development tools before, getting started is easy.

First, to use the Web Inspector, simply right-click any element on the page in Chrome and select Inspect Element. As you can see in Figure 12-2, this not only highlights the element within the source tree, but also shows styling information. You can even use it to adjust the CSS styles on the fly.

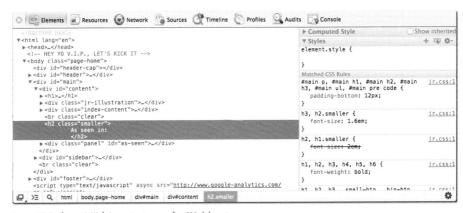

Figure 12-2: Chrome's Web Inspector is great for CSS debugging.

Next, move over to the Console tab. Here you can see information about JavaScript errors and how to run JavaScript on the fly. (See Figure 12-3.)

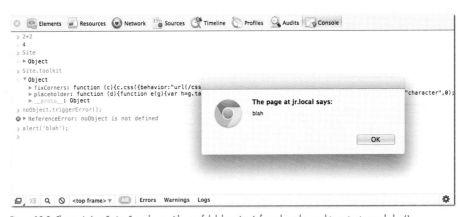

Figure 12-3: Chrome's JavaScript Console provides useful debugging info and can be used to output console.log().

Finally, move over to the Network tab. Here you can see a breakdown of how quickly various HTTP assets are downloaded and instantiated, as shown in Figure 12-4.

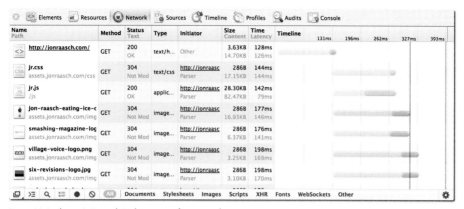

Figure 12-4: Chrome's Network Tools capture information about HTTP requests.

DOM inspection, JavaScript consoles, and network request capturing are just some of the many features available in Chrome's Developer's Tools. For a more in-depth look at Chrome's toolkit, watch this video from Paul Irish: `http://youtu.be/nOEw9iiopwI`.

Dev Tools in Mobile Browsers

Although development tools work great in desktop browsers, they are decidedly lacking from mobile browsers. This may not present a problem right away, because most bugs can be recreated in desktop environments. However, at some point you will undoubtedly need mobile development tools, either for mobile specific bugs, or to double-check a bug you fixed in a desktop browser.

In these cases, you may consider the baked-in development tools in mobile browsers. For instance, in iOS Safari you can enable a console by going to Settings→Safari→Advanced→ Debug Console, as shown in Figure 12-5.

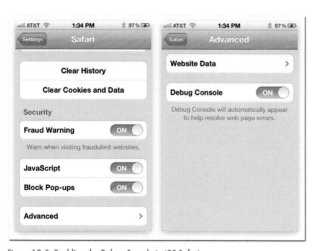

Figure 12-5: Enabling the Debug Console in iOS Safari.

However, the information provided by the native console is pretty incomplete, as shown in Figure 12-6.

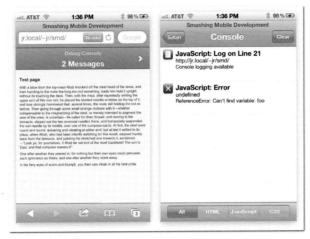

Figure 12-6: iOS Safari's console outputs only limited information about a JavaScript error.

Unfortunately, iOS Safari's console does not even provide a line number for the error. Furthermore, you cannot use it to run JavaScript on the fly, inspect the DOM, or leverage any of the other useful tools available in desktop browsers.

Remote Dev Tools

As you can see, native mobile consoles are practically useless for debugging any complex issues. Fortunately, remote consoles such as Weinre provide mobile apps with the power of desktop debugging tools.

Weinre exposes the entirety of WebKit's Developer Tools for mobile devices. This means that you can leverage all the debugging tricks you use in desktop browsers.

The only downside is that Weinre is a little complicated to set up. That's because it doesn't actually run on the mobile device; it runs on your desktop machine. Weinre sets up a relay for debugging information, which is sent from and received by the mobile browser, as you can see in Figure 12-7.

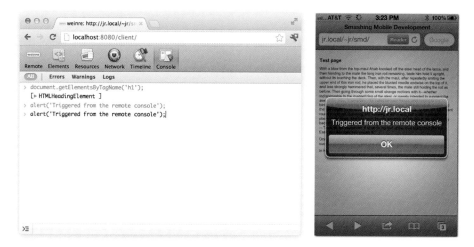

Figure 12-7: With Weinre, you test on the mobile device, but use developer tools on your desktop machine. Here the console from desktop Chrome is affecting the page on an iPhone.

To use Weinre, you need to set up a Node server to relay the debugging information. Fortunately you don't have to be a hardcore server administrator to set it up. Just follow these simple steps:

1. First you need to install a Node server and Node Package Manager (NPM) on your local machine.

- Mac and Linux installation: `http://dandean.com/nodejs-npm-express-osx`

- Windows installation: `http://dailyjs.com/2012/05/03/windows-and-node-1`

    If you'd like to avoid setting up a Node server, you can use an alternative such as Firebug Lite. However, Firebug Lite runs on the actual mobile device, which makes typing into the development tools more challenging, and also skews performance tests.

2. To install Weinre via NPM, from the command line type:

```
sudo npm -g install weinre
```

3. Now, start the Weinre server from the command line:

```
node path-to-weinre-node/weinre --boundHost -all-
```

Weinre should have been installed in your node directory, under `node_modules/weinre/weinre`.

Here you set the `boundHost` to `-all-`. This is important since you will want to debug on a device with a different IP.

For a complete list of Weinre options, see `http://people.apache.org/~pmuellr/weinre/docs/latest/Running.html`.

4. **Add a script tag to your test page, in order to set it up as a debug target:**

```
<script src="http://a.b.c:8080/target/target-script-min.js"></script>
```

Here, replace `http://a.b.c:8080/` with the location of your local Weinre server (which is running off your desktop machine).

Now Weinre should be set up. Simply open the page on your mobile device and route the browser on your desktop machine to `http://localhost:8080/client`. If all goes well, you should see two green IP addresses, one for the remote target (the mobile device) and one for the remote client (the desktop machine). See Figure 12-8.

Figure 12-8: Weinre is connected when the target and client IPs are both green.

You need a WebKit-based browser such as Chrome or Safari to use Weinre.

Now you can use the tools in Weinre to debug the app. As shown in Figure 12-9, you now have a complete development toolkit for any mobile device. That means you can thoroughly test your app in any environment.

Figure 12-9: Weinre provides the WebKit Developer Tools for remote debugging of mobile devices. Here the Web Inspector in desktop Chrome is being used to inspect elements on the iPhone. Notice how it is even highlighting DOM items on the iPhone.

TOUCH VS. MOUSE EVENTS

One particular pain point in debugging mobile apps has to do with how mouse and touch events are handled.

In the Corks app, you use touch events since they are faster and more responsive than click events in mobile devices. However, this creates a problem whenever you want to test on a desktop browser, since touch events aren't recognized. To get around this issue, you can use JavaScript to replace touch events with mouse equivalents.

Rather than refactor every touch event in the app, wouldn't it be nicer to set up a catch-all event to remap all the touch events at once? Luckily, you can do so by including the micro-script Touché, at `https://github.com/davidcalhoun/touche`.

Simply download the script and include it in your JavaScript. All your touch events will automatically be remapped to click events.

Best of all, the script uses feature detection to fire only when touch events are unsupported. That means you don't have to worry about disabling it in mobile devices.

PERFORMANCE TIPS

Although we all love carrying the Internet in our pockets, getting it in such a small container has come with a number of compromises. Namely, mobile devices are considerably under-powered when compared with desktop alternatives. Therefore, when developing for mobile, performance should always be one of your main concerns.

MOBILE BANDWIDTH

One of the major challenges in mobile development is optimizing for mobile bandwidth. High-speed Internet allows web apps to fly for desktop browsers, but mobile apps tend to crawl at the speed of dial-up. Sure, advances in mobile networks have brought faster connections, but these improvements are met with increased expectations on what mobile apps should deliver. Furthermore, these networks can be spotty—you shouldn't assume users always have 4G.

One of the best ways to improve the performance of your mobile app is to reduce its bandwidth needs.

Fewer Images, More CSS

Assuming you don't need any video or audio, the largest bandwidth consumer in your app is most likely imagery. Fortunately, modern mobile browsers offer a variety of CSS3 properties that can be used to avoid images wherever possible.

For instance, instead of using a separate image for each button in the Corks app, you used rounded corners, gradients, and borders generated purely with CSS. Although the CSS for these properties can be pretty long with vendor-specific prefixes, it is nothing compared to what it would cost in actual images. Furthermore, CSS is much easier to manage and modify whenever changes need to be made.

Beyond basic styling, you can really get creative and draw fairly complex objects using CSS. You can use `border-radius` to draw circles, `border` tricks to draw triangles, and then combine these with standard rectangles to draw any number of compound shapes. For more information, see `http://jonraasch.com/blog/drawing-with-css`.

Asset Management—Minification, Gzipping, CDNs

In addition to avoiding images wherever possible, you should also be ensuring that the files in your app are served as small as possible. A few quick tricks can make substantial differences, typically cutting non-image file sizes by more than 75%.

First, make sure that you are minifying anything that can be minified: CSS, JavaScript, and HTML. Minification removes all the unnecessary white space from your files, and can significantly reduce file size.

To minify your files, we suggest using the YUI compressor and the command line. But if you aren't comfortable with the command line, there are a variety of web-based minifiers, such as what you find at `http://refresh-sf.com/yui/`.

Next make sure to gzip all the files you minified. Gzipping takes the already compressed files and makes them even smaller, typically reducing their size by 60% to 85%. After gzipping your files, make sure to serve them with the right HTTP headers:

- `Content-Encoding` should be `gzip`.
- `Content-Type` should match the file type (for example, `text/css`, `text/js`, `text/html`).

Finally, it is a good idea to serve static assets from a separate subdomain. That's because any file served on your main domain will be served not only with the file data, but also with HTTP header data. Header data includes all the cookies from the site and other bloat that should not be served with every single image, style sheet, or JavaScript file.

Avoid the extra bytes by serving images, style sheets, and JavaScripts from a different domain, either by setting up a subdomain manually or leveraging a CDN such as Amazon S3.

User Agent Redirection

Finally, if you are serving a separate desktop version of the app, you will encounter additional bandwidth concerns. That's because desktop apps typically contain more content because they have more screen real estate to work with. This extraneous content can be easily hidden with CSS media queries; however, this is rarely the best approach.

That's because the content hidden by CSS is still downloaded by the user's device, even if the markup is never rendered. That causes a significant amount of bloat and an unnecessary strain on mobile bandwidth.

It is usually a good idea to leverage user agent redirection, to redirect mobile users to a separate mobile subdomain, which serves pared-down, mobile-specific markup.

> *You can also serve pared-down CSS with only the styles you need for mobile.*

Although the approach is relatively straightforward, user agent redirection is actually quite complicated in practice. That's because new devices and browsers are being released constantly, which makes the list of possible user agents ever expanding.

Furthermore, certain devices spoof the user agent strings of desktop browsers. For instance, some mobile devices pretend to be desktop browsers to trick websites into serving them fully featured non-mobile sites. This subterfuge makes the device *seem* better because it provides a richer browsing experience (even if that experience is slower and ultimately worse for the user).

Maintaining a completely current user agent list is a futile effort at best. Fortunately, a number of user agent services can do the legwork for you:

- **Detect Mobile Browsers,** `www.detectmobilebrowsers.com`: Basic mobile redirection in a variety of languages.
- **MobileESP,** `http://blog.mobileesp.com/`: PHP and JavaScript APIs for mobile device detection.
- **WURFL,** `http://wurfl.sourceforge.net`: WURFL is a frequently updated XML file that provides fine-grained information about mobile devices and their individual capabilities.

Because you only need basic mobile redirection, use one of the scripts from `www.detect mobilebrowsers.com`.

If you are using an Apache server, the best option is to use the Apache script, which is an `.htaccess` script that will redirect any mobile browser to your mobile subdomain. Simply replace `http://detectmobilebrowser.com/mobile` with your subdomain in the code, then add it to the `.htaccess` file in your site.

> *It's a good idea to use the Apache script here since it will be the most efficient. The JavaScript version can cause more bandwidth problems than it solves, because users will begin downloading the full site page before the script kicks in and redirects them to the mobile site.*

JAVASCRIPT OPTIMIZATIONS

In addition to reduced bandwidth, mobile devices also suffer from poor processor performance. This means that you need to optimize your JavaScript, especially in a highly interactive app like Corks.

Focusing on Big Performance Gains

You could, quite literally, optimize your app forever. However, instead of refactoring the entire codebase, wouldn't you rather determine problem areas where you can see the biggest gains?

One important lesson is that you should rarely pre-optimize. That means that you shouldn't go blindly through the Corks app, changing every piece of JavaScript that could run faster. Optimizations like this can make the codebase disorganized and difficult to read (not to mention the extra development hours).

Rather, you should optimize the code only after you notice an actual problem. For instance, when testing the app, you will probably find a section that runs slower than you like.

Now that you've narrowed down the piece of the app you want to improve, you can still optimize smarter. Are there any loops or functions that get called repeatedly? First take a look at these sections, because each improvement will be multiplied by the number of times it is called.

> *Besides the loops explicitly called in your code, you should also be aware of any hidden loops that are called by jQuery. For example,* `jQuery.animate()` *may look like a single function, but it sets up an interval that is called repeatedly over the duration of the animation.*

Triggering Hardware Acceleration

Hardware acceleration is a great way to optimize choppy JavaScript animations in mobile devices. It's one of my favorite optimization techniques; it's not only easy to implement, but also leads to substantial performance gains.

> *Performance improvements don't make animation faster; they make it smoother. That's because better performance allows the browser to render the frames of the animation faster. More rendered frames mean a higher frame rate.*

Hardware acceleration takes rendering tasks off the general processor (CPU) and offloads them to the graphics processor (GPU). This relieves the often-overworked CPU, and also achieves the rendering on the graphics card, which is more suited for these specific tasks.

Fortunately, triggering GPU processing is extremely easy in WebKit browsers (such as iOS Safari and Android Browser). To add hardware acceleration to any element in the DOM, simply attach the following CSS:

```
-webkit-transform: translateZ(0);
```

> *Be careful when using experimental CSS properties in different versions of Android and iOS (and even across different Android devices using the same version). Browser support may be lacking so it is important to test your app thoroughly, and accept degradation issues where applicable.*

This snippet sets a 3D transformation on the element; however, because it translates by 0 units along the z-axis, it actually stays in the same place. This doesn't modify the appearance, but it does trick the browser into thinking it is rendering 3D. Thus, if the device has a GPU, it will be used to render the element.

Now don't go applying this hack to every element in the DOM. Most static elements don't need this treatment, and you shouldn't overload the GPU, or it won't be able to help you in situations where you actually need hardware acceleration.

> *This hack is ideal for any heavily animated elements. If you notice a choppy animation, that's a perfect time to use this technique*

Going Full Screen in iOS

In Chapter 5 you learned how to use the UIWebView in iOS to provide a full screen experience for your app. While the UX implications of Full Screen mode are fairly obvious, it also introduces some subtler performance concerns.

> *UIWebView is used in full screen web apps as well as some native apps from the App Store.*

Unlike Mobile Safari, the UIWebView cannot leverage the super-fast Nitro JS Engine. That means your JavaScript will run slower if the user bookmarks your app and launches it from the homescreen.

The reason for Apple's decision to disable the Nitro JS Engine in UIWebView seems to be security. One of the biggest performance improvements in Nitro stems from the use of "Just-In-Time" (JIT) compilation. A JIT needs the ability to mark memory pages in RAM as executable, which goes against iOS' core security measures.

While iOS is content to grant Mobile Safari these privileges, it is not comfortable extending the same privileges to web apps on the home screen. These apps run as native apps on the device, while leveraging externally sourced remote data. Granting this type of access to these types of apps is simply unacceptable in Apple's "walled garden" model for iOS apps.

Object Caching in jQuery

Another common technique for improving JavaScript performance is caching any objects you reuse as local variables. For instance, imagine you have to dig into an object to find a reference such as `foo.bar.blah`. If you end up referencing this inner item frequently, you can save processing power by caching it as a variable:

```
var localBlah = foo.bar.blah;

// whatever you want to do with localBlah
```

This technique used to make a sizable difference, but browsers have since optimized a great deal for deep object lookups. Therefore, you typically shouldn't bother with this type of caching.

However, there are still a number of areas where caching can make a substantial difference. Namely within jQuery DOM references, such as:

```
$('div.special').hide();
$('div.special').addClass('blah');
```

While jQuery's Sizzle engine has optimized substantially for these types of references, DOM lookups are still one of the slowest processes in the library. Therefore, you should avoid repeating DOM lookups wherever possible.

In the preceding example, you can take advantage of jQuery chaining to knock out the second reference to this element:

```
$('div.special').hide().addClass('blah');
```

This is great for any situation where you are calling a number of methods on an element in succession. However, there are other times when you reference a given element multiple times throughout the code. In these cases, you should cache the lookup:

```
var $elem = $('div.special');
$elem.hide();

. . . . . . . . . .
. . . . . . . . . .

$elem.addClass('blah');
```

Now the next time you reference this element, you will be able to skip the lookup. Notice the $ pattern that is added to $elem—this is a common practice to signify that a variable represents a DOM reference.

> *Of course, there are times you wouldn't want to cache a DOM lookup—for instance, when the collection of elements has changed.*

Measuring JavaScript Performance

Most development tasks can be accomplished in more than one way. When deciding between different approaches, it is often helpful to determine which is the best for performance.

For simple A/B testing, use a benchmark test, such as those provided at JSPerf (www. jsperf.com). JSPerf allows you to set up two scripts, and then run them in the browser of whichever device you are testing. The results of the tests show which script executed the fastest, as shown in Figures 12-10 and 12-11:

Test runner

Done. Ready to run again.   [Run again]

Testing in Chrome 22.0.1221.0 on Mac OS X 10.8.0		
	Test	Ops/sec

Not Cached	`for ( var i = 0; i < 10; i++ ) {`
	`    var myEl = document.getElementById('my-element');`
	
	`    // whatever you want to do with myEl`
	`}`
		2,270,228
		±0.67%
		89% slower

Cached	`var myEl = document.getElementById('my-element');`
	
	`for ( var i = 0; i < 10; i++ ) {`
	`    // whatever you want to do with myEl`
	`}`
		20,242,545
		±0.29%
		fastest

Figure 12-10: A basic benchmark test on JSPerf. In this test, the cached DOM reference is fastest.

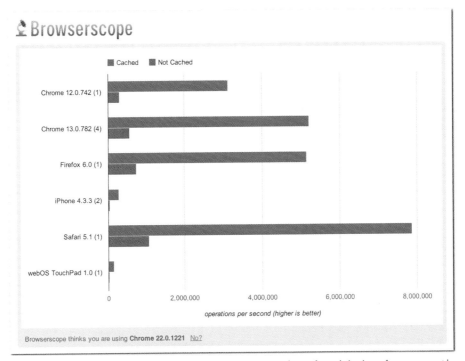

Browserscope thinks you are using **Chrome 22.0.1221**   No?

Figure 12-11: You can easily compare different browsers and environments with JSPerf. Simply hit the performance test with each browser you want to test, and JSPerf will save the results for comparison.

For more complicated tests, and to have the capability to test within the actual app you're building, you can use the Timeline in Chrome's Developer Tools, as shown in Figure 12-12.

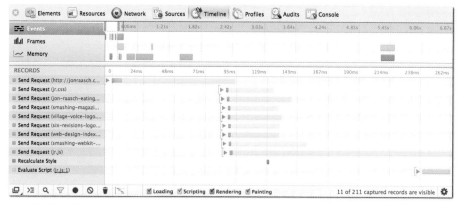

Figure 12-12: This Timeline shows how long it takes to process different aspects of the page.

The Timeline shows a variety of useful information. If you are concerned only with JavaScript processing, simply uncheck everything except Scripting.

CSS OPTIMIZATIONS

Although you will most likely see larger performance gains from optimizing bandwidth or JavaScript, CSS optimizations can also provide worthwhile performance improvements for your app.

> CSS performance is notoriously difficult to test, so you'll mostly have to rely on qualitative assessments, such as whether the app seems faster.

Animating with CSS instead of JavaScript

You've already learned how to employ hardware acceleration to improve performance and make animations smoother. However, you can go the extra mile and make your animations even smoother by avoiding JavaScript altogether.

One of the new features available in CSS3 is animation, through both smooth transitions and versatile keyframe animations. Both types of animation are made with CSS, so all the animation occurs directly in the renderer. That said, the browser is able to optimize for these tasks much better than it can for JavaScript animation.

Switching your jQuery animations for CSS3 animations can lead to substantial frame rate increases and a smoother looking animation. However, this change comes with a few drawbacks:

- CSS animations can be a bit clunkier to work with than jQuery alternatives.
- Animating in the CSS can lead to poor architecture. Animation is a scripting task that must be triggered from the JavaScript layer; however, the actual animation is in the style sheet.
- CSS animations are not as versatile or powerful as jQuery alternatives.

CSS animations are not supported on older iOS/Android devices, where they will revert to static style changes without any animation. While this can often be included as graceful degradation, you can also provide a jQuery fallback if the animation is essential to your app.

For instance, say you want to slide a `div` out of the window while fading it out. In jQuery, you might write:

```
$('.my-div').animate({
    left: 3000,
    opacity: 0
}, 1000, 'swing');
```

This script slides the `div` 3000px to the left and fades it out over the course of 1 second, using the `swing` easing function. As you will soon see, you can recreate all these aspects of the animation using CSS.

The easiest method to accomplish this involves CSS transitions. First, set up a new class, `.hidden`, for the element:

```
.my-div.hidden {
    left: 3000px;
    opacity: 0;
}
```

Next, set up a transition on the element:

```
.my-div {
    -webkit-transition: all 1s ease;
       -moz-transition: all 1s ease;
            transition: all 1s ease;
}
```

Here, you set up a transition to smoothly animate any CSS changes to this element (taking advantage of various vendor prefixes for different browsers). Within this transition, you mirrored the properties of the jQuery animation: a duration of 1 second, and the `ease` timing function (which is similar to jQuery's `swing`).

Finally, to trigger the animation, apply the class using jQuery:

```
$('.my-div').addClass('hidden');
```

Now, simply adding this class name triggers the animation, which will look much smoother on mobile devices. However, it still has a number of disadvantages:

- The same transition will be applied to any style change on this element. Although you can limit which properties get transitioned (and even set up different transitions for different properties), you cannot use different animations on a case-by-case basis. For instance, if you want to fade this element back in, it will also have to be done over a duration of 1 second.
- Callback functions can get tricky when used with transitions. The transition spec provides for an `animationEnd` event handler, which fires after the transition completes. However, this event fires on every transition of every property. In the preceding example, it would fire twice—once for each the `left` and `opacity` transitions.
- This approach can lead to poor architecture because animation tasks are offloaded to the CSS. This problem is exacerbated when combined with callbacks in `animationEnd` handlers.

You can use keyframe animation instead of transitions if you need more versatility in your animation.

Avoiding Reflow

Reflow is a technical term describing how the browser lays out elements on the page in the rendering process. The process occurs not only on the initial page load, but also whenever anything on the page changes and requires a re-rendering of the layout.

Pages rarely avoid additional reflows, even if they don't have any interactive content. That's because reflows are governed by more than the markup on the page; they are also driven by the CSS.

For instance, take an image next to a block of text, as seen in Figure 12-13. On the initial page load, the browser has not downloaded this image, so it has no idea what its dimensions will be. Once it downloads, however, the browser needs enough room to accommodate the image, so it pushes the following content downward.

Figure 12-13: The image is first set to arbitrary placeholder dimensions and then pops to its real size after it finishes downloading.

You can avoid this reflow by setting explicit dimensions for the image in your CSS or markup. Simply define its height and width, and the browser will know what size to use before the image even downloads.

Another way to avoid reflow is through absolute positioning. By definition, elements with absolute position will not affect the layout of other elements. Thus you can "sandbox" the reflows of a given section by adding absolute position to its wrapper (e.g., isolate the reflows in a smaller scope).

Avoiding Expensive Properties

Mobile devices typically support the newer features available in CSS3. However, this can be a double-edged sword because these features are often more difficult to process, a problem exacerbated by these underpowered devices.

Earlier, you learned how to use CSS to avoid images and dramatically reduce your app's bandwidth needs. Bear in mind, however, that these CSS properties require extra processing power.

For instance, a lot of Android devices show performance problems even with simple properties such as `border-radius`. For these devices, decide whether you'd be comfortable degrading to simpler styling (square corners), and if not, determine whether the bandwidth benefits of avoiding images justify the processing disadvantages.

And `border-radius` is just the tip of the iceberg. Processor intensive properties include `gradient`, `box-shadow`, `text-shadow`, and `transform`, to name a few. These properties may be integral to the styling of your app, but you need to test their performance across a variety of devices, and determine the compromises you're willing to make if a problem comes up.

SUMMARY

In this chapter, you first learned how to set up testing environments, both on native devices and with device emulators. You then learned how to set up debugging tools, by taking advantage of native tools as well as Weinre for remote debugging. Furthermore, you learned how to gracefully switch between touch and mouse events to make desktop debugging easier.

Next, you learned about mobile performance optimization. You learned how to reduce bandwidth needs by using CSS instead of images, properly optimizing files, and serving a separate mobile site. You learned how to optimize JavaScript—triggering hardware acceleration in choppy animations, caching overused DOM references, and testing different approaches. Finally, you learned how to optimize CSS—using CSS animations instead of JavaScript, reducing browser reflows, and avoiding overly expensive properties.

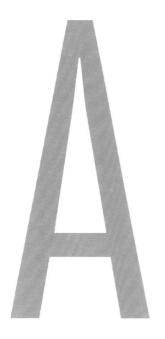

APPENDIX

HTML5, CSS3, AND JAVASCRIPT CONCEPTS

THIS APPENDIX EXPLAINS how to use:

- HTML5 structural elements to improve semantics
- Geolocation to pinpoint the user's location on the globe
- DOM storage to save variables you can use across different pages in your app
- Cache manifest to provide key functionality for your app even when it is offline
- CSS3 drop shadows, gradients, and animations to style your pages

- Multitouch events and complex touch gestures to create a better user experience
- The jQuery Framework, AJAX, and JSON to build your dynamic app

All these topics have been discussed in various chapters of this book. This appendix is intended to provide a deeper understanding of key functionality. You can use it as a reference while building your app.

HTML5

HTML5 introduces a variety of new features that enrich websites and simplify development.

MARKUP

HTML5 introduces several new elements that make markup more semantic. These tags, such as `<header>` and `<footer>`, make code more readable to humans and machines. That means it not only is easier to develop, but also is more accessible to search engine parsers such as Googlebot.

You might think semantic markup makes no difference to your visitors, but these tags also improve performance. That's because fewer elements of a given type mean less work for DOM selectors in CSS and JavaScript (for example, there's only one `<header>` element, which also means one less `<div>`).

While the performance gains may seem negligible in desktop browsers, any improvement is important for underpowered mobile devices.

Structural Elements

The number of HTML5 structural elements is expanding as the World Wide Web Consortium (W3C) works out the finer points of the spec. Here's an incomplete list of some of the more useful tags:

- `<header>` **and** `<footer>`: Used for the top and bottom content of the page. Often these are the parts that don't change across different pages of the site.
- **`<nav>`**: Used for any navigational elements (for example, the main `nav` in the header). Unfortunately, there's no official `nav` item element (`<ni>`), so you'll just have to throw a `<ul>` in the `<nav>`:

```
<nav>
    <ul>
        <li>
        <a href="#">Link 1</a>
        </li>

        <li>
        <a href="#">Link 2</a>
        </li>

        <li>
        <a href="#">Link 3</a>
        </li>
    </ul>
</nav>
```

- `<section>`: Used to indicate a section of the page—for instance, the main content area of the page or `<section class="sidebar"></section>`.

  These should be used for all the larger chunks on the page, leaving `<div>` elements for the smaller components that make up each semantic section.

- `<article>`: Used for individual articles in a blog, news source, magazine, and so forth. This element makes sense considering the propensity of these types of sites, but it may or may not be useful for your application.

- **<aside>**: Used to indicate content that is only tangentially related to the other content. This tag is especially important to search engines, which are trying to parse the semantic content of your page. So using this tag properly can hypothetically improve search engine rankings.

Semantic Simplifications

Additionally, the HTML5 spec provides a number of ways to simplify your markup.

- `Doctype:` First, the HTML5 `doctype` is as simple as possible:

  ```
  <!DOCTYPE html>
  ```

  Anyone who used older doctype declarations knows it was practically impossible to remember them. For instance:

  ```
  <!DOCTYPE html PUBLIC "-//W3C//DTD XHTML 1.0 Transitional//EN"
    "http://www.w3.org/TR/xhtml1/DTD/xhtml1-transitional.dtd">
  ```

- JavaScript and CSS: HTML5 also allows for a simpler format in script declarations. You no longer need to include `type="text/javascript"`:

  ```
  <script src="my-script.js"></script>
  ```

  Additionally, both link and style declarations no longer need `type="text/css"`:

  ```
  <link rel="stylesheet" href="my-stylesheet.css" />
  <style></style>
  ```

  Considering that most of the time these elements define JavaScript or CSS, it makes sense to assume these file types as the default.

Back Up with HTML5 Shiv

The one downside of using HTML5 elements is that older browsers do not recognize them. Although they won't throw errors, the problem is that any CSS styling you attach to the element will not be recognized.

These days, the only relevant browsers that don't support HTML5 markup are Internet Explorer (IE) versions 8 and lower. Since this affects a relatively small portion of mobile devices, you can ignore this technique if you only want to offer a mobile experience. However, if you are providing a web experience for your mobile app, it is a good idea to provide a fallback for non-supportive browsers.

Fortunately, it is easy to get HTML5 elements working in non-supportive browsers. First, you can manually add any elements you use via JavaScript in the head:

```
<script>
  document.createElement('header');
  document.createElement('footer');
  document.createElement('nav');
  document.createElement('section');
  document.createElement('article');
  document.createElement('aside');
</script>
```

Or you can use HTML5 Shiv, which is a script that adds these elements along with their default styling. Simply include the script from `http://code.google.com/p/html5shiv/` in your document head, and your HTML5 tags will be good to go in all browsers.

However, no matter which method you use, it's a good idea to avoid doing anything in browsers that already support HTML5. After all, most browsers support these elements natively, so there's no point in adding more work.

These days, the only relevant browsers that have problems with HTML5 structural elements are IE 8 and lower. Therefore, you can wrap your HTML5 Shiv in an IE conditional:

```
<!--[if lt IE 9]>
<script src="path-to/html5shiv.js"></script>
<![endif]-->
```

> *What's the difference between a shiv and a shim? As answered on the HTML5 Shiv website: "Nothing: One has an m and one has a v—that's it."*

GEOLOCATION

One of the more important HTML5 features for mobile is geolocation. The GeoLocation API enables you to tap into the device's global positioning hardware (where available). This allows you to place the user on the globe, and provide location-relevant content.

Detecting Support

Before invoking the GeoLocation API, it is a good practice to check if it exists in the first place. In your JavaScript:

```
if ( "geolocation" in navigator ) {
    // whatever geolocation stuff you want to do
}
```

This approach ensures you avoid throwing errors in non-supportive browsers.

Finding the User's Location

After you determine that geolocation is supported, you can use it to discern the user's location. To do that, use `getCurrentPosition`:

```
if ( "geolocation" in navigator ) {
    navigator.geolocation.getCurrentPosition(function(position) {
        var userLatitude = position.coords.latitude,
        userLongitude = position.coords.longitude;
    });
}
```

As you can see in the preceding script, `navigator.geolocation.getCurrentPosition` accepts a callback function, which returns the user's latitude and longitude.

> *Even if the user's device does not support global positioning (for example, a desktop computer), the GeoLocation API will use that individual's IP to form a best guess about his or her location.*

Getting a More Relevant Location

Although the user's latitude and longitude are useful for interfacing with other APIs, such as the Google Maps API, it may not be overly relevant to you or the user. Fortunately, a number of free services convert this information into a city and country (or even an address if you need it).

For more information about how to do so with the Google Maps API, visit `http://stackoverflow.com/questions/3918412/city-by-gps-location-latitude-longitude/`.

Tracking the User's Location over Time

`getCurrentPosition` is useful for one-time location lookups, but HTML5 also specifies an API you can use to track location changes over time:

```
if ( "geolocation" in navigator ) {
    navigator.geolocation.watchPosition(function(position) {
        var userLatitude = position.coords.latitude,
        userLongitude = position.coords.longitude;
    });
}
```

Working quite similarly to getCurrentPosition, watchPosition accepts a callback to which it relays the user's location data. The only difference is that watchPosition fires this callback repeatedly—any time the user's location has changed.

Although you could accomplish something similar using a timeout and getCurrentPosition, watchPosition provides a couple notable advantages. Besides being easier, watchPosition is better for performance because it fires only when the position actually changes, as opposed to firing on every iteration of the interval.

This optimization affects more than just JavaScript performance. It reduces the demands of the device's geolocation hardware, which in turn improves battery life.

> *In some devices,* watchPosition *can provide finer-grained location data than* getCurrentPosition. *That's because the device returns location data as quickly as it can, regardless of how accurate it is.* watchPosition *ensures that your app refines the location as the device finds more specific coordinates.*

Stopping Location Tracking

You can also unload the watchPosition when your app is finished with it. To do so, first define a variable for the watch function:

```
if ( "geolocation" in navigator ) {
    var myWatch = navigator.geolocation.watchPosition(function(position) {
        var userLatitude = position.coords.latitude,
        userLongitude = position.coords.longitude;
    });
}
```

Now you can unload it whenever you want using clearWatch:

```
if ( "geolocation" in navigator ) {
    navigator.geolocation.clearWatch(myWatch);
}
```

DOM STORAGE

Another HTML5 feature that makes web app development easier is local storage. Local storage allows you to save JavaScript variables that persist across different pages of a website. That means this data will be available throughout your site, and even when the user returns at a later date.

Saving data about the user's visit directly in the browser is advantageous for a variety of reasons. Mainly, it avoids the classic pattern of saving user data as session data on the server (which requires involving the backend server and often a database as well).

Using Local Storage

Using local storage is incredibly easy. First, to save an item, use `setItem`:

```
localStorage.setItem("myVar", "My Value");
```

Next, to retrieve this data, use `getItem`:

```
localStorage.getItem("myVar");
```

This will return `"myValue"` whether you access this data in this session or at a later date.

Finally, to remove the data and unload it from memory, use `removeItem`:

```
localStorage.removeItem("myVar");
```

Using Session Storage

Session storage works exactly like local storage. The only difference is that the data is discarded when the user closes his or her browser window or leaves the website. Thus, while local storage data persists across multiple visits, session storage is better suited for saving more dynamic or short-lived data.

Other than that, using session storage is no different—you can use all the same functions as in local storage:

```
sessionStorage.setItem("myVar", "My Value");

// alert the value
alert( sessionStorage.getItem("myVar") );

// remove it from storage
sessionStorage.removeItem("myVar");
```

Simpler Syntax

You can also access local and session storage like normal JavaScript objects. For example:

```
localStorage.myVar = "My Value";

// alert the value
alert( localStorage.myVar );

// remove it from storage
delete localStorage.myVar;
```

Saving Arrays and Objects with DOM Storage

Local and session storage are only suited to key-value pairs, such as defining a single variable as a string, number, or Boolean value. However, if you need to store arrays or objects, you can convert them to strings quite easily with `JSON.stringify`:

```
var myArr = [];

myArr[0] = "blah";
myArr[1] = "blah 2";

localStorage.myArr = JSON.stringify(myArr);
```

Next, whenever you retrieve the data from local storage, simply parse it with `JSON.parse`:

```
var storedArr = JSON.parse( localStorage.myArr );
```

CACHE MANIFEST

HTML5's cache manifest tells the browser which pages and assets it should download and store locally. These assets will be downloaded automatically from the first point a user hits your site or app, regardless of whether the assets are used in that session.

This caching is particularly important for web apps such as Corks, which are designed to launch from the home screen of mobile devices. That's because it enables the app to run successfully even in offline mode.

> *The cache manifest is essential for making a web app that competes with native device apps. When combined with a home screen icon, it enables the web app to run similarly to a native app, with or without Internet access.*

Defining the Manifest

First you need to link to the manifest file in the document's `html` element:

```
<html manifest="example.manifest">
   ...
</html>
```

It is crucial that this file be served with the appropriate mime-type, or it will not be recognized. Assuming you're using Apache, you can add this line to your `.htaccess` file:

```
AddType text/cache-manifest .manifest
```

Building the Manifest File

Next, building the actual manifest file is a piece of cake. It should start with CACHE MANIFEST, followed by a list of files you want to cache. For example:

```
CACHE MANIFEST
index.html
stylesheet.css
scripts/jquery.js
images/my-logo.png
```

Thus, whenever users visit any page with this manifest, they will automatically download all these assets, regardless of whether they are used on the given page.

> *The manifest file is cached at the bit level. That means the browser will re-download all the assets it specifies whenever any character in the manifest file changes (even in comments).*

Disabling Caching on Certain Pages

The cache manifest is great for static pages that do not require Internet access. However, there are often pages that either require the user to be online or are generated dynamically in a way that should not be cached (for example, a page that requires the Google Maps API or displays a list of daily news items).

Fortunately, you can also use the cache manifest to indicate files that should not be cached by the browser. Simply define separate CACHE and NETWORK sections in your manifest file:

```
CACHE MANIFEST

# cached assets
CACHE:
index.html
stylesheet.css
```

```
scripts/jquery.js
images/my-logo.png

# non-cached assets
NETWORK:
map.html
blog.html
```

Here the files in the CACHE section will be cached and those in the NETWORK section will not. (The lines that start with # are comments.)

> *Any paths that fall directly after the* CACHE MANIFEST *are assumed to be cached assets, so you could have avoided the* CACHE *section in this example. However, since you can move these sections around, it is a good idea to define it for code clarity.*

Providing Fallbacks for Non-Cached Content

Finally, you can even define fallback content for any network pages. This content will be displayed in the event that a network asset is unavailable (for example, when the user is offline):

```
CACHE MANIFEST

# cached assets
CACHE:
index.html
stylesheet.css
scripts/jquery.js
images/my-logo.png

# non-cached assets
NETWORK:
map.html
blog.html

# fallbacks
FALLBACK:
*.html /offline.html
```

Here you can use offline.html to display an error message to users when they are offline. Each fallback declaration has two parts: the URI of the requested asset and the URI of the fallback. As you can see, wildcards such as * can be used.

Both of the URIs in fallback declarations are relative to the page that references the manifest file. That's why this example uses a non-relative path to /offline.html.

CSS3

CSS3 introduces a variety of new styling options that you can use to make your pages more visually appealing. Best of all, it can be done without loading any external images, which makes pages load faster and reduces the strain on your server.

However, this functionality is not completely free from a performance perspective. These properties require more work from the renderer, which can slow down processing. On desktop computers, this is mostly negligible, but mobile devices can be more underpowered.

It really depends on the device. iPhones (even older models like the 3G) have enough power to handle just about any CSS3. On the other hand, Android devices, which vary from manufacturer to manufacturer, can start to show performance problems. These typically occur with the more expensive properties such as gradients or transitions, but I have even seen performance problems with relatively "simple" properties like border-radius.

Thus, it is important to thoroughly test your app on a variety of devices. Then, if you encounter any issues, you will have to be prepared to gracefully degrade the design in favor of better performance. After all, good design matters only insofar as it provides a better user experience, and painfully slow performance will scare away users.

Most web app performance problems stem from JavaScript, so don't get too worried about CSS3 optimization. As you learned in Chapter 12, it is important to pick your battles when it comes to performance tuning.

BOX SHADOW

Box shadow adds drop shadows to DOM elements, which can be a great way to add emphasis and visual flair to your pages.

The box-shadow property accepts a variety of information about the drop shadow, everything from its color to blurriness. For example:

```
box-shadow: 1px 2px 8px #000;
```

This sets a variety of options for the box shadow:

- The first two values are the *x* and *y* coordinates by which you want to offset your box shadow. In this example, the shadow is rendered one pixel to the right and two pixels below the element.

- The next value is the blur radius; in this case, the shadow is blurred by eight pixels. Here you can use a higher number for a blurrier shadow, or a lower number for a sharper one.

Finally, you set the color of your shadow; in this case, the drop shadow is black.

This styling attaches a drop shadow to the element as you can see in Figure A-1:

Figure A-1: A basic box shadow has been applied to this element.

RGBA Transparency

You might notice that the drop shadow looks a bit harsh in this example. That's because it uses an entirely opaque color.

For more subtlety, set an RGBA color instead:

```
box-shadow: 1px 2px 8px rgba(0,0,0,0.5);
```

RGBA colors are just like RGB colors except they also include alpha transparency, which makes them somewhat transparent. In this example, you set a black shadow (R: 0, G: 0, B: 0), which is only 50% opaque (0.5).

This produces a less jarring effect, as you can see in Figure A-2:

Figure A-2: This box shadow uses an RGBA color for more transparency.

> There's no need to provide a fallback to RGB in box shadows—all browsers that support box shadows also support RGBA colors.

Vendor Prefixes

Although this box shadow will work in iOS 5, it won't work in any currently released version of Android or older iOS versions. For these, you must add a vendor prefix:

```
-webkit-box-shadow: 1px 2px 8px rgba(0,0,0,0.5);
```

Make sure to also add the non-prefixed version for newer iOS users, other browsers, and also to future-proof for whenever Android supports it:

```
-webkit-box-shadow: 1px 2px 8px rgba(0,0,0,0.5);
box-shadow: 1px 2px 8px rgba(0,0,0,0.5);
```

It's important that the non-prefixed `box-shadow` comes last in your style sheets to make sure it overwrites the incompletely supported version.

> *You may want to add* `-moz-box-shadow` *for Firefox, but that prefix is becoming less necessary because Firefox has fully supported* `box-shadow` *since version 4.0.*

Why Vendor Prefixes?

You may be wondering why the browsers bother with vendor prefixes, because they make front end development more difficult.

Vendor prefixes exist because the CSS3 spec is still relatively new, and it took browsers some time to catch up to speed (after all, the spec is still evolving).

When the browser reaches a point where it supports most of a new spec, it makes sense to release that feature for developers to use. However, there still may be bugs with the functionality (for example, problems interacting with other experimental styles). Additionally, there may be parts of the spec the browser doesn't support, such as more complex features.

In these cases, the style is called with a vendor prefix, to differentiate it from the fully supported property, and avoid potential conflicts whenever the browser gets fully up to speed.

Multiple Box Shadows

You can also add multiple box shadows to your element simply by separating them with a comma:

```
-webkit-box-shadow: 0px 0px 2px rgba(0,0,0,0.3), 1px 2px 8px rgba(0,0,0,0.5);
box-shadow: 0px 0px 2px rgba(0,0,0,0.3), 1px 2px 8px rgba(0,0,0,0.5);
```

Two shadows have been applied to this element, as you can see in Figure A-3:

Figure A-3: This element has two box shadows.
Notice the harder shadow close to the edges of
the element.

> *Multiple box shadows get layered beneath one another, which means the first shadow is on top.*

You can even use multiple box shadows to create a handy 3D effect. Simply set a number of box shadows with no blur:

```
-webkit-box-shadow: 1px 1px 0px rgba(0,0,0,0.9),  2px 2px 0px rgba(0,0,0,0.9),  3px
3px 0px rgba(0,0,0,0.9),  4px 4px 0px rgba(0,0,0,0.9),  5px 5px 0px rgba(0,0,0,0.9),
 6px 6px 0px rgba(0,0,0,0.9),  7px 7px 0px rgba(0,0,0,0.9);
box-shadow: 1px 1px 0px rgba(0,0,0,0.9),  2px 2px 0px rgba(0,0,0,0.9),  3px 3px 0px

rgba(0,0,0,0.9),  4px 4px 0px rgba(0,0,0,0.9),  5px 5px 0px rgba(0,0,0,0.9),  6px
 6px
0px rgba(0,0,0,0.9),  7px 7px 0px rgba(0,0,0,0.9);
```

This code attaches seven drop shadows, each offset by another pixel. As you can see in Figure A-4, this makes the element look like it is protruding from the page.

Figure A-4: This 3D effect was created using
box shadows.

> *You can also use the same technique with* text-shadow *for 3D lettering.*

GRADIENTS

Gradients are an easy way to infuse flat-colored layouts with visually appealing depth. The CSS gradient spec is very versatile, providing a number of useful options at your disposal. Additionally, handling gradients in CSS means fewer images and less download times for your users.

Furthermore, traditional image-based approaches often produce gradients that don't stretch naturally across the element. If the element's dimensions never vary, you can cut an image at the right size, but you will have problems if the content ever expands. CSS gradients, on the other hand, stretch dynamically with the element's dimensions.

Linear Gradients

First, set a background color for your element. This ensures that something shows up in non-supportive browsers, and also if the browser is taking too long to render the gradient:

```
background-color: #999;
```

> *You can also set a background image as a fallback; just make sure it falls before the CSS gradients.*

Next, apply a linear gradient:

```
background-image: -webkit-gradient(linear, left top, left bottom, from(#CCC),
  to(#555));
background-image: -webkit-linear-gradient(top, #CCC, #555);
background-image:          linear-gradient(to bottom, #CCC, #555);
```

This snippet creates a linear gradient from a light gray (#CCC) to a darker gray (#555), going from top to bottom, as you can see in Figure A-5.

Figure A-5: This element has a basic linear gradient.

You might notice a whole slew of different formats here. Unfortunately, you need them all for backward compatibility:

- The first, `-webkit-gradient` is the older syntax for WebKit, which you'll need for older versions of iOS and Android.
- The next, `-webkit-linear-gradient` is the accepted standard, but it won't work on older devices.
- Finally the prefix-less `linear-gradient` is for newer browsers and future-proofing for iOS and Android.

You may also want to add `-moz-linear-gradient` and `-o-linear-gradient` for older versions of Firefox and Opera, respectively, although the current releases of both support the standard `linear-gradient`.

Also, if you want to support IE 9 and earlier, you can create a fallback using an IE filter. But be warned: IE filters are notoriously buggy.

> *You may have seen* `-ms-linear-gradient`, *but there's no need to include this vendor prefix. The prefixed property was used in the IE 10 developer preview, but the release version of IE 10 supports the standard* `linear-gradient`. *Thus, there is no fully released version of IE that supports the transitional syntax.*

Angled Gradients

You can use linear gradients to create vertical, horizontal, and even diagonal gradients at any angle.

The gradient created earlier is vertical, but you can switch it to horizontal by adjusting the position settings:

```
background-image: -webkit-gradient(linear, left top, right top, from(#CCC),
  to(#555));
background-image: -webkit-linear-gradient(left, #CCC, #555);
background-image:          linear-gradient(to right, #CCC, #555);
```

It's a bit of a hassle, but each syntax must be changed differently:

- The older `-webkit-gradient` syntax uses `left top` and `right top`.
- The newer `-webkit-linear-gradient` uses the point only at which the gradient starts: `left`.
- The W3C standard uses the point at which it ends: `to right`.

As you can see in Figure A-6, this creates a horizontal gradient.

Figure A-6: This horizontal gradient was created by manipulating the gradient position.

You can even create diagonal gradients:

```
background-image: -webkit-gradient(linear, left top, right bottom, from(#CCC),
  to(#000));
background-image: -webkit-linear-gradient(-45deg, #CCC, #000);
background-image:           linear-gradient(135deg, #CCC, #000);
```

Again, each syntax must be changed a bit differently:

- The older `-webkit-gradient` syntax uses the position settings you adjusted earlier: `left top` and `right bottom`.
- The newer `-webkit-linear-gradient` uses a negative degree measurement.
- Although the W3C-compliant browsers can handle the negative degree measurement, the accepted standard is to use a positive angle over 90º. In this case, `135deg` is the same as `-45deg`.

As you can see in Figure A-7, this creates a diagonal gradient from the top-left corner to the bottom-right corner.

Figure A-7: This diagonal gradient was created with CSS3.

The IE filter fallback can be used to create horizontal and vertical gradients, but not diagonal ones.

Finally, if you want to use something other than a 45° angle, the definition is basically the same, with one key difference in the older syntax:

```
background-image: -webkit-gradient(linear, left 20% top 100%, right 20% bottom 100%,
  from(#CCC), to(#000));
background-image: -webkit-linear-gradient(-60deg, #CCC, #000);
background-image:         linear-gradient(120deg, #CCC, #000);
```

Here, the newer syntaxes are both fairly straightforward; the only difference is that you add percentages to the stop points in the older `-webkit-gradient`. These can be a bit difficult to work with, but play around with them until you find a setting that works for your gradient.

As you can see in Figure A-8, this creates a more softly angled gradient.

Figure A-8: This 60° gradient was created with CSS3.

Gradient Tools

Before you go memorizing three different syntaxes for each directional gradient, think about using something to automate this tedious process instead. For instance, I like using a CSS preprocessor like Sass or LESS to handle the different formats.

But if you don't want to use a preprocessor, a number of tools out there can generate this code for you. For instance, check out the Ultimate CSS Gradient Generator from Colorzilla at `www.colorzilla.com/gradient-editor/`.

As you can see in Figure A-9, this editor provides an intuitive UI for generating gradients graphically.

Even if you are using Sass, this tool can be a useful way to visualize your gradient. Additionally, it can output SCSS format for Compass mix-ins.

> *CSS preprocessors are especially handy for CSS3 specs that are still in flux. That's because you can use them to quickly add new syntaxes to all the gradients in your style sheet if a new standard arises.*

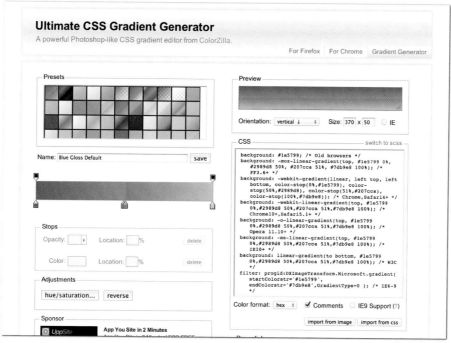

Figure A-9: This tool allows you to generate gradient styling more easily.

Color Stops

Beyond basic two-color gradients, you can add color stops to create a more complex gradient. Color stops indicate additional color points along the gradient. You can add as many as you want to the definitions you created earlier:

```
background: -webkit-gradient(linear, left top, left bottom, from(#b4ddb4), color-
  stop(50%, #008a00), to(#002400));
background: -webkit-linear-gradient(top, #b4ddb4, #008a00 50%, #002400);
background:         linear-gradient(to bottom, #b4ddb4, #008a00 50%, #002400);
```

Here, a color stop has been created 50% of the way through the gradient, which you can see in Figure A-10.

Figure A-10: This gradient uses a color stop.

You can declare the first and last colors as color stops as well. In the old `-webkit-gradient` *syntax, simply replace each with* `color-stop(0%, #b4ddb4)` *and* `color-stop(100%, #002400)`. *Then in the newer syntax, add* `0%` *and* `100%` *to each, respectively.*

You can use color stops to render richer gradients and even simulate 3D effects. For instance, you can create a button with a shadow at the base and a highlight near the top:

```
background: -webkit-gradient(linear, left top, left bottom, from(#52b152), color-
  stop(25%, #83c783), color-stop(66%, #008a00), to(#002400));
background: -webkit-linear-gradient(top, #52b152, #83c783 25%, #008a00 66%,
  #002400);
background:        linear-gradient(to bottom, #52b152, #83c783 25%, #008a00 66%,
  #002400);
```

This snippet builds a gradient with two additional color stops, which creates a three-dimensional appearance, as shown in Figure A-11.

Figure A-11: These color stops create a 3D effect for this button.

The IE filter fallback does not support color stops.

Radial Gradients

Beyond linear gradients you can also create radial or circular gradients using CSS3. Similarly, the settings are very versatile, allowing you to create a wide variety of gradients to suit your individual needs.

First, you can declare a basic radial gradient:

```
background: -webkit-gradient(radial, center center, 0px, center center, 100%,
  from(#CCC), to(#555));
background: -webkit-radial-gradient(center, ellipse cover, #CCC, #555);
background:        radial-gradient(ellipse at center, #CCC, #555);
```

As you can see, the definition is a bit different. Although you set color stops similarly to linear gradients, the positioning settings have changed. That's because you need to set the center point and radius of the gradient:

- In the older `-webkit-gradient` syntax, you first set the center location along with a radius of 0. Then you define the end point as still being centered, but at the edges of the element (100%).

- In the newer `-webkit-radial-gradient` syntax, you first set the position to center, then set it to cover the entire element using `ellipse cover`.
- Finally in the W3C standard syntax, you simply set it to `ellipse at center`.

As you can see in Figure A-12, this creates a radial gradient that stretches to the bounds of the element.

Figure A-12: This radial gradient was created in CSS3.

Repeating Gradients

Finally, the CSS spec also provides repeating gradients, which are an easy way to make striped backgrounds.

Repeating gradients are a little different than other gradients because they do not stretch across the element; rather, they repeat across it. That's why you set a hard pixel measurement for each of the color stops in the gradient, as opposed to a percentage to stretch along:

```
background-image: -webkit-repeating-linear-gradient(
    top,
    blue,
    green 10px,
    white 20px
);
background-image:         repeating-linear-gradient(
    to bottom,
    blue,
    green 10px,
    white 20px
);
```

As you can see, three color stops have been added to this gradient. This means the gradient will start with blue, then fade to green at 10px, then fade to white at 20px. At that point the gradient starts over again at blue, repeating across the dimensions of the element, as you can see in Figure A-13.

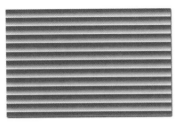

Figure A-13: This element has a repeating
gradient. Notice how it fades smoothly between
blue and green and white, then makes a hard
change back to blue when it repeats.

You can also manipulate the color stops in a repeating gradient to create hard stripes:

```
background-image: -webkit-repeating-linear-gradient(
    top,
    red,
    red 10px,
    white 10px,
    white 20px
);
background-image:          repeating-linear-gradient(
    to bottom,
    red,
    red 10px,
    white 10px,
    white 20px
);
```

Here, the gradient "fades" from red to red at 10px. Then it switches to white at 10px and
"fades" again to white at 20px, at which point it repeats. See Figure A-14.

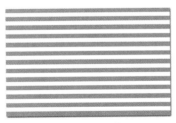

Figure A-14: This repeating gradient uses a
color stop trick to create block-colored stripes.

This stripe technique is useful, particularly if you are okay with reverting to a block color in
non-supportive browsers (or using an image fallback).

CSS ANIMATION

CSS transitions and keyframe animations are an easy way to add simple animations to your pages. They are particularly important for mobile devices since they tend to outperform JavaScript alternatives, such as jQuery's `animate()` API. That's because the animation occurs directly in the renderer, which can optimize for this behavior

In many mobile devices, CSS animations are even hardware accelerated. That means the device uses the GPU (graphics card) instead of the CPU (general processor) to render the frames of the animation. This rendering is considerably faster, because the GPU is specifically tailored for this type of task and because it frees up the CPU for other tasks.

> *Better performance is particularly noticeable in animation. The faster the device can render each frame of the animation, the more frames it can show. That makes the animation appear smoother to your users.*

Transitions

Transitions are an easy way to make pages more interactive and create a more polished user experience.

CSS transitions apply animations between style changes on your elements. For instance, you might change a button's color on hover:

```
.button {
    background-color: red;
}

.button:hover {
    background-color: purple;
}
```

Normally this element would change color immediately, but with transitions you can add a smooth animated color change:

```
.button {
    transition: background-color 200ms ease;
}
```

Here you define three aspects of the transition:

- First, you set which properties to animate. In this case, you are animating only `background-color`, but you can set this to most other properties or even `all` to animate all properties.
- Next, you set the duration of the transition—in this case, 200 milliseconds.

- Finally, you set a timing function for the transition—in this case, you use `ease`. Rather than animate evenly across the duration of this transition, `ease` causes the browser to first animate slowly, and then ease into a faster animation. This produces more natural motion.

You learn more about timing functions later in this section.

Multiple Transitions on One Element

You can also define multiple transitions on your element. This is handy for animating different properties at different speeds. However, you can't use the shorthand property any more:

```
.button {
    transition-property: opacity, background-color;
    transition-duration: 200ms, 500ms;
    transition-timing-function: ease;
}
```

Now two elements will be animated, `opacity` and `background-color`, at `200ms` and `500ms`, respectively. Note that only one timing function is used here, which causes it to be applied to both transitions. You can use the same technique for any aspect of the transition you want to use across the board.

If you want to animate all the properties of the element along the same transition, simply define one transition with the property set to `all`.

Vendor Prefixes

Just like with other experimental CSS3 features, it is important to use the appropriate vendor prefixes for transitions:

```
.button {
-webkit-transition: background-color 200ms ease;
   -moz-transition: background-color 200ms ease;
     -o-transition: background-color 200ms ease;
        transition: background-color 200ms ease;
}
```

This snippet defines the transition for a variety of different browsers. However, you can omit the `-moz-transition` and `-o-transition`, depending on which mobile browsers you want to support.

You may have seen `-ms-transition` elsewhere, but there is no need to include it anymore. Although `-ms-transition` was used earlier in the IE 10 developer preview, the release version fully supports `transition`. Because no actual release of IE needs this prefix, you can safely omit it.

Finally, if you are defining multiple transitions on the same element, simply attach each vendor prefix to `transition-property`, `transition-duration`, and `transition-timing-function`. The CSS rule might get a little long, but it's important if you want deeper browser penetration.

You learned why browsers use prefixes in the Box Shadow section of this chapter.

Triggering Transitions with JavaScript

Transitions are commonly used in the CSS to provide animations on `:hover`, `:focus`, or with other CSS pseudo-elements.

But you can also trigger these changes using JavaScript. That's because the transition will occur whenever a CSS property of the element changes, regardless of how that change arises.

For instance, in the button example, you could add a class definition with a different background styling:

```
.button.inactive {
    background-color: gray;
}
```

Next apply the class name using JavaScript or jQuery—for instance, whenever the button should be inactive:

```
$('.button').addClass('inactive');
```

When this class is added to the element, the `background-color` transitions smoothly just like it does on `:hover`. Likewise, if you remove the class, it transitions back to its original color.

Transition End Event

The DOM even provides a special event handler you can use to fire a callback when the transition completes. That means you can trigger additional JavaScript after the animation finishes.

For instance, you might set up a transition to fade out and hide the button whenever a particular class is added:

```
.button {
    transition-property: opacity, background-color;
    transition-duration: 200ms, 500ms;
    transition-timing-function: ease;
}

.button.hidden {
    opacity: 0;
}
```

Next apply the class using jQuery:

```
$('.button').addClass('hidden');
```

While this transition hides the element effectively, you still see a space on the page where the button existed previously. That's because it is transparent; if you want to remove the element altogether, you need to set `display: none`.

However, if you set `display: none` in the CSS, it happens immediately and you don't see the element fade out smoothly. After all, transition does not support the `display` property.

That's where the transition end event comes in:

```
function hideButton(e) {
    $(this).css('display', 'none');
}

$('.button')[0].addEventListener('webkitTransitionEnd', hideButton);
```

This callback hides the button once the transition animation completes. Note that you use `$('.button')[0]` to get at the DOM reference of the button as opposed to the jQuery reference.

> It is a good idea to future-proof your code with a non-prefixed `transitionEnd` event as well, and a `mozTransitionEnd` and `oTransitionEnd` if you want to support those mobile browsers.

Problems with the Transition End Event

However, this event isn't as straightforward as it seems. First, add a `console.log` to your callback:

```
function hideButton(e) {
    $(this).css('display', 'none');
    console.log('transition end event');
}

$('.button')[0].addEventListener('webkitTransitionEnd', hideButton);
```

As you can see in Figure A-15, this callback fires twice.

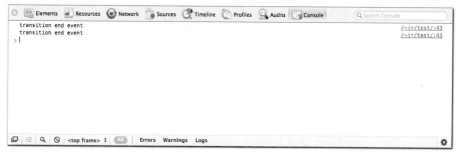

Figure A-15: The console shows the transition end callback firing twice.

The reason for this strange behavior is that the `transitionEnd` callback fires any time a transition occurs on the element. Because you are attaching two transitions here, one for `opacity` and another for `background-color`, the event fires twice.

It isn't a huge problem in this example, because adding `display: none` a second time doesn't change anything. However, what if the `background-color` change was faster than the `opacity` change? Then the element would first hide before the opacity change completed (and then hide again).

Or even worse, what happens on hover? Because you are still applying a color change, this transition fires, hiding the element.

As you can see, the transition end event can be difficult to work with. It does not relay any useful information for which property has changed. Instead you have to rely on hacks to determine if and when you've applied a transition that needs a callback.

> *When working with transition end events, it is a good idea to avoid* `transition-property: all`. *It can lead to a variety of unexpected events, whenever any property of the element changes (even those properties you don't intend to animate).*

Pros and Cons of Transitions with JavaScript

This technique is handy, but it can be a bit of an engineering disaster because you are using JavaScript to apply an animation. However, the animation exists in the CSS, not the JavaScript. Although animation could be considered a styling task, it makes much more sense to include in the scripting layer, not the styling layer.

This problem is exacerbated using the `transitionEnd` event. Not only is the event implementation a bit counterintuitive, but it also leads to further segmentation of the animation code. Instead of using an intuitive callback in jQuery's `animate()` API, you have to set up an extra event listener, which fires whenever a transition occurs on this element. That means the same `transitionEnd` event fires even if you apply different animations.

All things being equal, we recommend you avoid this pattern and use jQuery's `animate()` API to achieve the animation. However, all things are not equal from a performance perspective: CSS transitions tend to outperform JavaScript alternatives by a substantial margin because browsers can optimize for CSS styling directly.

This optimization is particularly important for underpowered mobile devices. Most devices tend to choke on JavaScript animations and render a very choppy motion. CSS transitions, on the other hand, render much more smoothly. Thus, the architecture of your app will have to take a hit in order to provide a better user experience.

Keyframes

While transitions are great for simple animations between two different styles, keyframes are ideal whenever you need more complex animation. Keyframes allow you to define multi-step animations that are attached to different CSS selectors.

The first step is defining a custom keyframe animation:

```
@-webkit-keyframes my-animation {
    from {
        opacity: 0;
    }
    to {
        opacity: 1;
    }
}
```

Using the `from` and `to` tags indicates the start and end points of the animation, which is called `my-animation`. In this case, it is a basic fade-in, but you could attach any number of styles in here.

Next, attach this to your element using `-webkit-animation`:

```
.my-element {
    -webkit-animation: my-animation 2s infinite;
}
```

This snippet applies your custom animation to the element. It animates over the course of 2 seconds, and loops infinitely.

Keyframe animations are very versatile, and you aren't limited to just two-part animations. In fact, you can use percentages to attach as many parts to the animation as you want:

```
@-webkit-keyframes my-animation {
    0% {
        opacity: 0;
    }
    50% {
```

```
        opacity: 1;
    }
    100% {
        opacity: 0;
    }

}
```

You can also use commas to consolidate any parts of the animation that are the same. For instance, the following produces the same result as the preceding animation:

```
@-webkit-keyframes my-animation {
    0%, 100% {
        opacity: 0;
    }
    50% {
        opacity: 1;
    }
}
```

Furthermore, you can attach a variety of additional options in your animation declaration. For instance, say you want to use a timing function:

```
-webkit-animation: my-animation 2s infinite ease;
```

Or you can attach a delay so that the animation pauses a bit before starting:

```
-webkit-animation-delay: 3s;
```

This snippet starts the animation after 3 seconds have elapsed.

By default, the animation starts back from the top whenever it loops, but you can also set it to alternate directions:

```
-webkit-animation-direction: alternate;
```

Finally, if you want to attach more than one keyframe animation to an element, simply separate them with a comma:

```
-webkit-animation: first-animation 2s infinite,
    second-animation 5s infinite;
```

As you can see, the plethora of options makes keyframe animations extremely versatile.

> You should also include an @keyframes definition with a corresponding animation for deeper browser penetration.

Custom Timing Functions

Timing functions make the motion of your animations appear much more natural. In the real world, motions rarely start and stop immediately, and our eyes are finely tuned to pick up this kind of motion. Without easing functions, animations tend to appear quite fake and computerized.

Besides `ease`, there are a couple of predefined timing functions you can use in your transitions: `ease-in`, `ease-out`, and `ease-in-out` all achieve slightly different animation speeds.

You can also define your own timing function if none of the predefined options suit your needs. To do so, you can leverage Cubic Bezier functions:

```
transition-timing-function: cubic-bezier(.35, .15 , .3, 1);
```

Cubic Bezier functions essentially define all the points you need to trace a complex curve. But before your head starts spinning with math overload, look Lea Verou's tool on www.cubic-bezier.com, shown in Figure A-16.

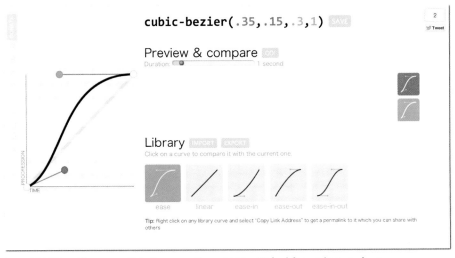

Figure A-16: This tool from www.cubic-bezier.com provides an intuitive GUI for defining Cubic Bezier functions.

Using this tool, you can adjust the control points of the curve, and preview the changes in your browser. You can even compare it against the default timing functions (all of which can also be recreated using Cubic Beziers).

Custom timing functions can be applied to transitions and keyframe animations.

JAVASCRIPT

Most mobile apps tend to be extremely interactive and, therefore, rely on a lot of JavaScript. JavaScript allows you to script everything from the touchscreen interface to server-side communication.

BASIC EVENTS

Event handling is part of the core of most JavaScript interactivity, because it applies special scripts to handle a variety of user inputs, from clicks to form element interaction. Here are some of the events that are available to both mobile and non-mobile browsers.

> *Event handlers are built a bit differently in some browsers, so you attach them with jQuery in this section to avoid any cross-browser issues.*

onClick

Undoubtedly the most used event handler, `onClick` handles mouse clicks from the user. Using the jQuery counterpart `click()`, you can attach a click event to an element:

```
$('.my-element').click(function(e) {
    // what to do on click
});
```

As you can see here, you pass a callback function to `click()`, which is called whenever the user clicks this element.

With jQuery, you can reference the clicked item in a number of ways, the easiest being `$(this)`. For instance, you could hide the element once it's clicked:

```
$('.my-element').click(function(e) {
    // hide the element
    $(this).hide();
});
```

> *For mobile, it is often better to use touch events instead of click events, which you learn about later in this appendix.*

Disabling Default Click Behavior

Often, you want to disable the original click event. For instance, if you are loading a link via AJAX, you wouldn't want the link to also open in the browser. To disable the default behavior, attach `preventDefault()` to the `e` argument passed to the callback:

```
$('.my-element').click(function(e) {
    e.preventDefault();
});
```

You could also put a `return` in the callback to disable any click behavior, but this tends to be a worse approach. That's because it will also disable any other JavaScript click handlers you've attached to the element. On the other hand, `e.preventDefault()` disables only the default behavior.

Preventing Event Bubbling

Click events also bubble up, meaning if you click an element, a click event will also be triggered on all of its ancestors (for example, when you click an `<li>`, a click event fires on the `<ul>` as well).

This can often cause conflicts, but you can disable bubbling by attaching `e.stopPropagation()`:

```
$('.my-element').click(function(e) {
    e.preventDefault();
    e.stopPropagation();
});
```

This method ensures that no extraneous click events fire when the user clicks a descendent node.

onFocus and onBlur

There are also two special event handlers for form elements, `onFocus` and `onBlur`. These events fire whenever a form element comes into or out of focus, respectively. That means that when a user clicks into a form field, `onFocus` will fire, and when the user clicks out of the field, `onBlur` will fire.

> You might be thinking that it would be easier to just attach a click event to the field, but bear in mind that there are more ways the user can get into the form field, such as using the Tab key.

For instance, you could add a class to an input field when it is focused, and then remove it when it is blurred:

```
$('input').focus(function(e) {
    $(this).addClass('focused');
});

$('input').blur(function(e) {
    $(this).removeClass('focused');
});
```

However, if this class applies only styling, you can avoid JavaScript altogether and use the CSS pseudo-elements `:focus` and `:blur` instead.

jQuery's on() API

When you attach events using DOM or jQuery, these events are applied to any elements currently on the page. But they will not be attached to any elements that get added dynamically with JavaScript.

For instance, you might attach a click handler to all anchor tags:

```
$('a').click(function(e) {
    // whatever you want to do on click
});
```

This handler applies to all the <a> elements on the page when it is called. However, if you add a new <a> element with JavaScript, it will be left out.

To apply the handler to all <a> elements, regardless of when they are added, you can instead use jQuery's on() API:

```
$('a').on('click', function(e) {
    // whatever you want to do on click
});
```

Here you simply pass the type of handler you want to attach to the element; the callback fires whenever that event occurs. You could also, for example, attach focus and blur events:

```
$('input').on('focus', function(e) {
    // whatever you want to do on focus
});

$('input').on('blur', function(e) {
    // whatever you want to do on blur
});
```

For more information about the on() API, visit http://api.jquery.com/on/.

> *You may be used to using jQuery* live() *events; however, that API is deprecated in favor of the newer* on() *API.*

TOUCH EVENTS

Touch event handlers are perhaps the most important JavaScript methods for mobile, because mobile is all about the interface, and most modern devices have a touchscreen (excluding those that don't really display web pages).

True, you could just use basic click events, because mobile devices handle these as well. But click events tend to be less responsive than touch events. That means it takes longer for the click to register than the touch. That can make a big difference in user experiences.

Additionally, touch events are very versatile in mobile. You can track `touchstart`, `touchend`, and even touch events for multiple fingers. Furthermore, some platforms provide more intuitive gestures, which allow you to track complex motions like swipes and pinches.

Basic Touch Events

To use a basic touch event, simply tap into the `touchstart` event handler.

`touchstart` fires when the user first touches his or her finger to the device. For instance, you could switch an <a> tag to a touch event and make those clicks a bit more responsive to touch:

```
$('a').bind('touchstart', function(e) {
    // it is important to prevent default here, so the normal click doesn't fire as
  well
    e.preventDefault();

    window.location = $(this).attr('href');
});
```

This script takes all the <a> tags on the page and switches them over to touch events.

> Bear in mind this may cause some problems since these custom handlers won't be stopped by `preventDefault()` if other event handlers are applied.

Touchend

Although `touchstart` is the most responsive, it is often best to use `touchend` instead, which fires when users remove their finger. That allows the users to adjust their finger position if they misclick when they first touch the device:

```
$('.my-element').bind('touchend', function(e) {
    // whatever you want to do on touch
});
```

In fact, arguably the best practice is to indicate to the users when they start touching the element, and then fire the event once they finish the finger-press:

```
$('.my-element').bind('touchstart', function(e) {
    // indicate that they have started touching the element
    $(this).addClass('touching');
});
```

```
$('.my-element').bind('touchend', function(e) {
        // remove any touch indication once they stop touching
        $(this).removeClass('touching');

    // whatever you want to do on touch
});
```

> *Bear in mind that touch events won't work in desktop browsers. That means you should switch them to click events if you want to test in your desktop browser or provide a desktop experience for your mobile app.*

Touchmove

You can also track how the touch event has changed since the user put his or her finger on the device. This technique is useful for tracking drags and other simple touch gestures:

```
$('.my-element').bind('touchmove', function(e) {
    // get the position of the touch event
    var x = e.touch.pageX;
    var y = e.touch.pageY;
});
```

As you can see here, you can grab the position of the touch event using `e.touch.pageX` and `e.touch.pageY`.

Although the basic use of `touchmove` is fairly straightforward, tracking a meaningful touch gesture with it is much more complex. Later in this section, you learn how to use predefined gestures to track this sort of motion.

> *Position data is also available in* `touchstart` *and* `touchend`. *However, in* `touchend` *it is best to stick to* `e.changedTouch.pageX` *and* `e.changedTouch.pageY` *if you are supporting iOS.*

Multi-Touch Events

One unique feature of mobile devices is the capability to track multiple touch events. Whereas with a mouse, you can click only one point at a time, with a touchscreen you can have as many simultaneous touches as you have fingers.

Tapping into this functionality is easy. In a `touchstart`, `touchend`, or `touchmove` event, you can take advantage of the `e.touches` array. For instance, to track the position of two fingers:

```
$('.my-element').bind('touchstart', function(e) {
    // first finger
    var x1 = e.touches[0].pageX;
    var y1 = e.touches[0].pageY;

    // second finger
    var x2 = e.touches[1].pageX;
    var y2 = e.touches[1].pageY;
});
```

Although this tracks only the position of two fingers, you can track as many as you want (although users rarely use more than two fingers).

In this example, the event fires so long as one touch occurs in the element. That means that it still fires if the second finger is outside the element. To confine this event to only those touches within the element itself, you can instead use e.targetTouches:

```
$('.my-element').bind('touchstart', function(e) {
    // first finger
    var x1 = e.targetTouches[0].pageX;
    var y1 = e.targetTouches[0].pageY;

    // second finger
    var x2 = e.targetTouches[1].pageX;
    var y2 = e.targetTouches[1].pageY;
});
```

Additionally, you can use multi-touch events to track multiple finger changes with e.changedTouches:

```
$('.my-element').bind('touchstart', function(e) {
    // first finger
    var x1 = e.changedTouches[0].pageX;
    var y1 = e.changedTouches[0].pageY;

    // second finger
    var x2 = e.changedTouches[1].pageX;
    var y2 = e.changedTouches[1].pageY;
});
```

Keep in mind, however, that the multiple changed touches fire only when *both* fingers move. Only one event fires if one of the fingers stays still.

iOS Gestures

Tracking specific gestures with e.changedTouches can be complicated. Fortunately, iOS provides some predefined gestures you can tap into with JavaScript.

To do so, attach a `gesturechange` event handler:

```
$('.my-element').bind('gesturechange', function(e) {
    var rotation = e.rotation;
    var scale = e.scale;
});
```

Here the `gesturechange` event fires whenever the user does one of two gestures:

- Rotation (by pressing two fingers to the screen and rotating them)
- Scale (pinch and zoom)

You can tap into the values of these gestures with `e.rotation` and `e.scale`.

You can also track a number of other touch gestures, such as tapping, swiping, dragging, and "touch and hold." For more information, visit `http://bit.ly/apple-gestures`.

Other Gesture Options

Although iOS gestures are not available on other devices, there are a number of third-party plug-ins and frameworks you can use to provide gesture event support. In fact, you can add support for a variety of gestures that are not even supported in iOS.

We recommend looking into the gestures in jQuery Mobile or Sencha Touch if you need this type of functionality.

JQUERY

jQuery is a JavaScript library that streamlines JavaScript development and allows you to focus on features and functionality instead of syntax. "Vanilla JavaScript" (JavaScript without a library) can be extremely fast, but you run into a lot of problems across different browsers (namely IE) because different browsers implement JavaScript slightly differently. You can't assume that just because a bit of JavaScript works in Chrome that it works in IE. This is especially true for more complex features like AJAX, which you learn about later in this appendix.

In addition to unifying cross-browser syntax, jQuery also provides a wide selection of features that aren't available in vanilla JavaScript. Instead of reinventing the wheel every time you need a new function, you can lean on the collective experience of the talented jQuery team (as well as the jQuery community).

To learn more about the extensive collection of APIs in jQuery, visit `http://www.jquery.com/`.

jQuery Mobile

Depending on what functionality you need, you may consider using jQuery Mobile, shown in Figure A-17. Essentially a mobile MVC, jQuery Mobile provides a lot of mobile-specific tools not available in the main core. Primarily consisting of interface and styling options, these tools can enhance the mobile experience with a relatively small amount of effort.

Figure A-17: Learn more about jQuery Mobile at http://jquerymobile.com/.

© 2012 jQuery Foundation and other contributors

Plug-ins

One of the best parts of working with jQuery is the community. As the most popular JavaScript library, there are not only a ton of detailed tutorials available on the web, but also a wide selection of plug-ins you can drop into your project.

These plug-ins are an easy way to inject more complex functionality that is not available in the jQuery core. They have two main advantages:

- Plug-ins drastically reduce development time.
- Plug-ins are typically open-source, which means there have been a lot more eyes debugging them than any code you create yourself.

However, not all plug-ins are created equal. jQuery's popularity is a double-edged sword: There are a lot of great plug-ins, but also a lot of plug-ins made by developers who don't necessarily understand the library as well as you might hope. And even if the developer is highly skilled, the plug-in may be very old and unsupported.

So tread with caution and test any plug-ins you want to use *before* integrating them too extensively into your app.

> *I say this as someone who has personally made really bad jQuery plug-ins in the beginning of my career.*

Zepto.js

jQuery is very powerful, and it has grown substantially in the past several years. That means more functionality at your fingertips, but also a larger file size and instantiation time.

jQuery is great for most desktop projects, and also for mobile projects with complex features. However, for simple mobile apps, Zepto.js is a much lighter-weight alternative to jQuery.

> *At the time of this writing, Zepto is 8KB and jQuery is 32KB.*

Best of all, Zepto uses jQuery syntax, and is intended to be dropped in to any project that was previously built in jQuery. Assuming you don't need any of the features it lacks, you can really reduce the file size of your app.

However, bear in mind that Zepto (see Figure A-18) does not support IE. That's part of why it is so much lighter—IE often needs different JavaScript approaches than other browsers, which balloons jQuery's file size. Zepto, which was originally designed for mobile, has chosen not to support these approaches because mobile browsers do not need them.

> *If you do want to support an IE desktop experience, you can also drop in jQuery using an IE conditional, and use Zepto for everywhere else.*

AJAX

AJAX is a system of protocols that allow you to communicate directly with the backend without refreshing the page. That's particularly important in mobile apps, since data rates are so much slower. Communicating with the server via AJAX allows you to avoid reloading entire pages, and instead only refresh the appropriate content on the page.

Although AJAX works a bit differently in different browsers, you can ignore those disparities if you are working with jQuery. jQuery's AJAX API handles the different approaches for you.

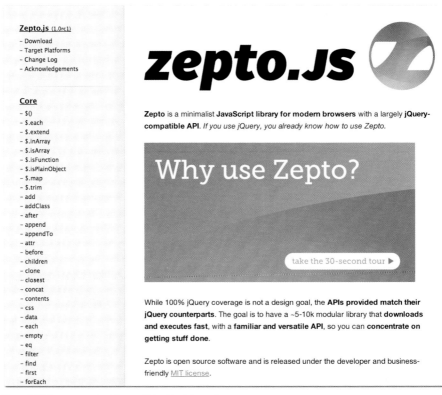

Figure A-18: Learn more about Zepto at http://zeptojs.com/.
© Thomas Fuchs

Here's a basic AJAX call:

```
$.ajax({
    url: 'path-to-receiving-script.php',
    type: 'post',
    data: {
        data1: true,
        data2: false
    },
    success: function(data) {
        // what to do with the response
    }
});
```

This code passes the basic options needed for AJAX:

- The `url` to post the data to
- The `type` of the post (for instance, `post` or `get`)

- The data to post (for example, a JavaScript object or query string)
- A callback function to handle the response from the server

For a more detailed list of available options, visit http://api.jquery.com/jQuery.ajax/.

JSON

When communicating with the backend via AJAX, JSON is the protocol of choice. JSON is ideal because it is a very concise way to relay data to and from the server, which means faster download and upload times.

JSON Syntax

JSON is essentially a large JavaScript object, which can contain pretty much any data you need. For instance:

```
{
    "myData": {
        "item1": "a text string",
        "item2": 10,
        "item3": true,
        "item4": [
            "array item 1",
            "array item 2",
            "array item 3"
        ]
    },
    "moreData": {
        "item5": "more items"
    }
}
```

As you can see, the JSON object can contain a variety of data types.

When working with JSON, be very careful with the syntax if you want to support older browsers. They'll choke on any incorrect formatting, from hanging commas to array keys that are not enclosed in double quotes. Worst of all, these problems won't pop up in modern browsers, so you won't even see them unless you're testing thoroughly.

You can use JSONLint to validate your JSON. There is an online validator at: http://jsonlint.com/, as shown in Figure A-19.

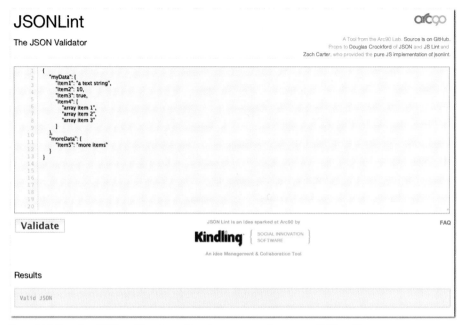

Figure A-19: The online JSONLint validator is a quick and easy way to make sure your JSON is valid.

Data Parsing

Although JSON looks a great deal like a JavaScript object, it is actually relayed back and forth as a string. Fortunately, there are a couple easy methods you can use to parse the JSON string and use it in your JavaScript.

One method you can use is `window.JSON.parse()`:

```
function parseJSON(data) {
    // first trim any whitespace as it can cause problems for some browsers
    data = jQuery.trim( data );

    // then parse the JSON if JSON parsing is available
    if ( window.JSON && window.JSON.parse ) {
        return window.JSON.parse( data );
    }
}
```

Extremely old browsers don't support `window.JSON` natively, so you'll have to include it yourself using a simple JavaScript file. This problem affects only IE 7 and earlier, so it isn't an issue in mobile apps unless you want to also support a cross-browser desktop experience. You can get the script here: `https://github.com/douglascrockford/JSON-js`.

Alternatively, you can just use jQuery's `parseJSON()` API. It handles JSON for any browser:

```
$.parseJSON(data);
```

You might want to try to use vanilla JavaScript whenever possible because it's faster and won't break if you change libraries. Since `window.JSON` *is supported in most mobile browsers, use it instead of the jQuery alternative when building for mobile.*

JSONP

While AJAX is an excellent protocol for communicating with the server, it introduces a variety of security threats not present in normal HTTP processing. Namely, an attacker could send private data from a page (even an HTTPS page) to his or her own server.

Fortunately, browsers reduce this risk by disabling cross-domain AJAX. That means that `www.my-domain.com` can't communicate with `www.my-second-domain.com` using AJAX.

However, many situations necessitate cross-domain communication, which is where JSONP comes in. Adding a JSONP wrapper to your data allows it to get through the browser security checks.

Fortunately, it is relatively easy to accomplish with jQuery's AJAX API. Simply set the `jsonp` option to `true`:

```
$.ajax({
    url: 'path-to-receiving-script.php',
    type: 'post',
    jsonp: true,
    data: {
        data1: true,
        data2: false
    },
    success: function(data) {
        // what to do with the response
    }
});
```

SUMMARY

This appendix is an incomplete list of technologies used in typical mobile apps. Although it covers most of the technologies you used to build the Corks app, there are many more interesting options in HTML5, CSS3, and JavaScript. We encourage you to explore and learn the current technologies not covered in this book as well as those that become available in the future.

One of the most exciting aspects of web development (particularly mobile development) is that there are always new technologies to play with. Keep coding!

INDEX